ALSO BY KAI T. ERIKSON:

Wayward Puritans: A Study in the Sociology of Deviance

*In Search of Common Ground: Conversations with
Erik H. Erikson and Huey P. Newton* (editor)

Everything in Its Path

Destruction of Community in the Buffalo Creek Flood

KAI T. ERIKSON

Simon and Schuster | New York

Copyright © 1976 by Kai T. Erikson

Published by Simon and Schuster
A Gulf+Western Company
Rockefeller Center, 630 Fifth Avenue
New York, New York 10020

Designed by Irving Perkins
Manufactured in the United States of America

1   2   3   4   5   6   7   8   9   10

Library of Congress Cataloging in Publication Data

Erikson, Kai T.
    Everything in its path.

    Includes bibliographical references and index.
    1.   Buffalo Creek, W. Va.—Flood, 1972.   2.   Disasters
—Psychological aspects.   I.   Title.
HV610 1972.E74   363   76-26462

ISBN 0-671-22367-4

Contents

Introduction

This report deals with the human wreckage left in the wake of a terrible flood that tore through a narrow mountain hollow called Buffalo Creek in the winter of 1972. I was originally drawn to Buffalo Creek as one of several consultants to a law firm that was about to file suit on behalf of some 650 survivors. Like everyone else caught up in that awesome event, I pursued the story with more energy than was required by the legal action itself—and in that sense, at least, the study to follow goes well beyond the commitment with which it began. But the legal action set the rhythm and scope of my research for the better part of three years, and when I try to explain what kind of book I imagine this to be, I have to say a word about its origins.

I first read about the Buffalo Creek flood in the morning newspaper the day after it happened. The account made enough of an impression on me that I could vaguely recall it a year later, although I managed to forget all about it in the meantime. In early 1973 I was approached by the law firm Arnold and Porter and was asked whether I might suggest the name of a sociologist who could spend some time in West Virginia and survey the situation at first hand. We decided that I should make a brief visit to Buffalo Creek myself so as to make a more informed recommendation about the matter.

I came back from that visit so awed and depressed by what I had seen that I volunteered my own services to the firm. There was a certain element of presumption in that act, considering that I knew very little about Appalachia, very little about coal mining, and very little about the character of human disasters. But I could at least claim the virtue of being available, since I was about to take a year's leave from my university anyway and needed only to clear my desk of other research plans.

I took extensive notes on that first trip to Buffalo Creek because my original intent had been to send a report to the law firm before passing on to other business, and there may be more method than self-indulgence in my trying to rephrase a few of those notes in order to convey something of the mood evoked by that first exposure.

Sociologists are often drawn to street corners when they try to get a feel for new locales, and the nearest thing to a street corner on Buffalo Creek is Charlie Cowan's gas station. I positioned myself there on my first morning, watching the coal trucks make their way up the scarred roads of the hollow and talking a little self-consciously with the people who came in to pass the time of day. At one point a leathery old man came in to get a soft drink and we exchanged a few words on the heat of the day. I looked up at the overcast sky and remarked (with a studied attempt at country shrewdness) that a storm might come up and cool the air. He turned away with a fierce "Haw," his face creased in irritation, and limped off to his car without another word. One does not mention storms casually on Buffalo Creek, and one certainly does not appear to welcome them as a relief from uncomfortable weather. I met the old man later at a large gathering, and he brought me a cup of coffee in what I took to be a shy act of penance. He did not say a word, but I had the impression that he was ready to make allowances for my insensitivity now that he associated me with Arnold and Porter.

The gathering mentioned above involved a large group of

lawyers and legal assistants collecting information from their clients. Tables had been spaced at intervals across a gymnasium floor and the room was filled with people awaiting their turn, lined along the walls on benches or standing around in quiet family clusters. The whole scene looked as if it had been painted in shades of gray. The children neither laughed nor played. The adults acted as if they were surrounded by a sheath of heavy air through which they could move and respond only at the cost of a deliberate effort. Everything seemed muted and dulled. I felt for a moment as though I were in the company of people so wounded in spirit that they almost constituted a different culture, as though the language we shared in common was simply not sufficient to overcome the enormous gap in experience that separated us. I got over that feeling before long, but the sense of being in the presence of deep and numbing pain remained an important part of the emotional climate in which this study was done.

I was driving down Buffalo Creek late that night when the storm that had been threatening all day finally broke with mountain vengeance. I pulled over to the side of the road near one of the several trailer camps on the creek and stayed there as half the lights in the camp flashed on, children began to cry, and small groups of men trudged out into the darkness to begin a wet vigil over the stream. Something of the mood of that camp reached across the creek to where I was parked, and I had to fight off a compelling urge to drive away, to escape. I had been in the hollow for only twelve hours.

These brief sketches can only begin to suggest what Buffalo Creek felt like to a stranger a year after the flood, but they do serve to introduce an important point. There was an urgency to this research quite unlike anything sociologists normally encounter in the course of their work, and it affected both the temper of the study to follow and the methodological cast it came to assume.

If the study had been organized along more conventional sociological lines, it might have been quite different. I might have chosen the people I interviewed more systematically, done a more thorough job of sifting through the available statistical data, looked harder for evidence of differences within the survivor group, tried to compare Buffalo Creek with other mining communities in the general vicinity, and taken better advantage of the opportunity I had to conduct formal surveys. I did not exercise those options as well as I might have. For one thing, I was not in a position to set the pace of this research because I had to be ready at a time of someone else's choosing to testify in a court action involving tens of millions of dollars. Yet I suspect that I would have had difficulty pursuing this study in the cool and measured way most sociological research is done even if the circumstances had been less pressing, partly because the event I was trying to understand seemed so much larger than the professional lens through which I was looking, and partly because the traditional methods of sociology do not really equip one to study discrete moments in the flow of human experience.

The problem is that sociologists usually select the scenes they study because those scenes shed light on some more general proposition in which they were interested beforehand. That is, the particular *case* is selected in the hope that it will inform and give support to a larger *generalization*. My assignment on Buffalo Creek, however, was to sift through the store of available sociological knowledge to see what light it might shed on a single human event, and this, clearly, reverses the normal order of social science research.

I think an argument can be made that sociologists should do this kind of work more often anyway. The search for generalization has become so intense in our professional ranks that most of the important events of our day have passed without comment in the sociological literature. The aim of any science, I agree, must be to move from particular observations to general findings, but there are times when the need for generalizations must yield to the urgency of passing events, times when the event must tell its own story.

Moreover, once one comes to know and respect a community of people, it becomes increasingly difficult to think of them as examples of a larger sociological proposition—all the more so if they are suffering in some sharp and private way. One of the first persons I met on Buffalo Creek said in a letter: "I feel as I'm sure a prisoner must feel who has been sentenced to prison for a crime he didn't commit." People like that have been the victims of so many different forces outside their control that one hesitates to imprison them once again between the cold parentheses of a theory. Much of what follows is theoretical, of course, since that is part of what a sociologist can contribute to human understanding, but I have tried to let the theory fall between the natural segments of the story rather than making it the main theme, the organizing principle, of the report.

The following study, then, may be difficult to place on the ordinary academic map. It is clinical in the sense that it tries to trace the source of a singular set of traumatic disturbances. It is historical in the sense that it tries to locate a particular event in its own time and place. And, of course, it is sociological in the sense that it was written by a person whose intellectual reflexes were tuned in that tradition and deals with the most sociological of all topics—the community. I would be content to think of these pages as an example of what C. Wright Mills called "social studies" and let librarians worry about the shelf on which they should be placed.

The report itself relies heavily on words spoken by the survivors of the Buffalo Creek disaster, and I should say something about the way those voices were recorded. To work for a firm like Arnold and Porter is to have the best research grant obtainable, not only because the firm underwrites the costs of the research with an absolute minimum of bureaucratic splutter, but also because one immediately falls heir to all the good will generated by a legal action of this sort. Social scientists who have ventured into Appalachia on research errands of one kind or another often testify that it is no easy matter to overcome the suspicion with which strangers are greeted there. But I was welcomed into Buffalo Creek with a warmth beyond anything I imagined or deserved. The people of the hollow share both the reserve and the hospitality characteristic of that part of the world, and my association with Arnold and Porter acted to peel away that outer layer of reserve all at once and to make me eligible for the extraordinary courtesy that lies underneath. My association with the firm also gave me access to a remarkable collection of documents—more than five hundred legal depositions averaging fifty or sixty pages in length, an equivalent number of psychiatric evaluations, and a thick file of statements and letters written by the survivors to their attorneys. In addition to all that, I was able to take advantage of my consultant role to conduct lengthy interviews with scores of people as well as to distribute a questionnaire by mail to all the adult plaintiffs in the action—more than 90 percent of whom responded.

The research, then, took two forms. I read thirty or forty thousand pages of transcript material, almost all of it in the form of words spoken by the survivors to inquiring attorneys, and I rounded out those long months of reading with periodic visits to Buffalo Creek, during which time I undertook a large number of additional interviews. I might add, finally, that I have read transcripts of interviews conducted by three of my partners in the Buffalo Creek action—Robert Jay Lifton, Eric Olson, and James L. Titchener—although I have quoted from those several transcripts sparingly. Unless otherwise indicated, quotations in the body of the text are drawn from one of four sources. The great bulk of them come either from legal depositions (which are on the public record) or from my own interviews (most of which are recorded on tape and stored for future reference); a smaller number are taken from written answers to the questionnaire I distributed to the adult survivors, and from the communications they addressed to the law firm. The speakers, of course, are not identified by their real names. All together, the words of 142 persons appear at one time or another in the text.

I have spelled out these details carefully because a number

of recent sociological monographs have used the voices of informants in a manner that can only be described as casual. A few authors, in fact, have admitted to the truly stunning generosity of "giving" words to the individuals they quote, either because the informants seemed to be having a hard time expressing what they "really" meant or because the authors decided to clean up their grammatical idiosyncrasies as a token of personal regard. I have no real objection to this procedure, although I suspect that it is often used without sufficient warning to readers. But it does place a new obligation on those of us who use quotations extensively to explain in some detail what liberties we have taken with them. For the record, then: the words represented in this book as having been spoken (or occasionally written) by the people of Buffalo Creek are reproduced here in their original form, the sole exception being that I have sometimes removed material from longer passages in an effort to condense them, and have sometimes strung sentences together that were really uttered at different times in the original interview. At one point I considered tidying up the grammar somewhat, which is exactly what I do when I am asked to edit some verbal remarks of my own so that they will look more presentable in print, but the thought did not last long. The language spoken on Buffalo Creek is marvelously expressive and often quite beautiful. A shrewd observer of mountain ways wrote fifty years ago:

> They have one gift that modern speech has largely lost, the ability to make phrases and even words fit the needs of the occasion; to express the fresh thought or feeling while it is fluttering over their minds. Their speech is still fluid. It is not yet congealed and fossilized into grammar.[1]

That remark is still true, and one might as well make the most of it.

I have gathered a number of debts in the writing of this book. The most compelling of them, obviously, is to the people of Buffalo Creek themselves, but that debt is difficult to acknowledge because I owe it not only to the kindness of a few special friends but to the generosity of an entire community. I came to Buffalo Creek a stranger, by which I mean not only that I was unacquainted with the people and their ways but also that I was a truly strange person from every point of view that made sense in their world. Few of them knew or cared what sociologists do for a living, so my professional titles could not really serve as a sufficient introduction; and there was nothing in my manner during those first few visits to dispel the very reasonable doubts they must have felt as to whether I had anything of value to offer. More than that, they were asked to accept me as an expert on community life, and yet it was apparent every time I asked a question that I was largely ignorant about the only forms of communality that mattered to them. I mention all of this because I benefited from a courtesy that comes naturally to the mountains but not in the flatter terrains where I have lived most of my life. It is true, of course, that I was trying to help people collect damages in a court action, so it is only reasonable to note that there may have been a certain method in their kindness; but their hospitality went so far beyond that consideration that I have a hard time thinking of it as any more than a minor factor. I would like to convey somehow that the gift of being treated with a degree of trust I had not yet earned meant a great deal to me personally and contributed enormously to this study.

I read the first draft of this study over several evening sessions to the most important group of critics I know—Joanna M. Erikson, Joan Mowat Erikson, and Erik H. Erikson. Their response emboldened me to distribute a second draft to several of my co-workers in the Buffalo Creek action, and I profited immeasurably from their comments—J. Bradway Butler, Harry Huge, Robert Jay Lifton, Ronald Nathan, Eric Olson, Sally Spencer, Gerald M. Stern, and James L. Titchener.

I sent a third draft, finally, to a number of colleagues who tried gallantly to rescue me from error and to help me understand more clearly what I was trying to do. Among them I should mention the names of Peter L. Berger, Gerald T. Burns, Cynthia Fuchs Epstein, R. W. B. Lewis, E. L. Quarantelli, Jonathan Rieder, and R. Stephen Warner. I have left one name out of that alphabetical listing because I want to make special note of his contributions to the study. Irving L. Janis reviewed the manuscript in each of its various stages and, in the process, taught me a great deal not only about the nature of human stress but about the value of academic colleagueship.

I owe a particular debt of gratitude to Gerald M. Stern, senior attorney in the Buffalo Creek legal action, for his understanding and support.

Those many authors who have shared a similar working relationship will know exactly what I mean when I acknowledge the wisdom and sensitivity of my editor, Alice Mayhew.

PART ONE

February 26, 1972

LOGAN COUNTY, West Virginia, lies on the western flank of the Appalachians. Most of its forty-five thousand inhabitants live in the watershed area of the Guyandotte River, spread along the edges of the river itself or wedged into the many coves and hollows that open on to it. Geologists call this region a "plateau" because once, when the surface of the earth was younger and the streams that trace through it like a network of veins had not yet done their work, the area formed an upland sloping away from the central crests of the Appalachians. With age, though, the plateau has become lined and wrinkled. The land is made up of sharp mountain ridges slicing high into the air and narrow creek bottoms in the spaces below, looking like creases in the folds of the earth. The slopes are covered with a thin growth of second-stand timber and a heavy mat of underbrush.

The ways of nature have done much to form the raw contours of this land, but men have made a contribution too. The warm greens of the surface world are now streaked with the blacks and grays and rusty reds of the underworld, for the debris from hundreds of mine operations spills down the slopes like ashes from long-dead fires and the walls of the hollows are slashed laterally with strip-mine benches, the oldest of them camouflaged by a layer of brush and the newest of them exposed like long gray scars.

Buffalo Creek is one of those mountain hollows, some seventeen miles in length. At the top of the hollow, where three small forks come together to form the creek itself, the valley floor varies in width from sixty to one hundred yards, barely enough room to accommodate the creek bed, the road, the rail line, and a row or two of houses crouched in the shadow of the slopes. As Buffalo Creek curls its way toward the Guyandotte, however, the flood plain broadens to a width of two hundred yards or more. Some five thousand persons lived on this narrow strip of land in the winter of 1972, stretched along the creek bed in what amounted to a continuous string of villages. The official state map gives names to sixteen of those villages and marks their location along the creek with crisp dots— Kistler, Crown, Accoville, Braeholm, Fanco, Becco, Amherstdale, Robinette, Latrobe, Crites, Stowe, Lundale, Craneco, Lorado, Pardee, and Three Forks or Saunders. But the people of the creek visualize their community as an almost unbroken line of settlement, with heavier clusters of houses here and there and an occasional church or store or post office to mark the center of recognizable towns.

Almost everyone on Buffalo Creek depends for a living on the mining of coal. More than a thousand men are employed in the mines themselves, and virtually everyone else in the hollow either lives off those wages, provides support services of one kind or another, or draws pensions as the result of disability, retirement, or death. The men work in underground mines cut into the mountains above the creek, and now that a certain prosperity has reached the coal fields they can earn wages of thirty or forty or even fifty dollars a shift—a far cry from the days, not so long ago, when men might work for twelve hours in the dim recesses of the ground for two or three dollars' worth of scrip.

Most of the houses on Buffalo Creek were built by the coal companies in the second and third decade of this century, be-

ginning in 1912 when the first spur line was laid up the hollow
by the Chesapeake and Ohio Railway. They were hammered
together with efficiency and speed, each a duplicate of its neighbor and each as spare as the circumstances permitted. As was
generally the case throughout the coal fields, these frame cabins
were rented out to incoming miners for a decade or more, and
then, when they had earned back their original cost at least
once, they were sold off to the people living in them for a clear
profit. Houses like these can be found all over the coal fields.
Most of them disintegrate into weathered shacks as the boards
begin to splinter and the roofs sag and the floors warp and
sink on their concrete-block pillars; but some of them are converted into handsome homes as owners invest time and money
and pride into the job of putting siding on the outside and
paneling on the inside, of shoring up the foundations from
underneath and fastening a serviceable roof on top, of adding
rooms and installing plumbing and replacing floors and putting
in new wiring—making change after change, in short, until a
wholly new structure has been built around the shell of the old.

A large number of houses had been renovated in this manner on Buffalo Creek. The percentage of home ownership is
difficult to establish reliably, but it compared favorably with
far more prosperous areas in other parts of the country and
was a source of continuing satisfaction to the people of the
hollow.

Buffalo Creek changed measurably over the years. Coal
booms came and went and the population fluctuated accord-
ingly, but the grim trend underlying all those momentary shifts
is that mechanization of the coal industry has cut deeply into
the character of the region. Old residents estimate that the
population of Buffalo Creek was once two or even three times
larger than was the case in 1972. Many of the people who left
the hollow to find employment in other parts of the country
were transient to begin with; they had moved in during good
times and were ready to leave when the tides of the market
shifted elsewhere. Among those who departed, however, were
a fair number of lifelong residents and an even more substan-

tial number of young persons who had grown up in the area. Some left because they were reluctant to follow their fathers into the mines (or to marry men who did); others left because opportunities for employment were shrinking with every new piece of machinery brought into the valley. As a result, the people of Buffalo Creek have both lost and gained.

When their children moved away, the people who stayed lost some of the sense of family continuity that meant so much to them. At the same time, though, they took advantage of their gradually thinning ranks to transform the grimy old coal camps into comfortable new neighborhoods. As properties became vacant here and there along the creek, they were bought up by people who remained, the houses torn down "for the wood that was good in them" and the cleared lots used for yards and gardens and a general sense of space.

So the residents of Buffalo Creek were fairly well off in the early days of 1972. Most of the men were employed and earning good wages, and if the hollow did not quite reach the national mean on the conventional indices of wealth, the people nonetheless owned their own houses, paid modest taxes, enjoyed a certain measure of security, and were generally satisfied with their lot. They had survived the crisis of automation and were even beginning to profit from it, and to that extent, at least, they were one of the most affluent groups in an otherwise impoverished region. Most of them had worked their way out of the hardships their parents had known in the old coal camps and the poverty their grandparents had known in the remote mountains of Appalachia. Looking back, the men and women of Buffalo Creek remember it as a secure, honest, comfortable life.

But all of this came to an abrupt end on February 26, 1972.

Buffalo Creek is formed by three narrow forks meeting at the top of the hollow, each contributing a thin trickle of drainage to the larger flow. The middle of these forks, reasonably enough, is called Middle Fork, and it has served for several years as the site of an enormous pile of mine waste, known by the local residents as a "dam" because it looks and acts like one, but known by spokesmen of the coal company as an "impoundment" because they have very sound reasons for being embarrassed by the former designation. Whatever its title, the mound of refuse in Middle Fork was there because it solved two important disposal problems for the company.

The first problem is that every time one digs four tons of coal out of the ground, one also digs up a ton or so of "slag," or "gob"—a heavy mixture of mine dust, shale, clay, low-quality coal, and a vast assortment of other impurities. The coal companies of Appalachia have traditionally disposed of these wastes by depositing them wherever the law of gravity and the logic of convenience might suggest, spilling them down the sides of the mountains, piling them at the foot of the slopes, or hauling them away by truck or aerial tram and dumping them into the nearest hollow. The slag itself is as black as the coal from which it is separated. When dry, it is crumbly and crisp like cinders; when wet, it is viscous and slushy, looking like an oily batter of mud. Wet or dry, it contains all manner of combustible materials and may smolder quietly for years on end or even explode in a moment of chemical irritation.

Middle Fork was full of slag. The Buffalo Mining Company, owned by the Pittston Corporation, had begun to deposit its wastes there as early as 1957, and by the winter of 1972 it was dumping about one thousand tons every day, the refuse from five underground mines, two auger mines, and one strip mine. Slag simply clogged up Middle Fork, forming a steaming bank of waste more than two hundred feet deep at the mouth of the fork, averaging six hundred feet in width, and reaching some fifteen hundred feet upstream.[1]

The second disposal problem involves the huge quantities of water it takes to prepare a ton of coal for shipment. The Buffalo Mining Company used more than a half million gallons of water a day to clean the four thousand tons of coal it loaded onto railroad cars, and this water, when it had done its work, was black with coal dust and thick with solids. In the old days, the companies solved their disposal problem by pouring this mess into nearby streams, but by the 1960's the coal operators were under a good deal of pressure to retain this water until at least some of the impurities had settled out of it. The companies were beginning to see the virtues of having a regular supply of water on hand anyway, so they responded to these pressures by dumping new refuse on top of the old in such a way as to form barriers behind which the black water could be stored and reused. In theory, at any rate, the water held behind these rough impoundments would gradually become clarified as the solids drifted to the bottom, and the water that managed to seep through those thick walls of slag would be filtered a good deal cleaner in the process.

The first impoundment built by the Buffalo Mining Company was begun in 1960, just a few feet up from the mouth of Middle Fork. It was a modest structure, no more than twenty feet high, and it soon proved inadequate. In 1966, then, another impoundment was formed six hundred feet farther upstream. This structure, too, was scarcely twenty feet high, and by 1968 a third impoundment was under way still another six hundred feet upstream. This new effort soon towered above its predecessors. It was constructed (if that is the word) by the simple procedure of dumping tons of new mine wastes into the back of the settling pond formed by the impoundment below and grading it from time to time with a bulldozer. The only compaction the structure ever experienced was the weight of the bulldozers and the dump trucks that passed across its surface. The dam, then, such as it was, rested on a spongy base of silt and sludge, the deposits from the reservoir of water held by the impoundment below, and it was composed not only of slag but whatever fragments of metal or timber—mine posts, crib blocks, roof bolts, wedges—that had been thrown aside into the refuse pile. At the time of the disaster, the barrier varied from forty-five to sixty feet high as it stretched across the hollow. It was fashioned from nearly a million tons of waste, graded into a huge flat tier 465 feet from side to side and 480 feet from front to back, and it trapped 132 million gallons of black water—a lake some twenty acres in size and forty feet deep at the edge of the impoundment.

And it was still growing in size. Middle Fork had become an immense black trough of slag and silt and water, a steaming sink of waste rearranged in such a way as to create small reservoirs behind the first two impoundments and a gigantic lake behind the third—sitting there, as Harry Caudill put it, "like a pool of gravy in a mound of mashed potato." [2] Each year, 200,000 tons of additional refuse were being dumped onto the impoundment, and each year another 100,000 tons of silt were settling at the bottom of the lake.

The days preceding February 26 were wet days. It was the middle of winter and rain mixed with occasional flurries of snow was to be expected. According to experts, the volume of precipitation was altogether normal for the season, but company officials in charge of the dam were uneasy because the lake of water seemed to be rising dangerously close to the crest. During the night of the twenty-fifth, officials inspected the structure every hour or two, measuring the level of the water by means of a notched stick placed at the edge of the dam, and rumors began to circulate throughout the length of Buffalo Creek that something was very amiss. Residents of the upper half of the hollow, long apprehensive about the mountain of slag looming above their homes, began to move to higher ground. Toward dawn, company officials were concerned enough to order a spillway cut across the surface of the barrier to drain off excess water and relieve some of the pressure. As the level of the water rose, however, and the level of anxiety with it, the company issued no warnings. Indeed, the senior official on the site dismissed two deputy sheriffs who had been called to the scene to aid evacuation in the event of trouble.

A few minutes before 8:00 A.M., an experienced heavy-equipment operator named Denny Gibson inspected the surface of the dam again and was alarmed to find not only that the water was very close to the crest, a fact he already knew, but that the structure itself had suddenly turned soft. "It was real soggy," he told an investigatory commission later, "it was just mush. . . . I had a funny feeling. I just wanted to get off of it." He wheeled his car around, tore down the dirt haul road to the valley floor, and rushed off to his family, honking his horn and yelling warnings at whatever passers-by he happened to encounter on his run home.[3]

At one minute before 8:00, the dam simply collapsed. There is little evidence that water came over the top of the dam, although that remains one of the obvious possibilities. It is a good deal more likely that the whole structure became saturated with moisture, dissolved into something resembling wet paste, and just slumped over on its foundation of silt and sludge. In any event, the entire lake of black water, all 132 million gallons of it, roared through the breach in a matter of seconds. It was already more than water, full of coal dust and other solids, and as it broke through the dam and landed on the banks of refuse below, it scraped up thousands of tons of other materials, the whole being fused into a liquid substance that one engineer simply called a "mud wave" and one witness described as "rolling lava." The wave set off a series of explosions as it drove a channel through the smoldering trough of slag, raising mushroom-shaped clouds high into the air and throwing great spatters of mud three hundred feet up to the haul road where a few men were returning from the mines. The rock and debris dislodged by those explosions were absorbed into the mass too. By now, there were something like a million tons of solid waste caught up in the flow.

All of this took only a minute or two, and then the wave shot out of Middle Fork and landed on the town of Saunders. It was not really a flood, not a straight thrust of water, but a churning maelstrom of liquid and mud and debris, curling around its own center and grinding its way relentlessly into Buffalo Creek. As the mass hit the valley floor with a sound that could be heard miles away, it destroyed a power line. The one surviving clock served by that line stopped abruptly at 8:01.

At about that time, a woman who lived in Amherstdale,

halfway down the hollow and out of earshot, looked out her window and thought the world seemed strangely quiet. "There was such a cold stillness. There was no words, no dogs, no nothing. It felt like you could reach out and slice the stillness." But nine miles upstream the carnage had already begun.

I was about a hundred and fifty feet above where the water came out. It was burning there, and when the water hit the fire, it shot right through the air about two hundred feet high, right through the air. There was a lot of dust and black smoke. And when we looked back down there [toward Saunders] and the water was down and the smoke had cleared up, we couldn't see nary a thing, not a living thing, nothing standing.

The wave demolished Saunders entirely. It did not crush the village into mounds of rubble, but carried everything away with it—houses, cars, trailers, a church whose white spire had pointed to the slag pile for years—and scraped the ground as cleanly as if a thousand bulldozers had been at work. At this point, the wall of mud and water was fifteen or twenty feet high when measured from the flood plain and thirty or forty feet high when measured from the creek bed. But it was erratic in its course, pausing for a moment to develop into a great frothing pyramid before plunging ahead toward a new cluster of homes, lashing up one side of the valley and then the other as it turned the corners like a bobsled in a chute, driving straight toward some helpless target only to change direction in a shower of black foam. The size of the wave, of course, changed a good deal as the mass churned its way toward the Guyandotte. It was a twenty-foot wall at Saunders; it was half that size by the time it reached such midway points as Amherstdale; it was hardly more than a conventional flood when it arrived at towns like Kistler, near the mouth of the creek. But this is to speak of averages, because the leading edge of the wave was renewed again and again as the mass became trapped momentarily behind a bridge clogged with the splintered remains of houses and telephone poles and sections of railroad track and then smashed through that barricade with new life and momentum. Moreover, the course of the water seemed a thing of almost uncanny whim. Clusters of homes on one side of the tracks were swept away altogether while clusters on the other side, lying at precisely the same elevation, were barely splashed.

This water, when it came down through here, it acted real funny. It would go this way on this side of the hill and take a house out, take one house out of all the rows, and then go back the other way. It would just go from one hillside to the other.

No wonder, then, that this writhing mass of water, driving houses before it and bouncing trucks on its crest "like beach balls," making a sound like thunder and belching smoke and sparks as it wrenched power lines apart—no wonder that people would remember it as a living creature.

I cannot explain that water as being water. It looked like a black ocean where the ground had opened up and it was coming in big waves and it was coming in a rolling position. If you had thrown a milk carton out in the river—that's the way the homes went out, like they were nothing. The water seemed like the demon itself. It came, destroyed, and left.

And another witness:

I can still see in my mind the houses floating on the water along with the cars and those gas tanks exploding in a big blast of fire. I'll never forget the loud awful sound of the big sub-station blowing up and shooting up in the air and crumbling down and over. Then the water hit another row of houses in that narrow valley and it started backing up Toney Fork. I felt as though the water was a thing alive and was coming after us to get us all. I still think of it as a live thing.

There are only a few eyewitness reports on the erratic behavior of the water as it passed through Saunders and upper

Pardee for the good reason that most of the people who survived it were not there to see it and most of the people who
saw it did not live to tell about it. One young but seasoned
miner who ignored warnings to evacuate and barely scrambled
up the side of the hill in time remembered:

*Well, there was one explosion, and that's when all the water
come, and then there was another big explosion and everything
come out, just like them houses wasn't nothing, just like bowl-
ing pins when you roll a ball against them.*

And his fourteen-year-old daughter, frightened and out of
breath, described the same scene.

*When we got up to the hill I saw all the camp just go, the
water took the whole camp. And I saw our house—it just
crushed up. And I saw the woman that lived down below us
in a trailer, I saw her trailer split right down the middle and
just fold back.*

As the edge of the flood turned the corner into Pardee,
armed now with the entire contents of the town of Saunders,
it had lost none of its original ferocity. One eighteen-year-old
man, the only survivor of a family of six, caught a brief glimpse
of the wave before it carried him off in the bed of a pickup
truck.

*I looked back and I saw, just around the corner of the barn
—nothing but water, that's all. It looked just like coal dirt. It
was real black. It was way above the creek banks, I'd say about
fifteen feet higher than the ground.*

And an older veteran of the mines, alone in his home when the
wave suddenly appeared a few feet upstream, could not remember anything that happened to him except that the water, as it
struck, "was just as high as my house."

Farther down the hollow, though, the flood was witnessed

by hundreds of people, some of whom were caught up in it and some of whom just managed to clamber up the nearby slopes and had to stand there helplessly as the torrent rushed by a few feet below them. Several miles below the site of the dam the water was still an awesome sight. It "towered high as telephone poles," said one witness, looking "like an ocean coming toward us." "To me it looked like it was tipping the sky," said another.

The view from the Lorado and Lundale area, about one-third of the way down the hollow: *

When I looked back, I saw the houses coming. They just looked like toy boats on the water, and they was abusting and hitting against each other and bringing the lines down there. But what scared me out of my mind was that debris up against the bridge going sky high. I went to screaming.

I jumped out of bed and I looked out the door and I couldn't believe it. It was a wall of water and debris. It looked like it was about twenty-five or thirty foot high coming running at us. And it was just black-looking. It was just rumbling and roaring and the houses was popping and snapping and they was breaking up.

I could see all the houses in Lorado just being kicked around like so many toys. I looked down at Lundale and it was completely gone, wiped out.

When I think about the flood, the first thing that hits my mind is the water. It just looked like a black mountain going down that hollow, and there was houses on top of it. A big tank blew up right on top of it, a gas tank from the trailers that was up there. It just blew completely. You could see fire in those houses and everything. There was a big transformer sitting

* Here, as throughout the report, each paragraph represents a different speaker.

down there close to where the old ball diamond used to be, and it just ripped out and crumbled those big steel beams just like you was twisting them around. And the wires! Electricity was shooting up the mountain, those wires were going bzzz, bzzz. . . . One mass of ugliness was all it was to me, the water and houses and the gas exploding and the electricity lines buzzing and things like that. Crashing sounds. Everything was completely out of control, and the sound of it, you know, was just a roar, a heavy roar.

The view from Braeholm, about two-thirds of the way down the hollow:

I could see Amherst Camp up there at the crossing right above me. It looked like the whole town just raised up and started moving down the hollow, just like it was sitting. I seen the first house hit the bridge, then the second, then the third and fourth. And then a mobile home hit those houses where they had done jammed up against the bridge, and I guess the pressure and the impact was rolling under and that mobile home just vanished underneath. I never did see no more of it. There were three women in it. They were standing in a big picture window and their mouths were moving. I gathered they were hollering.

When I looked back, our house had picked up, went over and hit the neighbor's house, and then it came out of there flying. It came down past two houses and then the other houses picked up and followed it. It set down at the railroad trestle. Two more houses came in against it and splinters went everywhere. We had nothing left.

Suddenly I looked up to the bend in the creek. A railroad bridge crossed the creek there, and at the instant I focused my eyes on the bridge I could see the boards were piling up against it and shooting up in the air, as if they were exploding. I began to run home as hard as my body would allow, screaming for my wife to get the children on the hill to safety.

I don't remember getting out of the building, but I remember getting to a tree. I remember hollering for somebody to help me, throw me a rope. They couldn't throw me a rope because they were too far away and they had no rope anyway. There were trailers and cars and logs and ties and everything coming at me. I was knocked down several times, knocked under the water several times by logs and everything. A trailer was coming at me. That's what I was scared of most, afraid it was going to turn over on me. Beyond the tree was where the roughest water was. It was boiling and the waves were bigger than this table, just over and over and over, and I couldn't get across that. No one was going to help me and the water kept rising and I couldn't hardly hold on to that tree. There was so much debris there I seen no way to keep holding on to it, and the force of the water was pretty strong.

And, finally, the view from Kistler, near the mouth of the hollow:

We watched some houses down below there. I seen one house— It was kind of funny. The water hit it and it looked like it went down a little bit and it just— Have you ever pushed a rubber ball down in the water and turned it loose? It'll jump up out of the water. When that house moved, it jumped plumb up like that, like a rubber ball, and down the creek it went.

Well, after I had gotten up on the hill, the water had already covered most of the entire area. But shortly thereafter, where I was standing, some of the houses looked as though they were lifted up. They looked like pieces of a puzzle moving, you know, a little ant farm. This one would float this way, that one that way. There was no wall of water where I lived. It was a gradual rise.

Middle Fork, looking downstream from the approximate site of
the dam

Saunders, West Virginia, February 27, 1972

Lorado, West Virginia, February 27, 1972

A mobile home carried downstream

Church on tracks, Lundale

All photos courtesy of Southern West Virginia Regional Health Council

The front edge of the flood knifed out of Middle Fork around 8:00 A.M. and passed through the town of Man, where Buffalo Creek finally empties into the Guyandotte River, at 10:00. An hour later, the last of the water was gone. During its seventeen-mile plunge down the hollow, the flood had moved slowly, almost deliberately, but its awesome forces were turning and twisting and seething inside the advance wave so that it pulverized everything caught in its path. The mass had come out of Middle Fork armed with a million tons of solid wastes, but by the time it had passed through places like Saunders and Pardee it had added buildings and railroad ties and vehicles and every conceivable kind of projectile to its arsenal. The dark wave that landed on the villages below, then, was more like a battering ram than a current of water. The edge of the flood churned down the steeper grades of the upper valley at something like twelve miles an hour and then slowed to half that velocity as it reached the lower valley and fanned out over a wider and more even plain.

During those hours, most of the homes on Buffalo Creek had been touched in one way or another and a large number of them had been wholly destroyed. Four thousand of the area's five thousand inhabitants were homeless.

It is difficult to imagine what the hollow must have looked like in the days that followed. Photographs offer only a hint. The wreckage of hundreds of homes and other buildings was strewn all over the landscape, much of it splintered into unrecognizable mounds of debris, and the entire valley was coated with a thick layer of sludge. Trees that still stood despite the force of the flood had been stripped of their foliage and the very contours of the land had been reshaped. Miles of railroad track had been torn loose from the roadbed and were now twisted around trees or bent into coils like barbed wire. And scattered somewhere in all this litter were 125 bodies, hanging from tree limbs, pinned in wreckage, buried under piles of silt, or washed up limp on the banks of the creek. It took a long time to recover the bodies. To this day, seven have not been found at all, and three—young children of identical size—lie in anonymous graves because they were too badly battered to tell apart. The story is that they were headless.

When the last of the black water finally melted into the Guyandotte, an aching silence fell over the hollow. The survivors were huddled together all over the hillsides, numb with shock, afraid to move. "We were like a litter of puppies," said one, "wet and cold, with no place to go." No one could believe that the worst was really over, and when rumors of a second dam rupture spread up and down the hollow, people accepted the news as if it were somehow inevitable. And as they waited, soft flakes of snow curled into the valley, as if to accentuate the blackness below and to mock their misery.

But soon people began to drift around in slow dazed circles, looking for missing relatives, seeking shelter, picking through the damaged stores for food and blankets and shoes, and trying to comprehend the sheer enormity of what had happened. A man of seventy, himself spared the worst of the flood, tried to convey the futility of that afternoon: "Well, the day of the flood we just milled around to see what we could find. Just drifted around. Nobody knowed what to do or what they was looking for." And a girl of fifteen said afterward:

Everybody was wandering around and asking if you had seen so-and-so, and I never saw a time like it. People would just stop to go to the bathroom right beside the railroad because there wasn't anywhere to go, and dogs that had been washed down and weren't dead were running up to you and they were wet. We walked up to the bridge at Proctor [above Amherstdale] and a bulldozer was starting to clear the debris from the bridge there. The bulldozer picked a little girl up, and when he saw he had her on, he dropped her off because it cut her back and her back was still pink. Her face was tore up so bad they couldn't tell who it was. Then we saw a hand under her, sticking up through the debris.

Bit by bit, in whispers, people heard that a spouse or a child had been washed ashore some distance downstream or that a loved one feared dead was somehow alive and safe, although many of the living bore the marks of death. A combat veteran of Vietnam, having just heard that his wife's whole family had been washed away, was surprised to encounter his father-in-law on the edge of the hillside. "He was in a shape where I could not recognize him, you know. He had to speak before I could recognize the man. He had silt all over his body and he looked like he was half frozen to death, you know. He just looked like a walking piece of dirt."

In the lower part of the valley, where most of the houses were more or less intact, people came down off the hillsides to survey the damage and begin the exhausting job of restoring a little order to their lives. In the upper half of the valley, however, where the devastation had been almost complete, survivors had no choice but to remain on the hillsides, crowding around campfires or wandering disconsolately among the ruins. There were those who could scarcely recall what had happened to them or where they lived, those who muttered vaguely or stared off into the distance with vacant eyes, those who jumped to their feet and started off on desperate errands only to forget what the urgency had been. For the most part, though, it was quiet. As the morning turned to afternoon and the winter light faded early, most people did nothing at all.

There wasn't anything to do but just sit there. We looked out over that dark hollow down there and it just looked so lonesome. It just looked like it was God forsaken. Dark. That was the lonesomest, saddest place that anybody ever looked at.

Within hours a local National Guard unit had sealed off the Buffalo Creek area and begun the difficult job of opening up an access road. Mobile medical units from nearby hospitals moved into the hollow along with Civil Defense helicopters to evacuate the badly injured, while organizations like the Red

Cross and the Salvation Army brought in needed supplies and began to prepare the first of what would become 200,000 meals and several million cups of coffee. Local schools were converted into temporary refugee centers, and a makeshift morgue was created in one of them. Bodies wrapped in black plastic bags were brought in on the back of Army trucks and were laid out in rows on the floor so that survivors could file by and claim their own. A number of volunteers from the surrounding countryside found a way through the roadblock into the area, most of them intent on the job of rescue, but some of them—or so the story goes on Buffalo Creek—to root among the wreckage for whatever valuables could be salvaged.

By Sunday, the pace of activity had picked up considerably. Details of the disaster were now being broadcast to the rest of the nation, and the roadblock at Man was crowded with survivors who wanted to get out, newsmen and relatives who wanted to get in, and a constant traffic of rescue teams passing back and forth. President Nixon was reached in Shanghai with brief reports of the disaster, and he responded with expressions of regret and a promise of Federal aid. The Office of Emergency Preparedness authorized $20 million for emergency relief and set up a field office to handle those funds, while the U.S. Army Corps of Engineers moved in with heavy equipment to clear away the mountains of debris. And, in the meantime, rescue teams continued the grim search for bodies, and public health nurses gave typhoid immunizations to everyone in sight.

Organized activity, however, was largely provided by outsiders. Most of the people of Buffalo Creek were still numbed by the savagery of the disaster, still trying to make sense of their shattered world. The first visitors to the hollow, aside from rescue workers called to the scene, were relatives who, made frantic by the early news broadcasts, hurried home to see for themselves. The following account by a twenty-three-year-old native of Buffalo Creek who was visiting in Florida and whose parents and brother lived halfway up the hollow is typical.

Well, it was Saturday morning. I was watching television and we got a flash that a twenty-foot wall of water ripped through Buffalo Creek hollow. I tried to get in touch with my family but the lines were all busy. I tried calling the State Police, but I couldn't get ahold of them. I tried the Red Cross and they did not know any details of it. I kept trying until about twelve or one o'clock. I finally got in touch with the State Police, you know, and I asked exactly where the flood hit. He told me everything in Buffalo Creek was either gone or destroyed. So I went home and packed a couple of shirts and pants and stuff and started coming home, hitchhiking. I arrived on Sunday morning, I don't remember exactly when, and I went over to the high school first. That's where all the people were at. I asked a couple of friends if they'd seen my parents, and they said no. I went over to the hospital and talked to some of the people over there where my mother used to work in the kitchen, and the lady over there thought my mother was in the morgue and my brother and dad were missing. I asked the lady where the morgue would be at and she told me in an old warehouse up there at Proctor. Then I started up Buffalo Creek, but they stopped me at Man and told me I could not go up the creek. I backtracked and went up the side of the mountain and went up the creek on my own. As I was going up through there I realized how bad it was then because I seen people taking bodies out of the creek and laying them beside the road. Right below where I live I seen a friend's house and they had three bodies in front of it. I went on up and finally got to the warehouse in Proctor and started in there and seen all them people there and I couldn't believe it. I turned back and went home to be sure, because I didn't want to go in there half messed up. I didn't really want to go in there and see what I thought I was going to see, I guess. I seen a neighbor of mine and asked him if he'd seen my mother and dad and asked him if they got out of the water. He said he seen them that morning and he said he was pretty sure they got out. So I just sat down and let it all out, you know. I started crying and stuff like that. After about an hour, just setting there, I met them in front of our house as they were coming up from Accoville. . . . We was walking around like everybody else, you know, looking for friends. We got to Amherstdale and they was just taking this young girl out of a bunch of debris. We seen her, and—well— we decided just to come back home. We went back home and went upstairs and stayed in our house. . . . The worst thing about the flood to me was walking across the mountain not knowing if I was going to find my mother in the morgue or find her home safe. And seeing that little girl being drug out of that pile of debris and her blond hair falling back on her shoulders. That's the two things I really think about. And when I dream, that's what I dream about.

Once the dead were lifted out of the wreckage and the injured were taken to hospitals, cleaning up became the big problem. In the upper half of the hollow this meant bulldozing the debris into great mounds so that it could be burned, while homes in precarious condition were marked with huge X's by the State Department of Health and were leveled by the Army Corps of Engineers. In the lower half of the hollow, however, where most of the houses were at least standing, cleaning up meant trying to dispose of an incredible mess.

The water was halfway up my curtains. Everything was full of mud and water. The mud was way up in the wardrobes, and the clothes, they wasn't no good. All the furniture was turned over except the sink and stove and stuff that was hooked up. My living-room floor had torn loose at the end and all my living-room furniture was hanging in the creek. Everything was wet and black. I went into the bathroom and stepped on a body at the door, so I just got out of there.

Well, there was mud all over the house, no place to sleep. There was mud in the beds, about a foot and a half of it on the floors. And I had all that garbage. It was up over the windows. In the yard I had poles and trees and those big railroad ties from where they had washed out at Becco—furniture, garbage cans, anything that would float in the water. They was all around the house and caught in the fence.

Both of the above speakers were middle-aged women, the first married to a disabled miner and the second widowed and alone. The carnage they were surveying those first hours after the flood would turn out to be their lonely burden.

Eventually, of course, the debris was cleared away from houses like these, the muck hauled away, the sewerage restored, the walls scrubbed clean, the yards stripped of rubbish so that grass might one day try to force its way through a drying crust of sludge. But a smell still hung in the air more than a year later and the warped boards continued to emit streaks of oily black mud from the deposits that had caked under the floors and between the walls.

When the initial rescue and cleanup operations had been completed, the valley was little more than a long black gash, devastated almost beyond recognition. But most of its inhabitants were still there. A few had left the creek for a time to seek shelter with relatives elsewhere; others were gathering what possessions they had left in order to move away permanently. But the majority found a precarious niche somewhere in the hollow itself and hung on—staying with friends, camping out in the school gymnasium, or trying to make the most of scarred and twisted homes. The most serious recovery problem, then, was finding adequate quarters for the many refugees, scattered as they were all over the territory they had once called home, and it was in response to this emergency that the most important outside agency of all moved into Buffalo Creek.

This was the U.S. Department of Housing and Urban Development. HUD went to work providing mobile homes for everyone without accommodations of their own, placing most of them on vacant lots in the general vicinity of Buffalo Creek and permitting them to be occupied rent-free for a year. The idea itself was sound in principle and the agency did a remarkable job of administering it. Within a short span of time HUD had established thirteen trailer camps, supplied almost seven hundred mobile homes, and found shelter for close to twenty-five hundred persons, half the original population of Buffalo Creek. Yet the long-range costs of this program turned out to be a good deal higher than anyone had anticipated. HUD assigned applicants to vacant spaces on a first-come, first-served basis, the theory being that people should be moved under a secure roof as soon as possible. The net result of this procedure, however, was to take a community of people who were already scattered all over the hollow, already torn out of familiar neighborhoods, and make that condition virtually permanent. Most of the survivors found themselves living among relative strangers a good distance from their original homes, and although they continued to be within commuting range of old friends and churches and stores, they felt alien and alone. In effect, then, the camps served to stabilize one of the worst forms of disorganization resulting from the disaster by catching people in a moment of extreme dislocation and freezing them there in a kind of holding pattern.

There were other complications, too, and we'll come to them later. But for more than two years, Buffalo Creek lay in a kind of suspension, unable to forget the dark torments of the past and unable to plan a brighter future. "You know what it's like?" said one survivor. "It's like you were watching the best movie ever made and it stops for a commercial or something like that. And the commercial just goes on and on and on . . ."

So most of the survivors remained on or near Buffalo Creek. But they were a very long way from home.

The purpose of this report is to try to convey what the Buffalo Creek flood meant to the people who lived through it and how it touched the course of their lives. Stories like the ones related in the last few pages, though, are but moments in a longer reach of time. They have no meaning, reflect no moral, until they are placed in a wider context.

In many respects, of course, the Buffalo Creek disaster was like all catastrophes of a similar magnitude. It was responsible for a great deal of human suffering and it left ugly scars, not only on the landscape, but on the minds of everyone who experienced it. Most studies of disaster in the social science literature focus on those elements in the scene of devastation that can be reasonably assumed to be common to human experience in general, and we will deal with some of those elements in Part Three.

But every disaster is also a unique private tragedy, inflicting its own special wounds, its own peculiar species of pain; and in order to understand fully what an event like this means to the people who survived it, one needs to know something about who they were and where they came from, how they organized their lives and what they asked of the future. In this case, we need to locate the people of Buffalo Creek in the larger sweep of history and on the wider social and cultural map, and that process begins with a look at Appalachia.

These are the matters to be dealt with in Part Two.

PART TWO

Notes on Appalachia

LEGEND HAS IT that the first settlers to make their way into the far reaches of Southern Appalachia were a special breed of men and women, raw in manner, nonconformist in religion, adventurous in spirit, independent in temperament. It is hard to know how much credit this legend deserves, but a sound case can be made for it.

Most of the pioneers who moved westward from the eastern seaboard as the eighteenth century drew to a close found a way around the mountains of what is now West Virginia, circling north across the more gradual passes of Pennsylvania or circling south through the Cumberland Gap into Kentucky and Tennessee. The main flow of migrants, then, continued westward, and only a few seemed to have turned back into the mountains they had just by-passed. This means that the far slopes of the Appalachians were largely settled from the west —by people who drifted down the Ohio River after passing through Pittsburgh and then turned eastward into the mountains or by people who looped north after crossing into Kentucky. They moved into the mountains along strange and angular paths, following the course of the larger rivers, then branching east along accessible creek bottoms, and finally working their way into the thousands of narrow coves and hollows formed by tributaries. Some of these people, presumably, found themselves more or less marooned on their way west, the victims of illness, fatigue, despair, or one too many broken axles. But the formidable mountains of Appalachia, for all their vastness and isolation, may have been immensely attractive to certain kinds of migrant, and it makes sense to suppose that they were a somewhat select sample of their fellow homesteaders.

A visiting French botanist, traveling down the Ohio River in 1802, described the territory along the left bank—then figured to be a part of Virginia—as "excessively mountainous, covered with forests, and almost uninhabited,"[1] but for the next three decades or so traffic into the region continued at a steady if slow pace. By 1830 it had slowed to a trickle; by 1850 it had come to an almost complete stop. And from that moment until recent times the original stock of settlers lived virtually alone in the remote hollows of Appalachia, untouched by the currents of change reaching across the rest of the country. There was movement in the mountains, to be sure, but it was created almost entirely by a re-sorting of the original population. The soil of the region proved thinner and more obdurate than the first settlers had supposed, so many of them had to strike out for other holdings when time and erosion had dimmed their hopes; and what the land lacked in fertility, the people made up in double measure. The result was that surplus children and settlers whose land had become barren were forced to press deeper and deeper into the mountains, wedging their way into ever narrower and more remote hollows, planting their crops and building their log cabins ever farther up the sides of the steep slopes. Hardly a hint of the outside reached into that vastness, however, and the rest of the world barely knew of its existence. Edgar Allan Poe spoke vaguely in 1845 about lands in the western part of Virginia "tenanted by fierce and uncouth races of men,"[2] but for the most part, the people of Appalachia were lost in an envelope of silence.

The land these settlers came to could be harsh and ruthless, but it was covered with timber, lively with game, and it had good enough pasturage for raising such livestock as hogs and good enough soil for raising such staples as corn and potatoes. Food could be hunted in the form of bears, deer, turkeys, raccoons, and squirrels, and it could be picked off the land in the form of berries or nuts or roots or honey. Life had its crude edges as measured by the more genteel standards of the seaboard, but a reasonably comfortable existence was possible in almost perfect freedom. An ax was the only tool necessary for fashioning a passable dwelling; a rifle or trap or barbed hook was the only implement necessary for getting dinner on the table; and a wooden plow, pulled by man or wife if no mule was available, constituted a full complement of farm machinery. The environment required almost nothing in the way of planning or innovation, almost nothing in the way of personal or social change. And so a cultural style came into being on this frontier that remained largely intact for the better part of a hundred and thirty years. There was no encouragement for change from within, since old habits and old traditions seemed wholly adequate for the simple realities of everyday life, and there was no encouragement for change from without, since new ideas and new people rarely penetrated that fastness.

It was fashionable in the early decades of the twentieth century, when Appalachia was more or less reintroduced into the nation's consciousness, to describe mountain folk as a living relic of the past, a people whose ways and outlooks on life had been preserved from the late eighteenth century as purely as if they had been sealed away in a time vacuum. According to this notion, travelers from the twentieth-century world should be able to walk into the hollows of Kentucky or West Virginia and come face to face with their own ancestors, hearing the accents of eighteenth-century speech, following the logic of eighteenth-century thought, observing the manners of eighteenth-century society. A remarkable traveler named Ellen C. Semple toured the highlands of Appalachia around the turn of the century and wrote an account of her observations in an English periodical. Of Appalachia, she said:

we find a large area where the people are still living the frontier life of the backwoods, where the civilization is that of Shakespeare's time, where the large majority of the inhabitants have never seen a steamboat or a railroad, where money is as scarce as in colonial days, and all trade is barter . . . an anachronism all the more marked because found in the heart of the bustling, money-making, novelty-loving United States.[3]

And Horace Kephart, who knew the mountains well, wrote in much the same vein a decade later:

Conceive a shipload of emigrants cast away on some unknown island, far from the regular track of vessels, and left there for five or six generations, unaided and untroubled by the growth of civilization. Among the descendants of such a company we would expect to find customs and ideas unaltered from the time of their forefathers. And that is just what we do find to-day among our castaways in the sea of mountains. Time has lingered in Appalachia. The mountain folk still live in the eighteenth century. . . . Almost everywhere in the backwoods of Appalachia we have with us to-day, in flesh and blood, the Indian-fighter of our colonial border—aye, back of him, the half-wild clansman of elder Britain—adapted to other conditions, but still virtually the same in character, in ideas, in attitude toward the outer world. Here, in great part, is spoken to-day the language of Piers the Ploughman, a speech long dead elsewhere, save as fragments survive in some dialects of rural England.[4]

This was a romantic notion at best and probably owed something to theories of cultural evolution which were then much in vogue, but there is a good deal to be said for it all the same. The games played by Appalachian children and the songs sung by their parents can be traced back to parts of the world where they have long since been forgotten, and there are expressions in mountain speech that sound virtually Elizabethan to the modern ear. Even in contemporary Buffalo Creek, surely one of the least remote parts of Appalachia, one can still pick out phrases that ring of Shakespeare, Spenser, or even Chaucer:

Our young'uns are all at home.

I don't like to be beholden to no man.

It come abusting against the bridge.

When it will happen, I know not.

There was a heap of people there.

He's mighty afeared.

I just sit there and study on it.

For the men, at least, it was a hunting life rather than an agricultural one. They ate the flesh and dressed in the skins of the animals they killed, and, like hunters everywhere, they came to respect and learn from the ways of their prey. In many respects, hunting was more than a form of work. It was a recreation, a measure of manhood, a part of being; it was a way of becoming absorbed into the rhythms of nature. And it helped to sustain a certain element of savagery in what was often a slow and monotonous round of life.

For mountain days were punctuated by moments of truly extraordinary violence. To begin with, the mountaineer's reflexes had been tempered in a land where the turns of nature could be sudden and cruel and where the reactions of animals might call for a brutal quickness of hand. And then the first settlers had wrested the land from understandably resentful Indians and had done so with a ferocity and cunning learned from those Indians themselves. Indeed, the first volunteers from West Virginia to join Washington's army, then encamped in the more genteel precincts of tidewater Maryland, were equipped with tomahawks and scalping knives as well as muskets and powder, and they demonstrated soon enough that they were expert in the use of those weapons.

The men of the mountains have generally distinguished themselves when they went to war, earning high marks for courage if dismally low marks for discipline, and the nation has engaged in enough wars over the past two hundred years to keep large numbers of them occupied. But they have found other wars to fight as well.

The Civil War broke the silence of the region in a number of crucial ways. The Appalachians, of course, form a hard peninsula of rock reaching down into Georgia and Alabama—right through the center of Confederate territory—and to the apparent surprise of both Confederate and Union strategists, a large number of mountaineers in Tennessee and West Virginia and Kentucky remained loyal. As a result, the western Appalachians became a scene of constant skirmishes and armed encounters, some of them vaguely military in objective, but others the product of simple animosity and restlessness. The mountains became a refuge for deserters and vaguely attached troops from both armies who foraged for food, settled old grudges, and sometimes remembered their military status long enough to bushwhack one another and maraud the countryside for supplies and horses. Mounted men on the verge of defeat or discouragement raided homes and burned crops and killed so indiscriminately that they soon passed over that thin line between guerrilla activity and sheer outlawry; and in a land so sensitive to insult, those indignities grew in the telling until no one could remember that they owed their origins to war. Appalachia never served as a real theater of the Civil War, but the echoes of combat reached into the mountains with a vengeance, and in one sense, at least, those echoes were not stilled for another seventy years or more. Warfare almost became a way of life.

For one thing, many of the mountain feuds that flared across the region during the second half of the nineteenth century and the first decades of the twentieth—as cruel and vindictive as Corsican vendettas—began with ill feelings generated by the war. The contending clans were not trying to extend the Civil War in the political or military sense, as local histories sometimes suggest. Randall McCoy and Devil Anse Hatfield, patriarchs of the most celebrated feud of all, both fought in the Civil War but returned home without any discernible interest in the issues over which it had been fought. Yet the mountains were dark with distrust. The sight of a charred barn, the memory of an ambush, the sound of an old challenge—these hung in the air like unanswered insults and had to be responded to in one way or another. Hundreds, perhaps thousands, of people lost their lives in the decades that followed.

Moreover, the Government that had profited so well from the loyalty of most of the mountaineers rewarded them after the war by imposing excise taxes on whiskey, and this innocent device for raising revenue—a Federal habit of long standing—touched Appalachian nerves to the core. Mountain people have always resented taxes on whiskey, partly because they do not like to be told what to do by any government, but mainly because whiskey plays a special part in the mountain economy. The anger that followed the Government's announcement of its intention to tax whiskey almost had the character of an armed insurrection—a sullen, sustained guerrilla resistance—and this continued in an intermittent way well into the twentieth century.

And, finally, the fierce struggles connected to the unionization of the coal mines in the first three decades of the twentieth century drew on all those years of experience. We are ahead of our story here, but the pitched battles fought in Kentucky and West Virginia between huge bands of armed men had all the ingredients of warfare.

But the sounds of violence did not end with these sporadic outbreaks of something very akin to war, for throughout the history of the region a savage brand of fighting characterized those moments when men were drawn together, especially if the occasion involved politics or called for drink. Knives and pistols were in common use, and hand-to-hand combat, sometimes staged like a medieval joust, might feature such gallantries as chewing off an opponent's ear or gouging out his eye with a sharp stab of the thumb. The visiting botanist quoted a few pages ago was extremely impressed by the manners of the mountain men he met on his travels: "With them," he wrote somewhat testily, "the passion for gaming and spiritous liquors is carried to an excess, which frequently terminates in quarrels degrading to human nature." [5] Now our botanist was a Frenchman, a true son of the Enlightenment, and he shared the strong views of his contemporaries as to what human nature consisted of; but the frontiersmen he was describing were equally sure that brawling in public places was as natural an activity as one could imagine. One hardy old mountain man, born about the time the above was written in 1802, remembered those more energetic days of his youth with a certain nostalgia.

> We always held an election on the first Monday in October; when would be seen a goodly array of hunting-shirts and moccasins, and almost every man with a big knife in his belt. A foreigner would have supposed that the voters were really some military party going to oppose a threatened invasion; and if a quarrel occurred, they would take off perhaps both coat and shirt, and fight until one or the other acknowledged that he had as much of a beating as he was willing to receive. Then their friends, if they did not get into a scrape among themselves, would take the combatants to the nearest water and wash off the blood.[6]

So moments of violence were frequent, but they served to accent the flow of everyday life rather than to provide its main theme. Mountain days were slow and uneventful, especially in the winter, and during those long silences, the members of a family would be virtually alone. An old storyteller from the Blue Ridge country begins one of his tales:

> *Away up under a mountain top*
> *Where the ravens wheel and the low clouds drop*
> *Lived Charlie Silvers and Frankie, his wife,*
> *A lonesome, hungry sort of life.*[7]

And in those lonesome, hungry stretches of time, the family came to assume an importance unlike anything known in less isolated parts of the land. For all practical purposes, the family was a community unto itself: it was an industry, a school, a church, a hospital. It was the only real shelter a person had. The bonds that were fashioned in this enclave were very close, and legends coming out of the mountains emphasizing the fierce loyalty of people not only to their immediate family but to the wider tracings of kin are not at all exaggerated. The clanlike society of the mountains may owe something to the Scottish Highlands and to the tribal organization of ancient Britain, but it was perfectly adapted to local conditions. In a country with no public institutions, no townships, no systems of social control, few stable congregations, and no other associations of any kind, membership in a family unit was the only source of identification and support one had.

The bonds of family were close, then, and we shall have occasion to hear more about that later. But those bonds were of a rather special cast. The family did not operate like an assembly of separate individuals, each of whom was expected to develop a personal bond of intimacy with each of the others. It was a generalized entity, a living tissue, from which every member drew some measure of warmth and to which every member offered some measure of allegiance. Brothers need not be close in the sense of knowing one another well as individuals or responding to one another's personal qualities; they were attached, bonded together, by a tie that often seemed almost impersonal. And the same was true of married couples. Visitors to the area have expressed surprise at the degree to which individuals will cherish, protect, nurture, and make particular allowances for their mates without appearing to know them very well as distinct personalities. Part of this is the celebrated individualism of the mountains: people will not presume to speak for anyone else, not even a husband or a wife. But part of it stems from a real indifference to the interior furnishings of another's mind, as if one's tastes and attitudes belong in a sphere of privacy to which no one else has access.

The report will have more to say on all this later. For the moment it is only important to point out that the mountaineers were so absorbed in the tissues of family life, so thoroughly a part of them, that they felt greatly diminished as persons when they were separated from them. More than that, they felt adrift, vacant, without a secure enough sense of their surroundings to know quite who they were.

A word should be said about mountain religion. So far as historians can determine, the people who ventured into the mountains came from a great variety of religious traditions, although broad designations like Scots Presbyterians and English Independents would account for a majority of them. Most of the settlers could have traced their spiritual ancestry back to dissenting strains of Christian thought, had they cared about such matters, and learned that their forebears went by such names as Lollard, Puritan, Separatist, Anabaptist, Antinomian, and a whole catalogue of other nonconformities. The settlers themselves did not use these terms or even know what they meant. They only knew that they were Protestants of a somewhat independent stamp and that the organized churches of Christendom often thought of them as vaguely anticlerical, suspicious of ecclesiastical authority, and too individualistic in spiritual judgments to fit the grain of any orthodoxy. It was a matter of policy in colonial Virginia to allow a greater margin of religious dissent in the back country than on the seaboard, a policy designed to promote the settlement of the western regions while encouraging the departure of dissenting elements from the Anglican communities of Virginia. So it is likely that a certain independence of thought and expression accompanied the first pioneers into the mountains, and those tendencies, no matter what their original form, were profoundly reinforced by the conditions of life prevailing there. Mountain life is the natural enemy of formalism anyway. It is a world of sharp and impending realities. It helps breed a social order without philosophy or art or even the rudest form of letters. It brings out whatever capacity for superstition and credulity a people come endowed with, and it encourages an almost reckless individualism. Yet it exacts a price for those freedoms in the form of loneliness, anxiety, and personal suffering. The mountains evoke an immediacy of experience, a resort to action as opposed to reflection, a respect for feeling and sensation; and the mountains also separate people into isolated hollows where they have little choice but to rely upon their own individual resources. It stands to reason, then, that the early homesteaders would become even more detached than they already were from old denominational connections and that their spiritual longings would become more personalized and internalized, more emotional and episodic.

Something like that, at any rate, appears to have been the general state of mind of the first arrivals, and no sooner had they become settled in their new households than the second Great Awakening reached Appalachia, confirming and giving substance to those uncertain inclinations. The new movement introduced a theology—a spiritual mood, really—entirely in keeping with the temper of mountain life. Its emphasis on revival and personal salvation was well suited to the frontiersman's self-centered individualism, and its emphasis on a haunting sense of sin was well suited to the darker sides of his nature. And so the second Great Awakening invigorated spiritual feelings at the very moment it helped erode the influence of the established denominations: it brought a deep piety to the mountains while undermining organized religion. The basic unit of worship was not a stable congregation, not a community of believers drawn together in fellowship, but an audience of individual souls called to hear a preacher at some kind of camp meeting. The basic expression of piety was not quiet prayer, but fevered revival. Our visiting botanist, to quote him one last time, must have been amazed when he came upon a backwoods camp meeting in 1802, just as the second Great Awakening was reaching its emotional height.

> The spirit of religion has acquired a fresh degree of strength within these seven or eight years among the country inhabitants, since, independent of Sundays, which are scrupulously observed, they assemble, during the summer, in the course of the week, to hear sermons. These meetings, which frequently consist of two or three thousand persons who come from all parts of the country, take place in the woods, and continue for several days. Each brings his provisions, and spends the night round a fire. The clergymen are very vehement in their discourses. Often in the midst of sermons the heads are lifted up, the imaginations exalted, and the inspired fall backwards, exclaiming "Glory! glory!" This species of infatuation happens chiefly among the women, who are carried out of the crowd, and put under a tree, where they lie a long time extended, heaving the most lamentable sighs. There have been instances of two or three hundred of the

congregation being thus affected during the performance of divine service; so that one-third of the hearers were engaged in recovering the rest.[8]

Because they best understood the nature of this piety, the Baptists and the Methodists made the greatest headway in Appalachia. They introduced a special breed of minister into the region, men qualified by the intensity of their passion rather than by the depth of their learning, who obtained their commission as the result of a divine call. They were often shrewd and energetic men, enormously gifted as orators, with an ability to use pitch and gesture as well as words to bring an audience to a high state of ecstasy. But they also tended to be harsh and illiterate; and instead of trying to bring a note of solace to the stern realities of mountain life, they talked about infant damnation, described the unrelenting tortures of hell, and did their best to inspire a distrust of Rome. A long-time friend of the mountaineers, picking his words with remarkable care, concluded in 1924: "Their religion, it is true, is not very dainty."[9]

It is no great secret that the austerity imposed by this kind of fundamentalism often creates a good deal of what outsiders tend to describe as hypocrisy and what insiders tend to experience as ambivalence. The voices of earnest preachers warned what might happen to those who drank or gambled or engaged in acts of fornication, and we may assume that quieter but no less earnest voices from within echoed the same grim alarms. But the mountaineer's convictions were episodic. What vigor there was in mountain life came from drinking and dancing and loving and making music—all of them the devil's work— and the tensions generated by this obvious asymmetry added to the anxieties of an already hard existence. People were born to suffer and to lapse into sin, to taste what joys life might offer and to repent having done so. A New England parson might be offended by the inconsistencies in all of this, but many a backwoods preacher, himself no stranger to hayloft or bottle, might find it easier to appreciate that the cycle of sin and cleansing, or backsliding and revival, of spiritual death and rebirth, is one of the natural rhythms of life. And if the constant tension sometimes produced a sadness close to melancholy and a guilt close to self-hatred—well, the ways of God were often mysterious. His judgments were awful and full of wrath, but maybe He knew His creatures well enough to understand their temptations and the overwhelming sorrow of much of their lives.

Religion in Appalachia, then, was strong in the sense that it induced a devout piety and a longing for spiritual grace, but weak in the sense that it did not result in the establishment of stable church congregations. For all the reverence expressed toward the Bible and all the fears held of the hereafter, the percentage of people who actually became members of the church in the formal sense was remarkably low—lower, in the estimate of Harry Caudill, "than in any other region of Christendom."[10]

As in religion, so in education. In many ways, mountain people were extremely fond of words. They told tall stories with exuberance, listened to political oratory as if it were an art form, were moved to their deepest moments of religious conviction by a barrage of spoken phrases, and created a gentle poetry in their songs that belied the fierceness of their reputation. Yet these mountaineers were one of the most illiterate people to be found in America. Whatever respect for books and learning the first settlers brought with them to Appalachia soon disintegrated in the mountain air, and formal education has remained low on the region's list of priorities until fairly recent times. For one thing, the knowledge necessary for survival in those parts was born of time and experience, and there was not a manual written in any language that contained as much practical lore or as many keen insights as were stored away in the mind of every man and woman around. Moreover, the fundamental Protestantism that took root in Appalachia did not attract attention to the kind of theological argument expressed in written form. It asked believers to consult the stirrings of their heart for answers to important questions about faith, and words—written words—were simply not an important part of that ethos. Indeed, they were to be suspected as dry abstractions, far removed from the world of feeling and action in which God intended His people to live.

There were practical reasons for the low estate of formal education in Appalachia, too. It takes money to establish a good school system and to keep it functioning properly, and there was never very much of that on hand. The people of the mountains did not know until too late what riches their land contained, and by the time the secret was out, they not only had failed to profit personally but had failed even to siphon off enough of the billions of dollars flowing by them out of the region to establish a fair tax base. What schools there were limped along with limited funds, inadequate staffs, and the sorriest of facilities; and this, combined with the noted reluctance of mountain folk to invest much faith in the value of book learning, spelled a gradual form of suffocation. Thus we come face-to-face with one of those cruel circularities that mark poverty everywhere: the obvious deficiency of educational programs in Appalachia, far from convincing people that more sustained efforts were necessary, instead convinced them that education does not actually confer the advantages claimed for it anyway. Nor can one argue that this is an unreasonable way to read the evidence, for experience has suggested again and again that the best education available in the mountains does not really change a person's prospects appreciably.

Everyday life in Appalachia, then, tended to repeat itself in slow cycles as one generation gave way to the next. People scratched a living from the narrow strips of land they occupied along the creek bottoms and up on the sides of the hills, growing Indian corn as their basic crop and keeping gardens near their homes which offered thin yields of cabbages, pumpkins, beans, tobacco, beets, and a sullen brand of potato that seemed to shrivel in the mountain soil. Livestock foraged for mast in the forests, and men hunted for venison, bear meat, and everything else soft enough to chew after a few hours of boiling. Most families kept stands of bees, housed in sections of hollow tree trunk, and the honey obtained from them, along with sorghum molasses, served as the main substitute for sugar.

It was a primitive life in every important respect and it required a remarkable degree of competence. There was little village organization, little community division of labor, few trades or professions, and this meant that every household had to provide a farmer, a carpenter, a blacksmith, an expert in preserving food, a mason, a weaver, a gunsmith, a spinner of wool, a barber, a dentist, a tinker, a cobbler, a tailor, and, when the end came, a maker of coffins. A mountaineer who lived along the eastern slopes of the Appalachians in the early nineteenth century remembered it well when he summed up his life in 1859.

> Mary was contented in her new home; and while I furnished meat and bread, she made us sweet butter as ever was eaten, and laid away enough for winter use. There were thousands of wild bees, and from each hive I discovered I got from two to ten gallons of honey. I could sell deer-skins at any time in the old settlement; for in those days many men, and almost all the boys, wore buckskin pants and hunting-shirts; which made skins bring a good price. In that way I bought flax and wool, and Mary carded it by hand, spun, wove, and made it into clothing. She done washing, knitting, house-work, milking and churning, besides keeping herself, her children, and myself cleanly and nicely dressed. This is the manner in which people lived in those days. . . . The early settlers, being but few in number, had a hard time to maintain themselves; and had they not used the greatest economy, they could not have lived in the wilderness at all. But they made all their own clothes. If a man wore a pair of boots, he was considered a gentleman.[11]

Housing in the mountains was provided by rude log cabins, fashioned by stacking huge trunks on one another, notching the ends, and then filling in the chinks with mud or clay. These were normally one-room affairs without windows, built small to conserve heat, and on any cold winter night those narrow precincts might provide shelter for a married couple, a normal mountain complement of ten or twelve children, an aging grandparent or two, and a scattering of dogs and chickens, all of them stretched out on the few available beds or making do with what remained of the dirt floor. There were no inns in that rough country, of course, so every cabin in the mountains served as a temporary hostel for whatever travelers ventured by, and they, too, were welcomed into that cramped space. The great Bishop Asbury, who included West Virginia in his vast ecclesiastical rounds in the late eighteenth and early nineteenth centuries, had many encounters with such accommodations.

> The house in which we live, at the springs, is not the most agreeable: the size of it is twenty feet by sixteen; and there are seven beds and sixteen persons therein, and some noisy children. So I dwell amongst briars and thorns; but my soul is in peace. . . .
>
> I lay on the floor on a few deer skins with the fleas. . . . O, how glad should I be of a plain, clean plank to lie on, as preferable to most of the beds; and where the beds are in a bad state, the floors are worse. . . . This country will require much work to make it tolerable. The people are, many of them, of the boldest cast of adventurers, and some of the decencies of civilized life are scarcely regarded. . . .
>
> The people, it must be confessed, are amongst the kindest souls in the world. But kindness will not make a crowded log cabin, twelve feet by ten, agreeable: without are cold and rain; and within, six adults, as many children, one of which is all motion; the dogs, too, must sometimes be admitted. On Saturday, I found that amongst other trials, I had taken the itch; and considering the filthy houses and filthy beds I have met with, it is perhaps strange that I have not caught it twenty times: I do not see that there is any security against it, but by sleeping in a brimstone shirt: —poor bishop! [12]

The narrow strips of land around those cabins were usually under cultivation, the gardens within the shadow of the cabins' very walls and the rows of corn not far away. The land itself had been cleared by the Indian method of girdling, killing the trees without felling them, and the sight so impressed William James on a tour of the mountains in the late nineteenth century that he included a stark description of it in one of his more important essays.

Some years ago, while journeying in the mountains of North Carolina, I passed by a large number of "coves," as they call them there, or heads of small valleys between the hills, which had been newly cleared and planted. The impression on my mind was one of unmitigated squalor. The settler had in every case cut down the more manageable trees, and left their charred stumps standing. The larger trees he had girdled and killed, in order that their foliage should not cast a shade. He had then built a log cabin, plastering its chinks with clay, and had set up a tall zigzag rail fence around the scene of his havoc, to keep the pigs and cattle out. Finally, he had irregularly planted the intervals between the stumps and trees with Indian corn, which grew among the chips; and there he dwelt with his wife and babes—an axe, a gun, a few utensils, and some pigs and chickens feeding in the woods, being the sum total of his possessions.

The forest had been destroyed; and what had "improved" it out of existence was hideous, a sort of ulcer, without a single element of artificial grace to make up for the loss of Nature's beauty. Ugly, indeed, seemed the life of the squatter, scudding, as the sailors say, under bare poles, beginning again away back where our first ancestors started, and by hardly a single item the better off for all the achievements of the intervening generations.[13]

James then goes on to make fun of his own first reaction, but the scene he describes produced similar feelings in many another traveler as well.

It was a hard life, and as time went on the mountaineers realized that nature held them in a tighter and tighter vise. The soil of Appalachia seemed to get thinner and more exhausted every year, each crop lowering the chances that the next would be sufficient for everyday needs, and the mountain people did not know enough about fertilization or prevention of erosion or crop rotation to protect their narrow holdings. In the meantime the growing population had to sort itself out on ever smaller parcels of bottom land or move off into more remote hollows where the land was too steep for proper care anyway. And to make matters even worse, the settlers had few opportunities to convert the natural riches covering their land into cash. Corn was the only crop that yielded a surplus, and it was too bulky to be carried down the uneven creeks or loaded onto pack animals for the trip to market; and by the time the scrawny cattle could be driven to river ports or to railroad stops—supposing they survived the journey at all—there was not enough meat left on them to supply a decent breakfast. So the settlers were left with few options. They might manage to float some logs downstream with a good deal of effort. They might scour the hillsides for ginseng or galax or bloodroot or wild ginger and find a willing buyer. Or they might convert their corn into the one product that could be transported to market profitably—whiskey. The mountaineers have received a very bad press on the subject of moonshine, and it goes without saying that a good deal of the local manufacture was consumed at home; but the fact remains that whiskey was sometimes the only cash commodity known in the mountains and an important part of the local economy.

The key to understanding modern Appalachia, however, does not lie in knowing who the original settlers were and what they did with their land, but in knowing what has happened to them since at the hands of outsiders. Whatever one knows about economic theory, wherever one stands on matters of political ideology, one still must conclude that the men and women of Appalachia are among the most truly exploited people to be found anywhere. In the beginning, they had rights to good land. It was covered with timber; rich seams of coal ran under its crust. It had soil fertile enough for the modest uses to which it was put and its forests were alive with fish and game. In the course of a few decades, however, dating from the last years of the nineteenth century, almost all of those valuable resources were cut or scraped or gouged away; and when the land lay bruised and exhausted from the punishment it had received, the people of the region had virtually nothing to show for it.

There had been minor raids on the mountains before, with salt, furs, feldspar, and other minerals as their object. But the first major assault on the riches of Appalachia took the form of a search for lumber. At one time, the mountain slopes had been covered by magnificent stands of timber—oak, walnut, poplar, beech, sycamore, maple, birch, and, above all, red spruce. The size of some of those giants would be hard to believe were it not for the evidence of old photographs. George Washington came across a huge sycamore on the banks of the Kanawha River measuring forty-five feet in circumference in 1770, André Michaux found one measuring more than that in 1802, and similar reports have been heard from working loggers elsewhere in the region.[14] In the space of a few years, though, all of that was cut away. The first damage was done by the original settlers themselves, since they looked upon trees as an encumbrance and cleared away many thousands of acres, but the real devastation took place between 1875 and 1925 as a vast lumber boom spread across Appalachia. At the height of the boom, in 1909, there were something like fifteen hundred lumbering operations and hundreds of mills in West Virginia alone; and by the time the rush was over, 8.5 million acres of virgin forest had been depleted—more than 85 percent of the timbered areas of the state. And these figures only tell part of the story, because the work of the lumbermen left stark ruins everywhere that were vulnerable to fire, and several million acres more were converted to scorched pasture land as a result. It is hardly an exaggeration to say that the forest reserves of Appalachia have been totally demolished, leaving in their stead a rough stubble of old stumps and second-stand timber.[15]

The grand prize, however, was coal, and the rush for that black fuel went into high gear during the second and third decades of the new century. The inhabitants of Appalachia had sold mineral rights to the land on which they lived for as little as fifty cents an acre, and, for many, it was years before they discovered that the deeds they had signed gave coal operators the right not only to bore holes deep into the ground but to use the surrounding territory as suited their purposes. They could take whatever timber they needed to shore up underground passages, they could build roads and rail lines wherever convenient, they could pollute the streams or dam them up or divert them from their natural course, they could dump slate and other forms of refuse wherever gravity dictated, not excluding occupied lands, and when the operations were complete and the coal was extracted, they could withdraw the supports holding up the mine shafts and leave an empty, ravaged mountain behind, filled with black water and so hollowed out that the land itself was in danger of collapse. In short, they could rearrange the lives of the persons living on the surface in any way that turned out to be convenient, and they could do so without owning one square foot of the land itself and without paying one nickel of taxes on it.

The final indignity, although this takes us somewhat ahead of the story, came with strip mining. Seams of coal run at odd angles, some of them reaching deep into the recesses of the earth where they can be mined only by underground methods. and some of them running so near the surface that the only practical approach to them is to scrape away the earth's crust and reach in from above. Now it is a critical part of this picture that mineral rights to the land had been obtained years before with the clear understanding that mine operators would move to a likely site, dig a shaft, and reach into the core of the mountain with men and machinery to take away the coal. All of this had a devastating effect on the surface, of course, which few had foreseen; but the opening of the strip mines on a large scale was nothing other than an atrocity, an insult to the land itself and an insult to the people who had occupied it for a number of generations. It is still the case that mine operators do not need to own the land in order to dig out the minerals lying underneath it, even if their method of extraction is to peel away the surface of that land altogether. What this process does is to tear enormous gashes into the sides of the mountains, scatter mine wastes all over the landscape, destroy vegetation, ruin what is left of the topsoil, sour the streams, leave the land vulnerable to rock slides and flash floods, and strand animals deep in the highlands by carving impassable strip benches across the slopes like ancient dry moats.

The residents of Appalachia have never placed conservation high on their list of personal priorities, and a portion of what has happened to them must be charged to their own accounts. Overwhelmed by the abundance of their land, they depleted the soil and thinned out the game and were willing accomplices to the pillaging of their timber, although they had no way of knowing what the consequences would be and derived only the barest profits from these activities. But what happened to them at the hands of others was simply plunder, and one cannot talk reasonably about the people of Appalachia without realizing that this has been one of the dominating themes of their history. They have been exploited by powerful interests far away and by the men who represent those interests closer to home—bankers, lawyers, politicians, landlords, sheriffs, and all the courthouse retainers who for years on end have run the mountain counties for the benefit of local and national coal corporations. This has had a pronounced effect on the economy of the region, obviously, but it has also had a pronounced effect on the mind and morale of the people who endured it.

It is said that change came slowly to Appalachia, and in one sense, at least, that is so. The people of the mountains were slow to adjust to the currents of industrialization and urbanization spreading across the rest of the nation and slow to develop a way of life in keeping with the rhythms of the new age. When observers remark that Appalachia did not change, however, they really mean that it did not "develop" according to prevailing American standards. It changed a great deal, in fact; but the direction of that change was downward and its end product was depression in both the economic and spiritual sense. For all the apparent steadiness of mountain life, for all its archaic manners and traditional ways, there is a sense in which no part of the country was more deeply hurt or more decisively changed by what Americans chose to call "progress" in the last decades of the nineteenth century and the first decades of the twentieth.

In general, then, life in old Appalachia mirrored a large variety of strains. It was a life of monotony and quiet, interrupted from time to time by lively celebrations, emotional revivals, and almost extravagant acts of generosity and daring. It was a life of isolation and individual self-sufficiency, tempered by a remarkable kind of neighborly cooperation when the time came nigh to roll logs, raise houses, shuck corn, or perform the other tasks too demanding for a single family. It was a life of sorrow, yet it was borne with dignity and pride. And it was a life of mystery: like people everywhere who stay close to nature and are sensitive to its enigmas as well as its predictabilities, the mountaineers were capable of chilling superstition, sure that ghosts sometimes skulked in the mountain shadows and that witches could do a great deal of harm if left to their own devices. It was a life of warm hospitality and deep distrust, a life that forever asked people to choose between resigning themselves to the futility of it all or rising up to collar the devil himself.

It was, in sum, a life made for caricature, and whole generations of observers, from casual tourists to professional social scientists, have left their marks on the standard portrait of the mountaineer. Like all caricatures, the image these observers produced is probably too sharp and simple in contour to serve as a reasonable likeness, but it captures the most prominent features well enough to be recognizable, even if it ignores those parts of the visage that are indistinct, lost in subtle shading, hard to focus on.[16]

The most striking characteristic of the mountaineer, according to this portrait, was his sturdy sense of individualism. He brought with him to the mountains a keen independence of mind and a distrust of organized society. The hollows offered him a natural shelter from the jurisdiction of state and Federal law and placed him far beyond the reach of any formal church authority. So he became something of a law unto himself, jealous of his autonomy, quick to defend his territory, constrained by no one, dependent upon his own personal resources, and self-centered to a fault. "To be free, unbeholden, lord of himself and his surroundings—that is the wine of life to a mountaineer," said Horace Kephart.

Even though hunger be eating like a slow acid into his vitals, he still will preserve a high spirit, a proud independence, that accepts no favor unless it be offered in a neighborly way, as man to man. I have never seen a mountain beggar; never heard of one.

Charity, or anything that smells to him like charity, is declined with patrician dignity or open scorn.[17]

The mountaineer also had a profound streak of fatalism. Life in the hollows was no easy matter. The caprices of nature and of other men always seemed to erode his efforts to become established on a secure footing, and whatever hopes he had entertained in the beginning of shaping the wilderness to his will and creating a comfortable future began to fade. Over a period of time, the self-confidence that had accompanied his move to the frontier gave way to a form of resignation and passivity. He might lose his children to illness, his kinsmen to feuds, his land to strangers carrying barely comprehensible deeds, but he learned to yield to the logic of it all as if it were somehow inevitable. This is not to suggest that he always bore his burden stoically; he mourned his dead and lamented his bad fortune and was capable of the sharpest resentments, but he appeared to feel that fate was the principal author of his miseries and his constant partner throughout life.

This helps explain a third mountain trait—the otherworldliness that seemed to pervade so much of Appalachian culture. The mountaineer took it for granted that salvation was available to anyone who experienced a real conversion and that there would be divine compensation some day for earthly suffering. This was a promise made in the Bible and repeated over and over again by the many preachers who patrolled the mountains on mules, and the mountaineer took it to mean that the sorrows of this world are transitory, not entirely real, something, even, of a dream.

And he was bound to ancient traditions by an attachment that was "stubborn, sullen, and perverse," according to Horace Kephart.[18] He longed for the past with a nostalgia bordering on bitterness and found virtue in almost any idea or custom that could be demonstrated to have descended from an ancestor. The past for which he yearned never existed, and he knew this to be so in his more reflective moments, but his reverence for it did not seem to be diminished at all on that account. He was conservative in principle, suspicious of change, and vaguely convinced that adherence to old ways would somehow stabilize the uncertainties of the life around him.

The mountaineer was also a creature of action rather than contemplation. By nature a hunter rather than a farmer, he avoided routine whenever he could and had a good deal more faith in actions executed today than in plans due to mature tomorrow. In religious expression, too, he preferred vigorous demonstrations of faith to quieter forms of prayer, almost as if he hoped to reach the Almighty by the urgency of his passions rather than by the cogency of his appeals. He was oriented to movement, impulse, locomotion, and his general approach to problems was to obscure them in a blur of activity. When he "set to studying," then, which was not too often, his ideas were quickly converted into emotions, and his emotions, in turn, were converted into something very akin to bodily states. A sense of gratitude, a feeling of affection, would turn into a great inner swell requiring expression; a feeling of resentment would turn into a dark humor clouding the heart until it was discharged by some act of vengeance. Ellen C. Semple put the matter well.

> Men who, from the isolation of their environment, receive few impressions, are likely to retain these impressions in indelible outline; time neither modifies nor obliterates them. Thus it is with the Kentucky mountaineer. He never forgets either a slight or a kindness. He is a good lover and a good hater; his emotions are strong, his passions few but irresistible; because his feelings lack a variety of objects on which to expend themselves, they pour their full tide into one or two channels and cut these channels deep.[19]

For reasons not hard to imagine the mountaineer could be terribly fearful and tense. Underneath the outer pose of bravado and self-assurance, he carried a deep anxiety with him no matter where he went, gnawing away at his confidence and sometimes even at the walls of his stomach, a fact testified to by concerned observers and by equally concerned physicians. The testimony of observers is in the form of comments like this:

> It is difficult and useless, perhaps, to try to name all the fears of the mountaineer, for apprehension pervades his whole life. One does not have to live long in the mountains to see that this anxiety affects persons of all ages, eating away at the relationships of person with person, even within families, at self-confidence, happiness, and health. The mountaineer lacks a confident sense of who he is and where he is going; instead, one finds a reluctant and anxious person who seems to ask for defeat by his very reluctance and uncertainty. Everybody who works in the mountains should be aware of this anxiety and its ramifications, for it determines in great measure the working of the group process as well as the kind and quality of response that can be expected from mountain people.[20]

And the testimony of physicians takes the form of clinical records where one can find countless references to nervousness and tension as well as to ulcers and all the other physical ailments that psychiatrists associate with emotional stress.

The mountaineer, finally, was deeply dependent upon his inner circle of family and his outer circle of kin. The people who made up those concentric circles were the world he looked to for support, and, more than that, the world from which he derived a refracted image of his own identity. Largely for that reason, he has always found it painful to leave home for any appreciable period of time, not simply because he feels lonely and insecure, but because he feels less than whole so far from the sustaining roots of his kin.

And that is the conventional portrait of the mountaineer as drawn by several generations of observers, its general accuracy certified by the sheer number of people who have contributed to it. But life is rarely as tidy as the pictures we draw of it, and this one, no matter how correct its larger contours, presents a number of problems.

First, the portrait deals for the most part with adult men, which is why I have used so many masculine pronouns in describing it. It is a fair bet when dealing with any character profile of this kind that the experience of the children and particularly of the women will not be represented fully, and we will have occasion to deal with that problem shortly. The women of Appalachia had a remarkably difficult life, not only because they were expected to do a disproportionate share of the work, but because they were also expected to free the men to exhibit the character traits on which their reputation rested. The average mountain woman married in her early teens and gave birth to as many as a dozen offspring in a childbearing career that might last thirty years. She did most of the work in and around the rough log home, spinning and weaving and knitting, making the family's clothes, feeding what livestock there was and slaughtering it when the time came, planting and weeding and harvesting the garden, milling the corn when it was picked, bringing water from the spring or creek, sawing the firewood, laying fences, dressing and salting the game her husband brought home, and, of course, nursing everyone through frequent bouts of illness. Mountain women often grew gaunt and leathery while still young, tough as rawhide but mistaken for aging grandparents at the age of twenty-five. The women may have been self-sufficient in the sense that they could cope with virtually anything, but the brawling independence and bravado that are supposed to have characterized mountain life were hardly their lot. Ellen Semple asked one of those mountain women what the men did with their time and got the laconic reply: " 'The men folks mostly sets on a fence and chaw tobacco and talk politics.' " [21] This may have understated the responsibilities of the men somewhat, but it certainly suggests that one has to look deeply into a cultural form to sense the experiences of all those bound to it.

Second, the portrait includes a number of features—especially the qualities of resignation and traditionalism—that are by no means local to Appalachia. Much of the portrait could serve as a passable description of people who live in the American South, of people who live in rural areas throughout the country, and of people gathered in ethnic ghettos elsewhere. When a minister named Jack E. Weller looked through the sociological literature for a people with whom he could compare his mountain neighbors, he found what he was looking for in Herbert Gans's study of Italian-Americans in the West End of Boston.[22] The resemblance is indeed remarkable.

Third, portraits like this appear to arrest the passage of time and thus offer single frames clipped from a continuous reel. The men and women involved are changing at the very moment their portrait is being done, and in that respect, at least, the portrait is instantly obsolete. The people portrayed here do not exist; their picture captures a moment in time, not a stable tableau, for there is a world of difference between trying to grasp the essential character of a scene in motion and trying to do so once it has reached a more settled state. All the evidence suggests that Appalachia is changing all the time, and, moreover, that this process was well under way when the studies on which this conventional portrait is based were being done initially. No matter how recent the portrait, it is a reflection of yesterday.

Finally, portraits like this tend to seek a measure of symmetry and homogeneity in the scene they portray and thereby understate the many contrasts. Any list of "traits" seems to have a certain consistency when the items are laid out one after the other in a written account, but human experience is not arranged in so linear a form. The items themselves are part of a continuous whole, an entire package; and when one looks back over the list of traits and tries to imagine how they would appear fused into a single configuration, it becomes hard to avoid the conclusion that there is a good deal of contradiction and discrepancy there. The mountain people are warm and hospitable, yet they are deeply suspicious of others. They are fiercely independent, yet they are so reliant upon family and kin that they scarcely know who they are when separated from that familiar surround. They are capable of an almost heroic ferocity when betrayed, yet they are passive in the face of misfortune and resigned to the inevitable futilities of existence. They are proud and resourceful and obdurate, yet they are often overwhelmed by their own vulnerability. They are profoundly individualistic, holding to a philosophy of life in which no one is beholden to the viewpoint of another, yet they are so bound by codes and so anxious to conform to the opinions of others that they are unwilling to stand apart even for the purposes of doing something out of the ordinary or enjoying an original thought. They are exuberant yet depressed, outgoing yet taciturn, steady yet impulsive, indulgent yet firm.

The conventional portrait of the mountaineer, then, is a study in contrasts, as is the case for any portrait of this kind. And that thought is important enough for our purposes to deserve a brief detour.

The Mountain Ethos

WHEN ONE TALKS about the "way of life," or "ethos," of Appalachia or Norway or any other place on earth where people seem to share a distinctive style of life and thought, one is talking about *culture*. The term itself has come to mean so many things to so many people that it is hard to supply a crisp working definition, but it is used throughout the social sciences to refer to those modes of thinking and knowing and doing that a people learn to regard as natural, those beliefs and attitudes that help shape a people's way of looking at themselves and the rest of the universe, those ideas and symbols that a people employ to make sense of their own everyday experience as members of a society.

On the face of it, at least, one would think this definition broad enough to handle almost any conceptual emergency, since all it really means is "the way a people live." A number of social scientists, however, seem to feel that the idea of culture is useful when one is dealing with distant societies but is rather unwieldy when one is dealing with all the diversities and complexities, all the conflicts and ironies and dilemmas, that figure so prominently in societies closer to home.

It is not difficult to imagine why this should be so. The idea of culture came into common currency through the work of ethnologists who made a special point of conducting their studies in remote corners of the world. The subjects of their research, for the most part, were people without letters, people without a strong sense of their own history, people who seemed —to a stranger, at any rate—to behave in remarkably homogeneous ways. Moreover, the field trips themselves tended to be brief sojourns in strange and different lands, which meant, first of all, that observers were rarely on the scene long enough to see very much in the way of historical change, and, second, that in their eagerness to understand the heart of the culture, they focused on the stabilities rather than the instabilities of the societies they were visiting.

As a consequence, early monographs from the field had the unintended effect of associating the concept of culture with simpler forms of social organization. "Culture" seemed to speak of South Sea islands where traditional ceremonies and ancient rituals fix the rhythms of everyday life, of peasant villages where new generations move gently into the places vacated by older ones, of tribal communities where clear systems of authority and austere codes of morality prevent the ambiguities one finds in more modern societies. "Culture," in short, seemed to speak of something timeless and unchanging in the lives of men, something orderly and secure, and when social scientists in other parts of the world could not find these qualities in the scenes they were observing, they often avoided the concept altogether. The problem is that students looking at modern societies are usually less impressed by the congruities than by the incongruities in what they see. They are sensitive to the fact that human life is frequently a thing of ambivalence and tension, of contradiction and conflict; and these are exactly the elements one hears the least about in most social science descriptions of culture.

Yet there are elasticities in the concept of culture that may go a long way toward bridging this gap, and I would like to consider one of them for a moment as we look for a road leading back to Appalachia.

Man is an exceptionally plastic animal. The range of behavior lying within his capabilities as an organism is essentially without limit, since he is a creature of few, if any, programmed instincts. In one sense, then, cultures can be said to set *moral* limits on the behavior of human beings to compensate for the fact that biology has failed to set many *natural* limits. Every people stake out a particular territory on the broad plain of human potentialities, drawing boundaries around that sphere of activity or thought and declaring it to be uniquely their own. Culture, then, is the moral space within which a people live, or, rather, the customary ways that develop within that space and make it distinctive.

So far, presumably, all this is familiar. To speak of culture is to speak of elements that help shape human behavior—the inhibitions that govern it from the inside, the rules that control it from the outside, the languages and philosophies that serve to edit a people's experience of life, the customs and rituals that help define how one person should relate to another. To speak of culture is to speak of those forces that promote uniformity of thought and action.

But there are other forces at work in a culture too. Cultural forms help determine how a people will think and act and feel, but they also help determine what a people will *imagine*. And it is one of the persisting curiosities of human life that people are apt to imagine the complete contrary of the ideas and attitudes that figure most significantly in their view of the world. The mind that imagines a cultural form also imagines (which is to say "creates") its reverse, and to that extent, at least, a good measure of diversity and contrast is built into the very text of a culture. Whenever people devote a good deal of emotional energy to celebrating a certain virtue, say, or honoring a certain ideal, they are sure to give thought to its counterpart. They conjure it up in those private chambers of the mind where dream and fantasy dwell. They act it out in childhood games. They view it in public ceremonials where the ideal and its opposite are both represented. And, most important, they become alert to it when individuals who behave in deviant ways are punished for doing so. Thus the idea and its counter-part become natural partners in the cultural order of things, setting up what I will call an *axis of variation* that cuts through the center of a culture's space and draws attention to the diversities arrayed along it. The dictionary defines axis as "a line passing through a body or system around which the parts are symmetrically arranged" and as "the principal line along which anything may extend, grow, or move." What I am proposing here, then, is that the identifying motifs of a culture are not just the *core values* to which people pay homage but also the *lines of point and counterpoint* along which they diverge. That is, the term "culture" refers not only to the customary ways in which a people induce conformity in behavior and outlook but the customary ways in which they organize diversity.[1] In this view, every human culture can be visualized, if only in part, as a kind of theater in which certain contrary tendencies are played out.

One's eye is sensitive to the characteristic tensions in the life of a people—the meaningful contrasts—one can see a good deal of cultural patterning there. These patterns should be seen not as flaws in the natural symmetry of culture but as the very stuff of culture itself.

These contrasting tendencies are reflected at many different levels within the social order. At the individual level, first of all, they are experienced as a form of *ambivalence*. When a person is caught between two competing strains in his cultural surround and can find no way to resolve the dilemma, he can be said to suffer from inner conflict. When he is able to attune himself comfortably to one or another of those strains, or manages somehow to combine them into a new and more coherent whole, he can be said to have achieved ego-integration. Whatever the outcome, though, both halves of the dilemma remain as active potentials in his consciousness, ready to assert themselves if conditions change.

At the societal level, these contrasting tendencies are experienced as a form of *differentiation*. The people of any culture sort themselves into a wide variety of groups and segments, each of them sharing something of the larger culture at the same time that each tries to fashion modes of living peculiar to itself. When these differences develop into competition for power or goods or are based on antagonisms of long standing, the result is apt to be social conflict; but when these differences develop into an implicit agreement to apportion the work of the culture as well as its rewards on the basis of the contrasting qualities that each group represents, the result is apt to be a form of complementarity.

The idea that people *do* different things in the service of some over-all pattern of coordination is entirely familiar to social scientists and is usually called "division of labor." It is a common observation in societies all over the world, for instance, that women perform other tasks than men or that the young have other responsibilities than the old. The idea that people *think* or *feel* different things in the service of an over-all pattern of coordination, however, seems a good deal farther fetched, but that is more or less what I am arguing. In the same sense that people contribute different skills and abilities to the organization of *work,* so people contribute different temperaments and outlooks to the organization of *sensibility.* When I noted earlier that men and women in Appalachia may be contributing different emotional strains to the general mountain ethos, I was anticipating the point being made here. To call this "complementarity" does not necessarily imply that all of the partners to the implicit agreement like the part they play in it. It only implies that they regard those parts as natural and inevitable, consonant with the social logic of their world.

Two points, then, before we return to Appalachia. First, the forms of contrast experienced by a particular people are one of the identifying motifs of their culture, and if one wants to understand how any given culture works, one should inquire into its characteristic counterpoints as well as its central values. Second, the axes of variation cutting across a culture are not only sources of tension but gradients along which responses to social change are likely to take place. When individual persons or whole groups of people undergo what appear to be dramatic shifts in character, skidding across the entire spectrum of human experience from one extreme to another, it is only reasonable to suspect that the potential had been there all along—hidden away in the folds of the culture, perhaps, but an intrinsic element of the larger pattern nonetheless. Such shifts do not represent a drastic change of heart, not a total reversal of form, but a simple slide along one of the axes of variation characteristic of that social setting.

I am going to suggest in a moment that a number of important changes in the life of Appalachia had essentially this history.

The Appalachian way of life, then, like any other culture, can be visualized as a tangle of contrary tendencies, and it would be an easy matter to take the list of mountain traits compiled by various students and rearrange it in such a way as to expose all the apparent incongruities. But our task here is to identify those axes of variation that seem most characteristic of mountain society, and at the risk of overlooking some obvious candidates, I will mention five.

First, mountain life seems to generate a sharp tension between love of tradition on the one hand and respect for personal liberty on the other. In some ways, the mountaineer is hedged in on all sides by constraints on his freedom of movement. He is so deeply indebted to the values of a long-dead past and so reliant upon old customs and habits that he often finds it difficult to entertain new options or to visualize new futures. He is more securely strapped in place by the traditional bonds of his cultural setting than is the case for most of the people whose lack of personal liberty he scorns. At the same time, though, he is extremely resistant to measures that seem to impose limitations upon him. He is apt to distrust the national government, the state government, and the county government with equal vigor, and his difficulties in establishing the most elementary kind of community government are legendary. So the mountaineer can be said to cherish freedom and to be wary of it, to protect the right to do as he pleases and then to consult aging traditions or the prevailing attitudes of his peers to find out what he *should* want to do. He is dubious of authority in any form, even when he is given the option to exercise it himself, and yet he is governed every minute of the day by tribal codes and community expectations and the voices of ancestors that have long since become silent echoes.

Second, the mountain ethos seems to be characterized by a deep contrast between self-assertion and resignation. The mountaineer likes to be in control of his own territory, and the history of his life in the region is marked by examples of his readiness to protect his home from marauders, his reputation from rivals, and his livelihood from such meddling outsiders as revenue agents. In that sense, it is hard to imagine anyone less submissive to circumstances. And yet the mountaineer submits all the time. For all his bravado, he has little confidence in his ability to influence outcomes and is apt to yield with surprising passivity to whatever fate has in store for him. He is helpless before the God who reigns over Appalachia, helpless before the crotchety ways of nature, and helpless before the crafty maneuvering of those who come to exploit him and his land. "What can I do?" is an everyday explanation for inactivity in the mountains, and, indeed, it is hard to argue that this is anything less than a practical estimate of the situation, for these are a truly vulnerable people. The resignation of the mountaineer, however, is not entirely like the stolid peasant fatalism one expects to find in other parts of the world; his reflexes may have been blunted over time, but he still flashes with indignation and still has sharp resentments. And so he has to find some midpoint between a rage that cries out for expression and a view of the world that calls for submission. "It takes a lot to rile a mountain man," said one teen-ager who lives on Buffalo Creek, "but when he gets mad, watch out!" When he gets mad, in fact, he usually does not do much of anything, especially if the object of his irritation is some powerful interest; but the potential for response is always there, eating away at his relationships with others and at his own sense of self-esteem.

Third, the people of Appalachia are self-centered and group-centered at the same time, and they live in such uneasy suspension between those contrary leanings that they find it difficult to develop either strong selves or effective groups. There is an irony here that is hard to describe, but the outlines look something like this: Mountain people, as we have seen, are quite dependent for emotional nourishment on their families, their kin, and their immediate peers. The family in particular provides a shelter in which people almost seem to huddle for warmth and security, and this degree of attachment and closeness can be extremely important. One's stature in the community as well as one's inner sense of well-being is derived largely from the position one occupies in a family network, and to step out of that embracing surround would be like separating from one's own flesh. The same is true for peer groups, according to Jack Weller.

> Because the mountain man finds his self-identification mainly in his relationship with others, he has never developed a satisfactory self-image as a single individual. He is only somebody in relation to his peers.[2]

The tightness of family and peer relations, then, does not leave room enough for the development of a sure sense of identity, and yet, in an odd way, the family does not appear to offer much security either. Mountain parents are kind and indulgent with their children, according to all accounts, but they are slow to express affection, provoke a certain measure of competitiveness within the family circle, and often try to earn obedience by warning younger children of the dark spirits out to get them if they go too far astray. In short, the anxieties of the parents are visited upon the children in endless ways, and many people emerge from their earlier years without the confidence to break new paths and without the security of belonging to a really supportive group. Thus the dilemma. The mountaineer is self-centered in that he is oriented to individual action and personal gratification, but he is group-centered in that he needs a thick tissue of people around him to know who he is and where he belongs. The problem is that these contrary strains almost cancel each other. The mountaineer cannot leave his group because he is not a whole person away from it, yet at the same time he is too isolated as a personality to participate in meaningful group processes or to put aside personal objectives for the sake of group goals—a quality of mind, by the way, that has served as a constant source of frustration to community organizers of one stripe or another who have passed through the mountains on their way to braver futures elsewhere.

Fourth, the people of Appalachia seem to be forever poised at some vague midpoint between ability and disability. On the one hand, they have earned a considerable reputation for physical sturdiness and an ability to survive hardship, and this is not hard to understand. A people who have hunted bears and fought Indians and scraped a living out of the flinty ground can be expected to be tough and durable. But for all the hardiness they showed in their everyday lives, the mountaineers were full of apprehension about health and suffered from a remarkable variety of aches and pains. Perhaps there is a special logic in this after all. People who depend upon their bodies to make a living—athletes and dancers are good examples—can be the most hypochondriacal specimens to be found anywhere, not because they are unreasonably concerned with their state of health, exactly, but because so much depends on it. In somewhat the same way, the mountaineers relied so heavily on their capacity to react physically and were so helpless when this capacity was dulled by illness or injury that the fear of disability became a prominent theme in their thinking. Their pharmacopoeia, featuring such preparations as bear grease and skunk fat, rattlesnake oil and sassafras, turpentine and the bark of the leatherwood tree, would have probably put a medieval surgeon to shame, and their clinical knowledge, a mixture of modern science and Choctaw medicine and Celtic folklore, was a wonder. All this meant that the mountaineers, despite their stubborn suspicion of science and learning, were particularly indebted to physicians of whatever school and particularly susceptible to tradesmen with medicines to peddle. It also meant that they had developed a sharp sensitivity to the vulnerabilities of their own bodies and were quick to declare themselves infirm. Perhaps one should not make too much of this because the ailments were real enough and the environment was truly dangerous. But it is hard to avoid the conclusion that these people could move with remarkable ease between the contrasting poles of ability and disability, coaxing their bodies into incredible acts of strength and endurance, and then spending inordinate amounts of time nursing symptoms that in another time and place might have passed unnoticed altogether.

The fifth axis of variation to be discussed here is so far-reaching in its influence that the first four can almost be subsumed under it. By all odds, the major source of strain in Appalachian life is the tension one finds between a *sense of independence* on the one hand and a *need for dependence* on the other, and this topic is important enough to deserve a longer discussion.

If one were to count the adjectives that appear most frequently in books and articles on the mountain character, the winner by quite a margin would be "individualistic." According to those sources, the people of the mountains are, above all else, free and independent spirits. They migrated to Appalachia in the first place to avoid external controls, and the style of life they fashioned for themselves in that isolated terrain is one long celebration of individual liberty.

"Independence" is a difficult concept to work with in any event. When one says that a people are independent, one is saying that they are free to do essentially as they please. This presumes, of course, that what "they please" is generated by sources from within and not molded by forces from without. Yet it is no easy matter to distinguish the inner will from the outer demand, and this is particularly the case when one is discussing the people of the mountains and the family groups in which they live.

Appalachian families, according to the testimony of virtually every interested observer, are patriarchal—and profoundly so. Fathers are the source of final authority within the family nest and exercise at least the theoretical right to dictate their every whim to wife and mother as well as children. But the word "patriarchy," like the word "independence," is not adequate to a context like this. For one thing, a very large part of what mountain men like to regard as their own individual authority is really a matter of tradition, so that when they issue an order or demand some act of obedience they are in effect repeating ritual words, an obligation imposed on them. Moreover, the proud sovereignty of the men, exactly because so much of it is dictated by an obligatory script, is a feature of the cultural setting to which others can sometimes respond more innovatively than the men themselves. In many portions of Appalachia, for example, the women are apt to be better educated, shrewder about money, and certainly the bulwark of the home itself, and in such situations it is not difficult to maneuver lightly around the predictable utterances of the men. "Any man likes to *feel* he's the head," said one woman to John B. Stephenson. "You know when to go along."[3]

George Santayana put the matter perfectly.

Perhaps in the flight of birds which Oliver had watched and wondered at in other days, the leader was not really a bold spirit trusting to his own initiative and hypnotizing the flock to follow him in his deliberate gyrations. Perhaps the leader was the blindest, the most dependent of the swarm, pecked into taking wing before the others and then pressed and chased and driven by a thousand hissing cries and fierce glances whipping him on. Perhaps those majestic sweeps of his, and those sudden drops and turns which seemed so joyously capricious, were really helpless effects, desperate escapes, in an induced somnambulism and universal persecution. Well, this sort of servitude was envied by all the world; at least it was a crowned slavery, and not intolerable. Why not gladly be the creature of universal will, and taste in oneself the quintessence of a general life: After all, there might be nothing to choose between seeming to command and seeming to obey . . .[4]

We have many reasons to suppose, then, that the individualistic posturing of the mountaineer is a part he is required to play, whether he is driven to it by "hissing cries and fierce glances" or accepts it because he knows no other way to relate to people. Could he act otherwise if he felt some need to do so? The chances are that he would fail that test quickly.

When we hear that someone enjoys a reputation for independence of thought or action, we should be ready to ask two related questions. First, what other *moods* complement that tendency in the person's own mind? That is, where does one look for the other half of the ambivalence within the emotional economy of the individual personality? Second, what other *roles* complement that tendency in the larger balances of society? That is, where does one look for contrary tendencies within the over-all pattern of social differentiation?

As to moods. It was clear from the beginning that the celebrated individualism of the mountain man (and here again I mean "male") was part of a gestalt that included strong undercurrents of dependence. These are reflected in the submissive way he related to nature as well as to the obligations of kinship, and they are also reflected in the stories he told and the songs he sang, some of which are the most plaintive to be found anywhere. The origins of that strain toward dependency lie somewhere in mountain patterns of child rearing, and while it is outside the scope of this study to dwell at any length on that subject, a brief word might be in order.

According to the testimony of observers, mountain parents are likely to be remarkably indulgent with infants, feeding them on demand, holding them in close physical embrace, and drawing a warm curtain of affection and intimacy around them. As children grow older, however, and begin to toddle off on their own pursuits, parents pay less and less attention to them —still indulgent in the sense that they permit a wide latitude in activity, but no longer so concerned or so solicitous. Parents seldom play with older children or offer them instruction, and discipline frequently becomes an episodic, almost whimsical matter. A good deal of misconduct is simply ignored, but when a certain line is passed, punishment is apt to be harsh, sudden, and sharpened by the kind of anger that often accompanies uncertainty and awkwardness. The upshot is that the child often feels expelled from the inner embrace of the family at an early age, and in that sense the major emotional problem he experiences is likely to be fear of separation. Children are drawn into the warm center of the family early, introduced to the family circle in style, and when they are nudged away from that center they devote a good deal of emotional energy trying to move back to it in order to recover the only real source of security they ever knew. So the apparent independence of the mountaineer is not altogether a welcome product. On the one hand, he has been forced to strike out on his own, foraging for new sources of nurturance, as it were; yet on the other, he has invested so much in the family and is so reliant upon it for protection and support that he often does not have the personal resources to join in emotional partnerships with others. His independence, then, is sometimes a form of sullen loneliness, masking a yearning to return once again to that original circle of warmth and intimacy.[5]

As to roles. It was also clear from the beginning that the surface independence of adult males was more or less subsidized by a corresponding dependence on the part of women and children. In much the same way that it takes a number of support troops to maintain one soldier on the front line, it takes a number of seemingly compliant people to supply and make room for one individualist at home—to honor his whims, provide an audience for his acts of self-expression, and populate the world over which he has dominion. In this, as in so many other respects, one person's freedom of action can easily become another's bondage.

So the axis running between a sense of independence at one pole and a need for dependency at the other is a prominent theme of the old mountain ethos, reflected in a kind of ambivalence at the personal level and in a kind of complementarity, however grudging, at the societal level.

The tension created by those contrasting tendencies stretched across the whole of Appalachian culture even in the old days, but the history of the region has drawn that tension even more tautly. Many volumes have been written about the way in which mountain people, so proud of their personal independence, turned out in the long run to be capable of an almost heroic form of acquiescence when the times called for it. The sight of tough and lean mountaineers yielding meekly to the paternalism of the coal camps or standing in line for hours on end to receive handouts did not fit the prevailing image, and observers were so impressed by what they took to be a complete change in Appalachian manners that they tended to see it as an index to the degree that the region had been devastated by circumstance. And so it might have been. But another way to read that scene—a no less tragic reading, for all of that— is to assume that the potential had been there all along and that the deterioration of mountain life was not so much a complete break with customary attitudes as it was a drift along one of the axes of variation characteristic of the culture in the first place.

There are other axes of variation one might add to this brief list, and some of them will figure in later portions of this study. For example, the mountaineers have been able to move back and forth with apparent ease from a fastidious sense of tidiness —"houseproud" is what their Scottish ancestors called it—to a remarkable degree of slovenliness. Within the soul of every mountaineer, or so it would seem, is a proud Highlander who insists on cleanliness and order as well as an unkempt hillbilly who can tolerate an incredible amount of disarray, and each of these creatures is seeking a chance at expression all the time.

For the moment, though, the important point to remember is that the sons and daughters of Appalachia, like people everywhere, are capable of reacting to new conditions in a number of seemingly divergent ways. They cannot sit still for a portrait because they are always in motion of some kind, sliding along the grids of their cultural field. They share a deep respect for personal freedom, yet they can be meekly submissive to others. They are resourceful, assertive, and competent, yet they have a tendency to yield easily to fate. They are individualistic in manner and thought, yet this state of mind can convert quickly into a mood of almost abject dependency. The emotional resources with which they walk into any future include a contrasting set of potentialities, and much depends on what those futures happen to have in store.

Beginning in the second and third decades of the twentieth century, the future of many mountain families was to move into coal camps.

The Coming of the Coal Camps

THE OPENING of the coal fields changed the face of Appalachia in a number of crucial ways. It brought mountain men and women in touch with a reality beyond their wildest imaginings, and it drew responses from them that often represented the most vulnerable of their emotional potentialities.

Some veteran observers of the Appalachian scene looked forward to the coming of coal as a way out of the cycle of poverty just beginning to appear in the early decades of the new century. One Presbyterian missionary, writing in 1906, after thirty years of traveling in and around the mountains, was almost ecstatic about the prospect.

> Much of the financial profit arising from this development of the natural resources of the mountains will go to the section where the investors live; but most of that profit will, after all, remain in the region that is being developed. . . . The development of the natural wealth of the section will vastly enrich it. . . . the mountains have been rediscovered, and ere long will yield forth notable contributions to human comfort and gain.[1]

But other observers felt that a terrible tragedy was about to engulf the mountains. When the mountaineer gets caught up in new forms of commerce, warned Horace Kephart in 1913,

then it is "good-by" to the old independence that made such charac-
ters manly. Enmeshed in obligations that they cannot meet, they
struggle vainly, brood hopelessly, and lose that dearest of all possessions, their self-respect. Servility is literal hell to a mountaineer, and
when it is forced upon him he turns into a mean, underhanded,
slinking fellow . . .[2]

And the forecast issued by James Watt Raine in 1924, after
the first of the coal camps had made their appearance, was
equally gloomy.

> There is unspeakable danger when manufacturing, mining, and
> other mass operations are thrust into a backward community by
> outsiders. They are conducted not primarily in the community's in-
> terest, but for the benefit of the exploiters. . . . The deadly sin is the
> thrusting of a ferocious and devouring social system upon an un-
> prepared and defenseless people. . . . A mountain man becomes a
> miner. He moves his family and a few household goods from the
> picturesque cabin in the cove or on the ridge to a desolate shack in
> the sordid village that has sprung up around the mine. He had not
> realized that he would have to buy all his food. A garden and corn-
> field had always seemed to him an inseparable part of a house. His
> cow starves as she roams at large. Milk and butter had heretofore
> seemed almost a part of the landscape. He can keep no bees for the
> honey. There is no acorn or hickory mast for his hog, so he puts it
> in a pen and tries to feed it on table scraps. . . . The life of nature,
> of which he has been a part, has been torn from him, and, stripped
> naked of all he has been accustomed to, he might as well be in a
> dungeon. The vices of our industrial progress fasten their tentacles
> upon him and soon suck out his life.[3]

Life in the mountain hollows had been spare, to say the very
least. People were bone-poor, generally illiterate, and easy prey
to all the ills of mankind which result from poor hygiene, inadequate diet, and general hardship. But there had been space
to move around in, clean air to breathe and fresh water to
drink, and reason to take pride in the orderliness of one's life.
The coal camps were quite another matter. The company-built
shacks huddled against one another in gray clusters, constrict-
ing the expansive manners of the mountaineers and drawing
them into an unfamiliar closeness. Large spirits often collided.

Sensitive nerves were often rubbed raw. Moreover, the worst of the camps were filthy and polluted, a degrading scene of air turned rancid by surface privies, hogs wallowing in the muddy streets, swarms of flies creating a great democracy of germs, mounds of decomposing garbage scattered everywhere, and raw sewage making a foul paste of the streams passing through the settlements. A Federal report on several representative coal camps in West Virginia, dated 1923, noted the following:

> The roads were usually rough and irregular, and in wet weather turned to black mud and puddles. There were no sidewalks, as a rule, and only such footpaths as had been worn by use. . . . In some settlements waste matter entered the creeks flowing through the center of the town, privies were tumble-down, and incredible amounts of garbage and rubbish lay on the ground. Chickens, ducks, geese, and hogs wandered about, adding to the general disorder and unwholesomeness. . . . Many privies were ramshackle, with doors lacking and pits broken. One was tied to a tree to keep the high waters of the creek from washing it away. . . . Garbage, tin cans, broken crockery, and other rubbish littered almost every road in some of the camps; in some, the almost stagnant creeks contained cans, wooden crates, bottles, and even old furniture, shoes, and clothing.[4]

In addition to all of this, smoke and soot and grime hung over the narrow settlements like a pall, and sulfuric fumes from mine waste joined forces with the odor of decay from human waste to sour the air and insult the remaining senses.

Another odor hung in the air too—the smell of danger and death. The mountaineers were no strangers to injury and they knew what it was to take risks, but there is no way they could have readied themselves for the sheer relentlessness of the perils they faced in the mines. Mountains do not give up their treasure easily. It takes a good deal of work to scrape and blast and bore one's way into the center of that huge, resistant mass; but once one is there, the mountain suddenly proves to be brittle and full of caprice. The roofs of the long underground passages may collapse in a shower of slate. Dangerous gases may become trapped in the dim interior of the rock. Electric wires may suddenly come alive with lethal currents, and explosive charges may misfire. And as the machinery grinds and pivots in those narrow confines and the mine cars shuttle along with their heavy cargo, they seem to reach out for unwary flesh.

Sixty years ago, when the Buffalo Creek mines first opened and the old-timers now in retirement first began their working careers, mining was almost a solitary contest between men and mountains. Miners were equipped with picks, shovels, tamping bars, augers, long iron needles, black powder in twenty-five-pound kegs, and head lamps along with cans of oil to fuel them. A man would begin the process of removing coal by cutting a narrow shelf at the base of the seam, a task usually accomplished by swinging a pick while lying on one's side, and then he would drive a deep hole into the face of the seam with the auger, a five- or six-foot drill looking like an oversize brace and bit with a breastplate at one end. He would pour powder into a paper cartridge, crimping the ends as if he were rolling a sausage, and shove that package into the hole with the needle, an iron bar five or six feet long and the width of a pencil. The hole was filled with damp dirt or clay and packed tightly with the tamper after a fuse had been inserted. And when all that had been done, the miner lighted the fuse, hurried to safe ground, and listened while the cartridge exploded and shattered a ton or so of coal from the face of the seam. The final step of the process was to shovel the coal onto waiting cars and push them along the hollow shaft to the main passageway, where mules hauled them to the surface.

From one point of view, at least, this was a simple operation, and one could learn to go through the mechanical motions in a matter of a few minutes. But the danger involved was horrendous, and the miner who could not only deliver a day's yield but survive the process in the bargain had to be highly skilled. The right amount of powder had to be used, the fuse properly inserted, the hole tightly packed; and the success of every step of the process depended on perfect timing and on a canny understanding of the condition of the rock itself. The interior of any mountain has to be respected like a living thing. One has to know its moods, listen for its warning sounds, and anticipate its sudden shifts in position.

In the years to come, of course, elaborate machinery was brought to the mines to chew the coal out of the ground and to process it once it reached the surface, but this machinery only served to introduce a new set of dangers into the life of the miner. So it can be said truly of either era that the mines have imposed an awesome penalty on the men who ventured into them. The available statistics are unreliable at best, but one can get some idea of the scale by noting that mine deaths must be calculated in the hundreds of thousands and incapacitating injuries in the millions since 1900 or so; and these figures tell only half the story, for mining leaves permanently cramped muscles and permanently damaged tissue even in those who never find a place on the casualty lists. The men who went into the mines may not have been aware of all the actuarial odds involved, but they knew that they would lose time for serious injuries several times in the course of an average career and that they were more likely to retire for reasons of disability than for reasons of increasing age. The men who die at home or in the hospital of "natural" causes—respiratory ailments like black lung or silicosis being an obvious example—are not included in any death figures, but that is how life ends for many. "He just ran out of air," said one veteran miner on Buffalo Creek describing the death of his brother, and complaints like the following can be heard in any part of the coal fields.

With this black lung, you smother continually, twenty-four hours a day, seven days a week. But there's times when you smother worse. It's on my lungs. It's rock dust. There's nothing I can take that gives me any ease—just stop, sit, lay down if I can, or just be still. I cough a lot and I cough up stuff, mostly in the morning. I'll cough up black and yellow mixed, and I smother bad until I do cough this all up.

And that is how careers in the mines often come to a close.

The speaker below had lived on Buffalo Creek for fifty years and had spent forty-five of those years working in the same mine.

I couldn't hardly get up to work of a morning. My legs would give out on me. I knew something was wrong, but I didn't know what it was. I just kept right on trying to work. And finally I took double pneumonia, and Dr. Craft, he put me in the hospital and he got hold of my charts and he come around to talk to me. He says: "Henry, you have silicosis." And I says: "No I don't, I chew too much tobacco." He says: "No, you got it, you won't be able to work no more." So I went on back home and I laid around about a month. I got to feeling pretty good, so I went back and begged him to let me go back to work again, and he says: "Well, I'll have to give you a work slip if you want to go back, but you can't make it." So he gave me a work slip and I went back, worked ten days that time, and fell out sick again. I went back to the doctor and he says: "Henry, I told you you can't make it, you are going to die in that mine." I said: "Well, Dr. Craft, let me try it one more time," because I had some debts I wanted to pay. All right, he gave me a work slip to go back and he said—now these are his words, I'm a Christian man and I don't lie—he said: "Henry, if you take sick in that mine, wherever you're at, you come out of there." Them was his words. I said: "Well, I promise you that." He said: "If you'll promise me that, I'll let you go to work." So I worked four days, took sick one night, didn't go out the next morning, and I went back to him. He said: "Now I done told you you can't make it." And so I haven't been back since. I went back and told the general mine foreman that I just couldn't make it, and he said: "Henry, I've known you for years, and you've spent enough time in the mines anyhow. You go out and get your pension."

None of this is unexpected. The men know that they begin to die the moment they enter a mine, and what songs are still remembered throughout the coal camps reflect that dark inevitability.

> *Rock dust has almost killed me,*
> *It's turned me out in the rain;*

> *For dust has settled on my lungs,*
> *And causes me constant pain.*
>
> *It's killed two fellow workers,*
> *Here at Old Pardee;*
> *And now I've eaten so much dust, Lord,*
> *That it's killin' me.*[5]

The mines left other permanent marks on the men who worked in them. Old miners who spend their time hanging around the stoops of Appalachia look out at the world through eyes blurred by years spent in darkness and singed red by decades of exposure to coal dust and other irritants. Their hearts are enlarged by the strain of working in the thin air of underground passages. Their hands are thick and callused, their shoulders sloped, their knees and thighs and lower backs stiff with years of bending. "Oh, anybody that works in the mines will have sore shoulders and sore legs," said one old miner matter-of-factly; "you wouldn't be a miner if you didn't." And many of them live out their remaining years with amputated limbs, sightless eyes, and torsos that have gone limp as the result of spinal injuries.

Partly in response to those circumstances, a way of life developed in the coal camps which naturally owed a lot to the traditional culture of Appalachia but represented something of a variant. The camps reverberated with the sounds and smells of industry. Trains pounded in and out of the hollows at all hours of the day and night, great masses of heavy machinery were spread across the open spaces, and industrial soot settled everywhere. But the miners remained a rural folk in almost every important respect, holding on to their old ways with real determination. For most of them, the move out of mountain cabins into company shacks did not represent an abrupt change of cultural manner. To city dwellers, coal is almost the perfect symbol of industrialization: it generates vast power, is used to fuel heavy machinery, and leaves a residue of black smoke and soot all over the urban landscape. To mountaineers, though, coal is a part of the earth, almost a crop, having more in common with roots and plants and other parts of nature's bounty than with the grimy factories to which it is bound. In the old days, miners would sometimes suck on small pieces of coal, as if it were rock candy, and this habit was deemed so peculiar by people from other parts of the country that one old-time miner felt moved to comment on it.

> This custom illustrates one thing about work in the mines which is not usually understood by non-miners. One of the first things that strikes the observer is that the miner comes out of the mine covered with coal dust: his clothes, his hands, his face, his hair, filled with it. He looks dirty, and it is true that he badly needs a wash. But to the miner the coal is not dirty. Other things may be—grease, for example —but there is no harm in good black coal dust.[6]

For most of the new arrivals in the coal camps, then, mining was more like an agricultural pursuit than an industrial one, and they saw themselves as having transferred from one rural activity to another.

The miners were soon to discover that they were virtually anchored to the coal camps, unable to drift back to the old hollows because the land would no longer support them there, yet unable to enter the mainstream of American industrial life because they had few skills to offer and no heart for moving away from the embrace of their familiar mountains and familiar circles of kin. One passing irony here is that coal operators in the early days imported a good number of immigrants from Europe as well as drawing people from the surrounding region, and those new recruits, despite the fact that they were largely unacquainted with their adopted land and its language, proved to be far more mobile than their mountain colleagues, the reason being that most of them were in contact with fellow immigrants in industrial cities to the north who could help in easing the way. The oldest European settlers in the eastern half of the country were more out of touch with modern America than were the newest arrivals. By the time the first coal boom ended in the late 1920's, most of the immigrants had gone elsewhere, although one still finds a sprinkling of Polish and Italian names on the long lists of Celtic and Anglo-Saxon ones.

The mountaineers were deeply affected by their experience in the coal camps, even in spite of the fact that most of the changes in outlook and manner that took place were well within the larger compass of the mountain ethos.

In the first place, conditions of life in the camps were so hard to cope with that many people simply went slack in behavior and thought, responding to the mess around them by slouching down into it themselves. The wives fought off the dirt and grime with what tools mountain living had equipped them, and then their spirits began to go limp as they yielded to the inevitable. The husbands tried to keep some semblance of order in their households and in the community generally, and then they too fell into the habit of dumping their trash into the creek, allowing their houses to deteriorate, leaving dead hogs to rot where they fell, and abandoning old cars and trucks along the side of the road like rusting hulks.

In the second place, new forms of fellowship began to develop among the working miners and their families, including a rough comradery often found where people face common dangers or common enemies. Life out in the mountain hollows had been clannish, almost tribal in its respect for kinship and family, but these feelings of association had never reached over a wide enough span to become the basis for a sense of community or a sense of neighborhood. An observer writing in 1924 put it well:

> There is no common vehicle, no fluid solvent for the easy dissemination of ideas throughout the whole community. Perhaps even the term "community" is a misleading name for the scattered people that live up and down the same creek, each family like a remote constellation, revolving in its own fixed orbit.[7]

But the mountain tendency toward strong family ties took on a new meaning in the coal camps. People were wedged together in very close quarters and their everyday lives were governed by virtually the same rhythms; and as time passed, the old feelings for kin began to shift focus and to embrace the people with whom one worked and the people with whom one lived as well as the people to whom one was related. Since these feelings of relatedness were drawn from so deep a well, they were strong, intimate, and enduring. People needed that support, too. For one thing, it was not long before the miners began to feel that they were really an excluded class in the American scheme of things and had to rely upon one another for security. One man with fifty years in the mines said:

Now I've been told that coal miners is the hardest people in the world to get along with, but I can't see it that way. In the first place, you've got two strikes against you if you're a coal miner and don't live among yourselves. You take the biggest part of the people who live away from the coal fields: they think you're a bunch of hicks or you have coal dust in your veins or something. We've got to stick together. It's the only protection we have.

And, indeed, the fellowship of the coal camps was for many years the only insurance available to those who lived in them, not only in the sense that it furnished a layer of emotional insulation against the pains and sorrows of a hard life, but also in the sense that it offered real help in moments of need. One woman who lost her husband to black lung and her son to a slate fall told the following story.

In a coal-mining town, it's like we're all one big family. When my husband died, I went someplace, to the store maybe, and when I came back home there was a pile of money that covered the table. And I said to the kids, "Lord, how'd I get this?" And they said, "Well, some of the neighbors came." The neighbors wanted to know if I had something to eat, and I said, "Yeah, I've got something to eat, and I've got a way to get some more, too." And I thought that was the end of it. But when I went out again and came back, the place was full of groceries, boxes sitting everywhere. So they really did take care of their own, the miners did.

In the third place, the old mountain tendency toward passivity and resignation took on an exaggerated new meaning in the camps. The miners felt increasingly helpless before the ruthlessness of the coal companies and the unreliability of the mountains from which they scratched a living, and they learned to accept the dangers of their new vocation and the condition of their living arrangements as if they were inescapable. Most miners liked the idea of drawing wages and many of them enjoyed the work itself, but they lived so close to the edge of disaster that they almost began to feel that death and injury were their natural fate, their own peculiar destiny. The same fifty-year veteran quoted a moment ago:

That slate, it don't have any respect for persons. It'll fall on anybody. It comes to you that the man working right beside you gets killed, say. For a day or two it bothers you, and after that, why, you know you've got a living to make so you go back and try to forget. But I think that ninety percent of the coal miners are scared to death all the time they're in there. You get hurt, you dread going back in there, but you try to forget it—or at least I did, and I don't think anyone is different from what I was.

In the fourth place, the coal camps brought mountain men and women in contact with a medium of exchange they knew very little about—cash. They had been accustomed to living off whatever they grew in the ground or took from the land; they might collect a few dollars a year from the sale of timber or from a sporadic trade in herbs or moonshine, but beyond that, cash was simply not a very important currency of everyday life. They were the shrewdest traders in the world, but they did not have enough experience with money to measure its worth or count its uses. After all, it takes a certain capacity for abstraction to understand deep in one's bones that a few disks of metal or a few crumpled pieces of paper can be a proper return for twelve hours of hard work, and urban people easily forget that it took their grandparents a number of years to fully appreciate the properties of money. The first important property of cash—that it can be converted into material goods almost immediately—is quickly learned. In the old days, of course, when wages were scarcely sufficient to keep food on the table, this is all one needed to know anyway; but later, when a degree of prosperity came to certain of the coal fields, this understanding of money was expressed in waves of spending for automobiles and appliances and all manner of other possessions. The second important property of cash—that it can be saved to buy a more secure tomorrow or can be invested to grow in value—is not so quickly learned. The idea that money has worth and meaning aside from its power to attract usable goods is lost on a large number of people everywhere, not because they lack the wit to understand the matter intellectually, but because they have no inner "feel" for it. Money is a symbol, not a substance. The peculiar tricks that bankers play with it have very little reality to people who still know the difference between work and play and who can still tell what they own and what they do not own by looking around their own households. One survivor of the Buffalo Creek disaster was trying to explain to an extremely dubious lawyer what assets his family had lost in the flood, and he said of his dead brother:

Yes, he had some savings, but how much I don't know. We talked about it a little bit a few times. He had roughly forty to forty-five thousand dollars in savings. And he kept that in the trunk of a car.

The details of this story may not be correct—the man who told it is not sure himself—and it is certainly not typical for Buffalo Creek or any other coal camp. But the indifference with which this huge cache of money was handled would not be regarded as a glaring eccentricity throughout the coal fields, even if most people saw it as something less than a sensible form of banking. Many people, though, do not save at all, in part because they have so little experience with surplus funds and in part because Appalachian miners have so many reasons to wonder whether there will be a tomorrow to save for.

Maybe I can explain it this way. There were these people running a grill up there and they was nice people. They was leaving, and so I went up there one evening to tell them good-bye. Him and me was standing outside the grill there and he asked me, he said, "The coal miners make good money, why is it that they don't save any?" Now I've heard that question before, and the only way I've ever found to explain it is that people say, "Well, what's the use of me working late, piling it up, and getting killed in the mines so that somebody else can have the benefit of it?"

And, finally, the people who drifted into the coal camps not only resigned themselves to the terrible dangers of their trade but yielded to a kind of paternalism unlike anything they could have dreamed of earlier. The coal operator owned the entire camp, of course, so he served not only as the miners' employer but as their merchant, landlord, mayor, chief of police, banker, and school superintendent. He paid the salaries of the physician, the schoolteacher, the minister, and, in all likelihood, every attorney for miles around. And he owned the local political apparatus, too, either in the sense that he exerted a great deal of influence over it or in the sense that he actually paid the salaries of county officers.

When the coal operators were benign and amiable patrons, as most of them fancied themselves to be, they nonetheless tended to see the camp as a private preserve over which they must exercise a kind of feudal dominion and the workers as raw, simple children who came into their charge. But when the coal operators were less than amiable, their power to coerce and intimidate was formidable. They could evict tenants without notice and have the eviction notices served by officers of the law on their own payroll; they could cut off a person's credit at the only store available and deny him access to even elementary medical and sanitary services—and all of that within the law. Outside the law, they could normally do whatever else they thought useful without any real fear of sanctions. And their record for mine safety, to hear the old-timers talk about it, was not one of their more prominent virtues either.

The coal companies didn't have any respect for the men. They wanted all they could get out of them. Why, they didn't pay any more attention to a man getting killed around a coal mine than they did a dog, not near as much as they did a pony. They valued a pony or a mule around the mines more than ten men.

What this meant to a miner in one of the good camps—and Buffalo Creek is supposed to have been one of those, as we shall see—is that he did nothing for himself but work his assigned shift. He lived in a house issued to him by the company and paid a fixed rent. His tools were selected by the company, sharpened by the company, inspected by the company—but paid for out of his wages. His family's entertainment was provided by the company. He was delivered by a company doctor, taught by a company teacher, and given solace by a company pastor who also said a few words over his body before he was buried by a company undertaker.

The coal camps were such isolated countries, such remote enclaves, that they even had their own currency. The economy of the camps rested on a checkoff system in which the only thing changing hands was "scrip," tokens or coupons issued by the company that in theory represented the amount of credit a miner had accumulated on the books. It was a kind of play money, for all practical purposes, and few people regarded it as being worth its face value—either because the companies that used it in trade charged inflated prices or because they treated it like debased currency in the first place. When Edmund Wilson visited West Virginia in 1931, he found scrip being sold on the open market at sixty cents on the dollar.[8] It was entirely possible, as the folk lament had it, that one's pay voucher at the end of a week of work and a week of trading at the company store would reflect a negative amount. In a study commissioned by the Federal Government in 1923, for example, fully 60 percent of the families surveyed were working at a deficit averaging more than three hundred dollars a year.[9] And the Depression was still five years in the future.

Wherever an individual coal operator may fall on a scale ranging from benevolent to vicious, wherever a particular coal camp may fall on a scale ranging from tidy to squalid, the dominant tone of the place was one of regimentation. Houses were arranged in straight files and were pressed closely together, virtually identical in size, contour, color, and trim. And the architecture of the camp gave physical expression to the spirit that ran through it. The tight symmetry of the settlement was reflected in an almost absolute conformity of personal rhythm and style, and everything of value was measured in discrete units—productivity by tons delivered and dollars paid, freedom by hours away from the schedule of work, living space by feet of frontage, and job security by tenths of a decimal point in the curious shifts of the market. Whatever else one may say about it, autonomy and self-respect do not flourish in a climate like this.

The most telling change to take place among the people who sifted into the camps was their gradual slide into passivity and dependency, a process accelerated by several important developments in the history of the region.

Whether one is talking about the old mountain hollows or the newer coal camps, Appalachia had been more or less sealed off from the rest of the world for a century and a half. Beginning in the 1930's, however, a number of events occurred that acted to puncture that seal in particularly sensitive places and to bring new currents of air into the mountains.

Among the many changes introduced into Appalachia by the New Deal, one of the most important may have been rural electrification. Throughout the whole of the Depression, the coal fields were among the most blighted regions of an already devastated country, but the percentage of households owning radios was way above the national average. And the radio opened up channels to the outside that provoked new aspirations and expectations all over the mountains. Slowly at first, but at an ever-growing pace, young people began to drift away. A few joined the Civilian Conservation Corps or took jobs in other parts of the country and never returned. A larger number joined the armed forces during World War II and took advantage of veterans' benefits and their new experience of the outside world to settle elsewhere. And, as if by an iron law of the mountains, the routes out of Appalachia seemed to work like a selective filter, drawing away the best-educated, the youngest, and the most energetic people in the region, while posing obstacles to the least endowed among them. Fully half of the mountain men who reported for induction in the military during World War II were turned down on other than occupational grounds, for instance, and the war industries naturally tried to recruit men and women with the most serviceable skills. By the end of the 1940's, however, when automation was brought to the coal industry in a big way, the flow of people out of the mountains in general and the coal fields in particular became something closer to a torrent. Automation of the mines acted to reduce the number of working men by half in the space of a decade, and this pressure from the inside, combined with an almost gravitational pull from the outside, helped to create what may very well be the largest proportional out-migration of persons in the history of this highly mobile nation.

In the decade between 1950 and 1960, the Southern Appalachian region had a net loss by migration of more than one million individuals, roughly one-fifth of the population, and the figures for the decade to follow were comparable. At the same time, the prodigious birth rate that had always been characteristic of the region began to decline. More than 40 percent of the people who lived in Logan County in 1950 had moved elsewhere by 1960, and this total, while high, is not unrepresentative of the area in general. As remarkable as these figures seem, however, they still tell only a part of the story, for the iron law of the mountains was at work here too: well over half of the young men and women of the coal fields left during this period to make their fortunes somewhere else, and their ranks inevitably included some of the most competent individuals around.

The population left behind, then, was thinned not only in number but in what the rest of the world took to be talent— high in disability and unemployment, low in literacy and industrial skills. It was ripe, in fact, for that other great innovation that had been originally introduced by the New Deal— welfare.

Welfare came to the mountains along with the Depression, and, to the surprise of seasoned observers, the people of Appalachia seemed to accept it without turning so much as a hair. Nearly 75 percent of the region's inhabitants received some form of Federal or state assistance in the years of the Depression, and it was not long before relief had become one of the standard modes of existence throughout the region. It goes altogether without saying that the people had strong claims to assistance. They were poor, they suffered from high rates of malnutrition and disease, they had been deeply victimized by others, and a very large number of them had been disabled as a result of occupational injury. But even so, the readiness with which those proud mountain folk took to the dole was both astonishing and profoundly sad. The potential had been there all along, perhaps, the natural counterpart to the individualism that had dominated mountain life, but the net effect of this skid into dependency was to sap what reserves of self-respect were left and to further demoralize an already devastated people. "I have never seen a mountain beggar; never heard of one," Horace Kephart had said many years before in a passage already quoted. "Charity, or anything that smells to him like charity, is declined with patrician dignity or open scorn." Now it may well be that many of the mountaineers visualized welfare as a part of nature's bounty rather than as a form of human charity, for they had long lived in an area where the necessities of life were taken casually from the land; but the long-range effects of the arrangement certainly took their toll on patrician dignity.

A reporter named Bill Peterson, having acquired a sense of the old mountain character from observers like Kephart, went to Appalachia in 1972 intent on finding "an untainted old hillbilly, someone who would represent the best traits of the proud, fiercely independent, Anglo-Saxon mountain man." He looked for two weeks before he found one—a stooped relic of ninety-one who had spent seventy years up the side of a mountain and had helped raise nineteen children there. Before he made his rare find, though, Peterson asked the local shopkeepers what had happened to the old breed of mountaineer, and they told him " 'the welfare done got them all.' " [10] Had he looked further he might have found what he was seeking, for the old ways are still respected in isolated corners of Appalachia, but they no longer constitute a dominant cultural strain.

The turn to welfare as a way of life was accompanied by a sharpened sensitivity to illness, and this characteristic, too, as we have seen, was rooted deep in the mountain experience. Welfare provided an ethic, as it were, in which people could come to terms with their everyday troubles by retreating into sickness and making the most of their disabilities. On the one hand, men and women who organize their lives around the dole learn soon enough to offer palpable symptoms when they petition for relief. This makes them eligible for additional benefits and lends a suggestion of concreteness and dignity to what otherwise can be a degrading transaction. Harry Caudill, who knows the mountains as well as anyone, puts the matter flatly:

> So the jobless forty-five or fifty-year-old miner with "a gang of young'uns" to support went through a demoralizing struggle. Bit by bit, his self-reliance and initiative deteriorated into self-pity. Seeing the hosts of pensioned old people and the swarms of dependent children whose parents were dead, fled or disabled, he came to the belief that he and his children ought to enjoy the same benefits. . . . He became, in countless cases, a welfare malingerer. In a nation that was seeking to lead, liberate and protect the world, men were reduced to the tragic status of "symptom-hunters." If they could find enough symptoms of illness, they might convince physicians that they were "sick enough to draw." Like dispirited soldiers who hope to avoid combat, they besieged the doctors, complaining of a wide range of

ailments. Their backs ached. They suffered from headaches. They could not sleep. They were short of breath and had chest pains. Their stomachs were upset and they could not eat. Above all, they were "nervous." . . . Half seriously, half in jest, some doctors referred to their malady as "chronic, passive dependency syndrome." [11]

This kind of behavior is vastly different from simple malingering, and we cannot understand it properly if we assume, as the above language almost invites us to, that it is somehow voluntary and deliberate. People who view the world as out of whack and themselves as broken, fragmented, and torn loose from their moorings often use illness as a way to signal to themselves and to others what the nature of their discomfort is. The process itself is unconscious, hidden from the awareness of even the most perceptive persons, and the pains issuing from it are every bit as sharp as wounds that leave more visible marks on the body. In a sense, illness or infirmity comes to serve as a recognizable name for the otherwise vague maladies that plague people, an identifying motif for lives that are otherwise empty of substance or hope. To be ill in some defined way (or to be known by some other negative quality) is often better than to be nothing at all. Dostoievski expressed the point superbly when he had a deeply estranged character say:

> Oh, if I had done nothing simply from laziness! Heavens, how I should have respected myself then! I should have respected myself because I should at least have been capable of being lazy; there would at least have been one positive quality, as it were, in me, in which I could have believed myself. Question: What is he? Answer: A sluggard. How very pleasant it would have been to hear that of oneself! It would mean that I was positively defined, it would mean that there was something to say about me. "Sluggard"—why, it is a calling and vocation, it is a career.[12]

To be compensated for injury or illness, then, quite aside from supplying a needed source of material support, legitimizes one's feelings of discomfort and apprehension. One gets a return for all the punishment one has had to absorb; one has a license not only to withdraw from the source of that pain but to explain to others why one has done so. The appeal of this solution, understandably, is all the greater for men who sense their bodies and minds deteriorating in the depths of the mines. To work in those dark corridors is to experience battle fatigue in every meaning of the term. Mining is more dangerous than service in wartime, and the constant anxieties that attend it work their way into the anatomy of the spirit as surely as other, more palpable agents work their way into the tissue of the body. The human mind has a secret strategy for dealing with that kind of anxiety, though: to end the gnawing fear of getting hurt by hastening the feared result itself. If one betrays a certain negligence at work, inviting the fates to do their worst, as it were, physicians will call it "injury proneness." If one is disabled by illnesses that seem to well up from some other legacy than the bodily tissue itself, physicians will call them "psychosomatic disorders." And both expressions appear often in psychiatric discussions of coal mining, as one might suspect.[13]

The point to be made, though, is that the aches and pains that bring petitioners into welfare clinics are quite real, even if they derive from a more subtle chemistry than is described in basic medical textbooks. In Appalachia, this chemistry has something to do with the way in which poverty and uncertainty corrode pride, the way in which emptiness of the spirit creates infirmity. The mountaineers moved into the age of welfare with a strong sense of their own sturdiness as well as a corresponding sensitivity to illness and disability, and the conditions they encountered in that new age served to reinforce the sensitivity while numbing the complementary strengths.

The coal camps seemed to activate potentialities that had always been a latent part of the mountain ethos and to give them new vigor. A brooding sense of resignation and submission, balanced in the old mountain character by a complementary sense of self-assertion, now began to dominate the mood of the camps. The tension between tidiness and disorder, which had once furnished a source of diversity in Appalachian life, was now more or less resolved in favor of the latter. The mountaineer's celebrated individualism seemed to slump all at once into a state of dependency—almost as if the old cast of mind had served as a bizarre apprenticeship for the newer one. As we go down the list, in fact, and watch the peculiar mechanics of culture at work, we are almost bound to observe that the coal camps appeared to bring out the weaker trait in every pair of contrary tendencies.

There is one exception to this rule, however, and it is an important one. The coal camps placed an enormous burden on the men and women who went into them, and as individual strengths began to buckle under the strain, the boundaries that sealed people off in their own private compartments seemed to diffuse. The coal camps acted to diminish the mountaineer's extraordinary self-absorption in many important ways and to increase his reliance on group structures. As a result, a new form of communality was fashioned in the coal camps as neighborhoods and villages began to replace families and clans as the basic units of social life.

Buffalo Creek

BUFFALO CREEK is located in the very heart of the Appalachian coal fields, but it represents a variant on the larger Appalachian experience because most of its people have managed to escape the poverty and general dispiritedness that hangs over so much of the region.

Logan County was first settled around 1800 by squatters who turned into the mountains on their way west and by recently discharged soldiers with land grants from the new national Congress. The names of those first arrivals are still prominent throughout the county generally and along the edges of Buffalo Creek in particular—Adkins, Bailey, Browning, Butcher, Dalton, Harvey, Hatfield, Maynard, McComas, Miller, Morgan, Mullins, Starr, Staten, Stepp, Toler, Trent, Vance, Vernatter, Workman. The first residents of Buffalo Creek itself drifted there in the neighborhood of 1810, establishing homesteads along the creek bottom and living there in relative isolation for more than a century. The Logan County historian tells us something about those early days as well as the way local people like to remember them.

The early settlers, while coming from every class of society, were fortunate in having among them no drones who are so often dubbed "gentlemen." . . . There were no "gold refiners and perfumers" among them, but they were rather sturdy farmers, carpenters and laborers, used to the axe and rifle, and perfectly at home in the wilderness.[1]

And this wilderness was well provided, at least at first. Sulfur and saltpeter could be found in hundreds of local caves, and from such raw materials the men fashioned ammunition to hunt the numerous animals spread out across the territory. Aside from small game, the main objects of the hunt were bear, deer, and buffalo. They supplied meat for the table and skins for clothing and footwear, and the latter of those animals left a name for Buffalo Creek before they disappeared entirely. Corn was the staple crop, supplemented by a variety of produce from local household gardens, and irregular quantities of furs, timber, ginseng, and moonshine were floated down the Guyandotte River by canoe.

Not much happened in those quiet environs for the better part of a century. Every now and then a moment of excitement punctuated the silence and left a trace on the county records, but they were passing episodes, flashes of color on a long, gray calendar. In 1864, a man named Henry Walker was hanged near the mouth of Buffalo Creek, the execution being accomplished in the direct mountain fashion of hoisting the culprit onto a barrel, placing a noose around his neck, and then kicking the barrel out from under him.[2] Later in the century, the Hatfield-McCoy feud ranged across the county, and one of its major battles was fought near Buffalo Creek.

The most important events in the history of Logan County, however, were the development of new rail lines and the opening of the mines at the turn of the century. In 1900, the county was very sparsely populated. A few small farms were scattered along the Guyandotte and its tributaries, and the only other industry worth noting was logging. In the census of 1900, the county was given credit for fewer than seven thousand inhabitants, although this may have been an underestimate. Engineers and geologists had realized for a number of years that the land was rich in coal, but no serious efforts had been made to bring it to the surface because the county had virtually no roads worthy of the name and not a foot of railroad track. The Guyandotte had served as the county's only highway for one hundred years.

In 1904, the Chesapeake and Ohio completed a rail line into the town of Logan, which was at that time a remote county seat of something like six hundred inhabitants; and in the following decade, spur lines sprouted from the main track like shoots from a stem and reached into the remote hollows off the Guyandotte. The line opening up Buffalo Creek was completed around 1912, and from that moment on, the business of Buffalo Creek, like the business of the rest of the county, was coal.

In the early years of the coal industry, the most difficult problem to be solved was the small local labor pool. There were scarcely more than one thousand able men in the county when the coal fields first opened, and many of them were otherwise occupied. In 1905, when the coal companies had to rely on the local supply of talent, there were only four hundred miners in the whole of the county; and as spur lines reached deeper and deeper into coal-rich valleys like Buffalo Creek, the need for additional workers became critical. The need was met, as it normally is, by a large influx from the outside, mainly by native mountaineers from surrounding areas, blacks from the rural South, and immigrants newly arrived from eastern and southern Europe. The labor force reached two thousand in 1910, climbed to ten thousand in 1920, and increased from that total in small and irregular increments until it reached a peak of fourteen thousand in 1950. By 1960, the total had shrunk to its 1915 level of five thousand as a result of automation. Substantial numbers of Southern blacks and European whites worked the mines of Logan County during the boom years of the twenties, but they were the first to leave when the Depression began to affect production in the thirties and they had practically disappeared by the time automation had done its work. Figures gathered by the West Virginia Department of Mines, based on a somewhat different set of estimates than the ones reported above, offer an interesting statistical silhouette of this picture. In the middle of 1921, the labor force of Logan County was 54 percent mountain white, 16 percent Southern black, and 30 percent foreign-born. Ten years later —the total number being somewhat smaller as a result of the Depression—the labor force was 62 percent mountain white, 19 percent Southern black, and 19 percent foreign-born. Clearly, the immigrants were leaving in greater numbers than their native-born comrades, and they were followed in their retreat to the industrial North by large numbers of the blacks a decade or two later.[3]

At the end of the 1950's, when automation had sliced the labor force by more than half, most miners along Buffalo Creek and in Logan County generally were either descendants of original settlers or migrants from nearby counties in West Virginia and Kentucky. The sample I know best, of course, are the 650 plaintiffs who joined the Buffalo Creek legal action, and I can report that not one of them has a recognizable middle or southern European name, although—and there is more than passing irony in this—the superintendent of the mine responsible for the fatal dam is named Dasovich and the president of the corporation being sued, a native of the area, is named Camicia. Virtually all the names on the plaintiff list correspond with the names of original settlers, but this may not mean a great deal by itself because most of them are really clan names, common throughout all of Appalachia, and the people who carry them on Buffalo Creek may have originated anywhere in the mountains. Roughly 10 percent of the people of Buffalo Creek were black on the eve of the flood, and that proportion was reflected in the plaintiff group, although it is worth noting that those same blacks did not constitute 10 percent of the work force. We do not have accurate data for Buffalo Creek specifically, but it is reasonable to suppose that one-fourth and maybe even one-third of the working population was once black. A black woman who came to Buffalo Creek in the 1920's as a child tried to explain:

There was quite a few Negroes when I was young, yes. We don't have too many now, because some of these coal companies, well, looked like they just hired whites, you know. The Negro men didn't have any work, and some of the younger men went on to those different cities, you know, like Detroit. One would leave, he'd come back and tell everyone how good he was doing in Detroit or Chicago there, and he'd get one or two more to go. Well, they'd all follow them out of there, and it looked like the hollow was just stripped of Negro people. Right now I'd say it's ten to one of white people to Negro people. You don't see too many. But there used to be quite a few Negro people, just scattered out all through the hollow. You didn't hardly go into any camp that they wasn't in. But now there's none at Lundale, none at all, because they moved them all out. I went to Logan one day and this woman asked me— one of the clerks—she said, "Mrs. Cartwright, would you tell me something if I asked you?" I said, "If I can." She said, "Could you tell me why there wasn't any colored people killed in that flood?" And I said, "Well, the way I see it, there wasn't any up there to be killed." I said, "These coal companies seen to it that the Negro people weren't there, that's why. And the few that was there, well, they've moved to the lower part of the community. The white people gave them the lower part of the community, so naturally they weren't in the flood area." I said, "They wouldn't give the Negro men jobs, they took them out of the mines. That's why."

For a time, when Buffalo Creek was almost one continuous boom town, it contained a rich mixture of ethnic strains and a virtual pageant of different languages and customs and moral tempers. The presiding officials of the county had never seen or even imagined such a development, and they responded by installing a police system of the most remarkable efficiency. The elected sheriffs of the county had at their disposal an armed posse of deputies, most of them paid by the coal operators, who maintained order in the teeming camps and did everything they could within and without the law to discourage union organizers. The best-known of those sheriffs was one Don Chafin, a man of extraordinary skill and ruthlessness, who patrolled the county as if it were a medieval fiefdom and earned such mixed reviews for his performance that he has since become the leading figure in a dozen local legends and at least one published book.[4] During that time, Logan County enjoyed an almost unblemished reputation for inhospitality to labor unions. " 'Among other things,' " said the ranking coal operator of the county to a committee of the United States Senate in 1921, " 'we kept out, and continue to keep out, the United Mine Workers of America.' "[5]

As a result of all this, Logan County became an extremely important symbol throughout the coal industry in the early 1920's. It was the largest nonunion field in the nation and surely the most tightly policed. For the United Mine Workers, organizing Logan County would have the effect of a military victory. It would act to inspire working miners everywhere, stabilize gains made in other parts of the country, and plant a flag, as it were, on the most stubborn terrain of all. For the coal operators, on the other hand, holding the line would act to promote their own brand of industrial management—a system they took to be remarkably enlightened—and perhaps even strike at the power of the union nationally. Most of the coal fields to the north of Logan County had been organized by 1920, while most of the coal fields to the south had not; so the northern border of the county became a boundary of immense strategic importance. It was like a line drawn in the dust, a challenge to belligerents on both sides to test the territorial claims of the other.

The official historian of Logan County wrote in 1927: "During the twenty-three years of development in this field the dove of peace has ever circled over the county."[6] He meant, of course, that labor struggles had never disturbed the heavily guarded coal camps, and to that extent he was correct. But the dove of peace experienced some anxious moments as it flew its rounds, and at one point, it even had to peer down at men fighting with machine guns and to share those peaceful skies with airplanes carrying bombs.

Until 1921, the war had been fought with more conventional arms. The weapons of the coal companies included injunctions against union organizers, yellow-dog contracts, and a vast arsenal of other legal aids provided by a friendly judiciary; and, in addition to those procedures, the companies knew a hundred ways to intimidate and coerce. There were evictions and beatings, both of them administered by uniformed deputies, and there were blacklists circulated by the coal operators that ended employment possibilities for anyone suspected of union sympathy. " 'Fifty percent of the men on Buffalo Creek would leave if the union came in there,' " said one operator to a reporter from New York in 1921,[7] but just to make sure he had judged correctly, he joined his fellow operators in stationing three deputies on the creek permanently. The reporter just cited called his dispatch "Civil War in West Virginia," and he was not the only correspondent to come back from Logan County full of alarm. A brief note in *The Nation,* dated 1920, concluded with the warning: "Today, wherever I have gone in southwest West Virginia, I find both sides armed. This section of the State is now a powder mine, ripe for blowing up." [8]

The explosion occurred only months after the two reporters had filed their stories. Logan County was by then in a state of armed readiness that might have been called martial law if it had been proclaimed by an official of higher rank than county sheriff, and coal miners from the organized fields to the north, long anxious about their southern flank, decided in the spring of 1921 to march in protest on Logan County. A large group of men gathered in Kanawha County for the purpose of organizing a peaceful demonstration, but as they discussed the matter around campfires and took stock of their collective strength, the project escalated into something resembling an armed invasion. Soon a ragged army of men, several thousand of them, began the long trip to Logan County, armed with an assortment of weapons and carrying provisions that the combat veterans among them were sensible enough to supply. In the meantime, Sheriff Don Chafin had been assembling an army of his own, deploying it along the northern border of the county, and paying special attention to the strategic passes on Blair Mountain. The two forces met there. Men skirmished all along that uneven line, dug into bunkers of every size and firing at one another with ordnance varying from old squirrel rifles to Army-issue carbines and even an occasional machine gun. Two airplanes were requisitioned by the sheriff to distribute leaflets on the other side of the enemy lines, but the pilots were observed to pause in these labors to drop several bombs. Before Federal troops were called in to restore order, hundreds of men had been wounded and an estimated forty-seven were dead.[9]

One seventy-five-year-old veteran of the battle of Blair Mountain who has spent most of his life on Buffalo Creek remembered the scene clearly.

In '21 on Blair Mountain back there, between the thugs and the mine workers, why it was a crying shame to see what went on over there. They loaded them up on coal cars and sent them out of there dead men. I was over there when they dropped a bomb. It went about three foot into the ground—it was headed, you know—and it wouldn't go off. It just lay there and smoked. Don Chafin dropped it. We were all armed with those big Craig rifles, and man, we gave it to him. . . . Shooting at him? You're not kidding we were shooting at him. Man tries to kill you, you'll try to kill him if you can, won't you? Well, that's the way it was then.

One of the main roads into Buffalo Creek passes over Blair Mountain, and it is certain that the people of the creek were aware of—and perhaps even caught up in—the events just described. At that time the camps up and down the hollow were alive with activity under the watchful eyes of the deputies stationed there, and while no reports exist of labor agitation on the creek itself, the old-timers insist that it was union territory in sympathy if not in fact. The old man quoted above who saw the skirmishing on Blair Mountain said, "I carried a pistol so long I had the prints of it on my hip." For some miners, at least, tension must have been high. By the standards of the day, though, the camps along Buffalo Creek were reckoned to be good ones. The same reporter who thought he could sense a civil war coming to West Virginia in 1921 was impressed by the quality of housing on Buffalo Creek, and he counted it among the best he had seen on his tour of the Southern coal fields. The houses were "neat frame structures," he said in his report, "painted red with white trimmings." Although they generally lacked plaster and other everyday comforts, they were furnished with coal-burning grates, electricity in the form of bare bulbs suspended from the ceilings, and private privies out back. Not luxurious, but the paint, the electricity, and the private toilet facilities were not common elsewhere in the coal fields, and the boardwalk in front of the dwellings as well as the plentiful water pumps were worth noting.[10]

The mood of Buffalo Creek, then, was not as somber as was the case elsewhere, and old residents look back on the twenties and thirties as a time of restless expansion and even a certain joy.

When I was a boy, we had a theater here, we had a pool room here, we had a drugstore, a company store, scrip offices and everything. They had a ball diamond down there and we used to play ball. The theater ran every night, you see, and it was run by the company. The whole thing was run by the company. I even remember many years ago on one Fourth of July they killed an ox and dug a pit and barbecued the whole thing right down there. . . . Now when you had the hand sections here, you had all those Italians and colored people and Yugoslavians and Hungarians and, well, all types, and from what I understand from my father, these people would come into New York and get their way paid to down here, you see. They'd give them a pick and a shovel and all the tools they'd need to go into the mines, and they would hold it out of their wages, so much per half, until they had paid for their transportation down here and also for their tools. And at that time we had a lot of boardinghouses, you know. We had an Italian boarding-house, we had a Yugoslavian boardinghouse, we had a colored boardinghouse—large buildings that maybe had twenty-two, twenty-three, twenty-four rooms. Two buildings put together, that's what they'd make the boardinghouses out of. . . . Back then there were fifteen hundred, maybe two thousand people in Lundale. Just before the flood there wasn't but seven hundred and fifty or so.

And another old-timer added: "Well, the whole creek was a city of its own. It was full of houses up through there."

The Depression struck Buffalo Creek hard, as it did all the coal fields, and the boom years of the twenties became something to reminisce about over the back fence as foreign-born workers began to depart and the mines began to lower production. The area was pinched but not strangled, and most residents of the hollow hung on for better times. One young mother remembered her childhood in the late forties and the stories her parents had told about the years before:

It was kind of referred to as "the good old days," but it wasn't so hot, you know. The Depression and all. . . . It was just rough wood floors in the thirties and forties, and news-papers on the wall for insulation. Momma talked about how they'd sit and read the funnies off the wall and everything like that.

The real problems came with the automation of the coal mines in the 1950's, when the entire industry had to regroup. There had been any number of improvements in mining tech-nique since the early days of the industry, but the effect of most of them was to increase the productivity of the men under-ground without replacing any of them. The new machinery introduced in the early fifties, however, was the first step in a drastic revolution, for new methods for extracting the coal it-self (principally the continuous miner) and new methods for processing it once it reached the surface (principally the endless conveyor) not only improved productivity but replaced men altogether. The labor requirements of the industry were more than halved, creating a surplus labor pool in the tens of thousands. The number of working miners in the state of West Virginia shrank from 125,000 to fewer than 50,000 in the space of a few years, and this jettisoning was a decision shared by the coal operators and the leadership of the United Mine Workers. In the twenty-year period between 1948 and 1968, the national membership of the UMW dropped from 350,000 to 128,000—the result of a deliberate policy to move into the second half of the century with a trimmer and more disciplined cadre of workers.[11]

It cost Buffalo Creek a large number of inhabitants when the industry was automated. Something like half the miners in the area lost their jobs, and the waves of out-migration that followed, composed largely of young people, created a fair amount of disruption and left huge holes in the generational structure of the creek. Yet Buffalo Creek was one of those communities with sufficient resources and sufficient good fortune to survive the effects of automation and even to gain a certain measure of strength. For one thing, the flow of people out of the hollow seems to have been gradual and steady, with the result that groups of jobless men did not collect in stagnant pools throughout the area and create a mass of unemployed hangers-on. For another, the mines operating along the creek maintained fair levels of production even during the occasional periods of slump, so the area was never entirely choked off.

In the end, the efficiency of the men who survived the cutbacks was increased considerably, and this, combined with the efforts of the UMW to protect its dwindling constituency, created higher wages and an unaccustomed level of job security. The labor force had been pared drastically, but it included a reasonable sprinkling of younger people and a skilled body of veterans who knew their business well and could command good pay in normal times and extra shifts when production happened to go up.

Quite a few persons were receiving some form of welfare assistance along Buffalo Creek on the eve of the disaster, but it had not become one of the major industries of the hollow, and it had not become an established way of life. The coal companies employed roughly one thousand people out of a population of five thousand, and almost all of them were earning fair wages. Sixty percent of heads of households were working regularly, some 15 percent were retired and living on pensions, and an additional 25 percent were drawing checks for disability, unemployment, death, and so on. When one considers that this last group included a large number of men who had left work for reasons of disability and a large number of women who lived alone, the total is not really very high.[12]

The people of Buffalo Creek do not talk much about the migration of their young men and women, in part because the pattern is so familiar to them by now. One gets the impression that the community as a whole was not seriously disrupted by the change and that the people do not feel a deep and compelling sense of loss. But it is hard not to wonder. On weekends, there seem to be as many Ohio license plates on the road as those of West Virginia, a sure indication of visiting children, while recent high-school yearbooks, with their pictures and descriptions of graduating classes, read like a roster of those who have gone away.

The facts are devastating. According to the United States census, the population of Logan County dropped 40 percent between 1950 and 1960 and another 25 percent between 1960 and 1970.[13] Since the birth rate remained fairly high during those periods, it is reasonable to infer that as many as a third or even a half of the adult population left, and this loss, of course, was concentrated heavily in the younger age brackets. As an example, 65 percent of those people who were between ten and nineteen years of age in 1960 no longer lived in the county by 1970, and when one remembers that the 1960 population had already absorbed a comparable loss in the preceding decade, the size and shape of the out-migration seem incredible.

These figures are for the entire county, of course, and do not necessarily reflect the state of affairs on Buffalo Creek. Nor do we have any way of knowing exact figures for the area, in part because the Census Bureau did not gather separate data on Buffalo Creek until 1970 and in part because the information collected even on that date is largely inaccurate. Knowledgeable old-timers, however, guess that the population of the hollow was once two or even three times larger than in 1970, as the man from Lundale testified, and spot checks of several residential neighborhoods tend to support that estimate.

As elsewhere in Appalachia, families on Buffalo Creek generally say that they want their sons to keep out of the mines, knowing that the only other option is to leave the area altogether. The wife of one miner said, "Well, I don't want either of my sons in the mines. I guess that's a normal feeling about boys," and her mother, who was listening in on the conversation, added quickly, "That's right. I had a son killed in the coal mines and then it was black lung that killed my husband, so the mines almost got me, too." Still, a number of teen-age boys insist that they want to remain on Buffalo Creek even if it means a career in the mines, and present indications are that there will be vacancies for at least a few of them when the time comes. Most of them will leave, however, no matter what their present inclinations, for that is becoming the way of the coal fields.

On the whole, the people of Buffalo Creek were doing all right before the flood. Long years of work were beginning to pay dividends in the form of comfortable homes, brighter futures, and reliable sources of income. The working miners and their families were about to join what Harry Caudill called "that favored class" in the social world of the mountains, "a sort of blue-collar royalty amid a population of industrial serfs."[14] And they were rich in skills, too. Buffalo Creek was still an old mountain hollow in the sense that most people depended on their own individual competencies to keep order in the world around them, and while there were specialists to consult in the event of real technical trouble—doctors and television repairmen, for example—the work of maintenance fell largely on the householders themselves. The women generally remained at home and managed that increasingly complex domain with skill and dignity, accepting a degree of responsibility for the welfare of their families beyond that known elsewhere. And the men, whose competencies were more visible to a stranger, knew a remarkable amount as well. Almost every man in the hollow, with or without the help of a neighbor, could wire a house, install a septic tank, repair an engine, shingle a roof, and build a garage. Almost every man was skilled with a rifle and a fishing line and knew his way around the woods. Almost every man had (or was retired from) a job requiring special training and demanding respect. And almost every man could defend his family, hold his own in any company, avoid demeaning debts, and generally call his life his own.

And yet the skills possessed by both women and men were local to the conditions of their home ground, and the irony of their situation was that they could not easily transfer those proficiencies to other terrains. Most of them are uncomfortable in those corners of the universe where words and symbols have replaced everyday experience as the coin of intelligence. For all their command of the intricate mechanics of mining, most of them do not have the kinds of skill required in foundries or shipyards or automobile assembly plants. And, in general, they do not know how to get along in the more urbanized regions of their own country where the ground is covered by a crust of concrete, where human traffic flows in straight lines or turns on sharp right angles, and where people relate to one another as if they were acting out the terms of a contract. All this is too abrasive, too angular, too quickly paced for the people of Buffalo Creek. They are not sure how to live away from the land or outside the embrace of a more secure communal surround.

When one asks the residents of the hollow what community they belong to, they normally respond with the name of the village in which they happen to live; this is their post office address, after all, and the site of a good many of their everyday activities. But it is evident that they think of Buffalo Creek in general as their real territory. This is where they come from. This is what they mean by "home."

Now sociologists have given a good deal of elaborate thought to what the term "community" does (or should) mean, and we will turn again to that subject later. For the moment, though, it should be noted that the kinds of human relationship that obtain up and down the creek reflect the spirit of *gemeinschaft* as much as anything one can expect to find anywhere in the land. Few status differentiations are made between people (although relations between black and white have a character all their own), and, in true Appalachian fashion, few people are ready to accept the responsibility of leadership. So far as a skeptical outsider can tell, the society of the hollow has become as level in respect to prestige and rank as human habits permit. This means that people are identified by the place they occupy in the larger linkages of family and community rather than by the work they do or the way they live. The assumption seems to be that everyone lives by the same values, knows the same lore, does the same tasks, is acquainted with the same people, and even shares the same thoughts. Relationships between people are thus based on a high degree of mutuality, and they emerge from a quiet agreement to look out for one another and to submerge one's separate sense of self into the larger tissues of communal life. In that sense, the sentiments that are supposed to be characteristic of families reach outward to embrace wider clusters of people—a neighborhood, a village, a whole valley—and this extension is explicitly recognized by the people of the hollow when they comment, as they regularly do, that their neighbors are "just like kin" or that Buffalo Creek in general is "just one big family." "Community," of course, comes from the same root as "communion," and the ancient meaning of the term is entirely apt here. The people of the creek feel that they are joined together in a common enterprise, even though they disagree often as to how that enterprise should be managed, and they feel that they are attached to one another by a common past, a common present, and a common future.

The residents of the hollow are attached to one another in deep and enduring ways, then, but they are also attached to the land. This tendency has roots deep in the Appalachian past and it is reinforced on the creek by the exaggerated contours of the ground. To begin with, the men earn their living by going down into the depths of the earth and delivering themselves to the uncertain mercies of nature. But in other respects, too, people do not so much live *on* the land as *in* it. Most of the terrain they see and relate to is either above them or below them, enveloping them on all sides, and the natural dangers they face, many of them connected with water, come at them from all directions. Danger lashes down on them from above in the form of rain, loosening the mounds of debris on the sides of the mountains; it reaches up from underneath in the form of swelling streams and flooding bottoms; and it pours in sideways when the mountains give way and send torrents of water and rock toward the settlements on the creek. The people of Buffalo Creek are more tuned to the rhythms of nature than a casual observer, impressed by the industrial character of their work, might imagine. The mountains are their security and their insecurity, their solace as well as their curse. They are a familiar, comforting part of the landscape, yet they can become a terrible threat with scarcely a moment's notice.

Right after the flood my sister came and she wanted me to go back to Michigan with her, and I told her I couldn't make it up there. She said, "Well, why can't you?" And I said, "I couldn't see no hills up there and I'd just die." So she said, "Well, them hills almost killed you," and I said, "Those hills just saved me, too." You know the song about West Virginia? Well, that's how I felt. Those hills were a real mommy to me that day.

The sense of attachment to land, particular parcels of land that make up one's home territory, is so important that people do not have a familiar vocabulary for talking about it, but the feeling is reflected clearly and simply in any number of casual comments. A sixteen-year-old boy, living only a few short miles from his original home, could complain: "Where I'm living at now, I don't know nobody around and I don't know my way around the hills up there." And a seventy-four-year-old man, asked what he did with his time before the disaster, could say crisply: "Before the flood was I'd get out and run the woods and deer hunt. And ginseng and bee hunt and squirrel hunt. . . . I was a regular wood hick."

On the eve of the disaster, then, Buffalo Creek was home for a close nucleus of people, held together by a common occupation, a common sense of the past, a common community, and a common feeling of belonging to, being a part of, a defined place.

Appalachian men and women moved into the coal camps balanced, as it were, between contrary inclinations built into their cultural heritage, and they lost a good part of that balance in their new surroundings. The people of Buffalo Creek, however, had found a way to restore much of the old equilibrium. The ways of the old camps were still there, submerged in some, prominent in others. But the complementary half of the contrast was beginning to reassert itself and even to constitute the dominating motif of life in the hollow. Self-assurance had reappeared in the form of a conviction that one could build and protect a satisfying life with one's own efforts. Orderliness had reappeared in the form of a deep pride in home and neighborhood. Independence of thought and manner had reappeared in the form of a commitment to hard work and a rejection of every kind of welfare that was not counted as just compensation. In short, the old mountain strengths were coming back, and with them a growing dignity of person.

The rest of this book will be concerned with the effects of a sudden trauma on the people of Buffalo Creek, but in order to fully understand the context in which this event took place, it is important to appreciate that life in Appalachia has been the source of a deeper and more sustained form of trauma for many years. If the Buffalo Creek flood is viewed as an acute disaster, a sharp and abrupt assault on the integrity of human lives, then the Appalachian experience in general has to be viewed as something akin to a chronic disaster that has worked its way into the human spirit in a more gradual fashion.

When we talked previously about the modern mountaineer, that numbed and dispirited creature shuffling off to welfare offices of one kind or another, we were talking about somebody who already suffers the effects of shock. And this revised portrait is not exclusive to Appalachia. It could serve as a reasonable likeness of people anywhere who seem to have lost out in the contest for status and a proportionate share of the land's wealth, so it should be no surprise if we sometimes catch fleeting glimpses in this portrait of the kinds of people who live in sharecroppers' cabins, on Indian reservations, in black ghettos, on skid rows, in immigrant quarters, or wherever it is that the victims make their home. I will argue in the concluding chapter that these people, too, are the survivors of disaster and that the pain reflected in their faces is a form of trauma. But in the meantime I only want to point out that the people of Buffalo Creek had to face the effects of the flood with reflexes that had already been dulled by a more chronic catastrophe, a catastrophe that is part of the Appalachian heritage.

This is the real measure of their accomplishment. They had not only worked their way out of the poverty and insecurity that had been the lot of their parents, but they had done so by beginning to erase the emotional and cultural deficits that have so long been the counterpart of want in Appalachia.

PART THREE

Looking for Scars

In some respects, the disaster of February 26, 1972, now belongs to the past. Most of the debris has been cleared away from the valley floor and new layers of grass have covered the worst of the physical scars. One needs a guide now to discover which of the open stretches of land was the original site of Saunders or Pardee, and where the homes were most heavily concentrated in Lundale or Braeholm. Occasionally, to be sure, even the most distant stranger is able to find traces of what happened here—half a brick chimney reaching stubbornly out of a grassy field, watermarks on the sides of old buildings, doors and windows boarded over in mute witness to the havoc of the past and the uncertainty of the future.

The worst damage, though, was done to the minds and the spirits of the people who survived the disaster, and it is there that one must begin the search for scars. Two years after the flood, one still met adults on the creek whose faces darkened in anguish as they told stories of "the water" and one still met children who had not spent a single night in their own beds since the flood or who still went to sleep fully clothed "just in case." The flood was with them always. When the weather was good, they found themselves thinking about the flood as every turn in the creek produced a new association. When the weather was bad, they expected the flood to return momentarily. And when they went to bed, poised on the edge of sleep, the black water would crash and smoke through their minds again—an apt prelude to the dreams that would follow.

The case can be stated flatly: Everyone on Buffalo Creek has been damaged by the disaster in one way or another. I was surprised and even a little suspicious during my early visits to the hollow by the remarkable uniformity of the complaints I heard, even though I knew that other students of disaster had noted the same thing. It was as if every man, woman, and child in the place—every one—was suffering from some combination of anxiety, depression, insomnia, apathy, or simple "bad nerves," and to make matters worse, those complaints were expressed in such similar ways that they almost sounded rehearsed. The speaker below happens to be a woman in her early thirties, but her lament could have been voiced by any number of other people on Buffalo Creek.

Well, I've got a nervous condition due to the flood. I am tense. I lose my temper easily. I have bouts of depression every now and then. I can't stand loud noises—they tear my nerves all to pieces. It seems like I've lost all confidence in myself. I am afraid to be alone. I'm afraid of storms. I have nightmares. I am just not the same person I was before. . . . When I have those bouts of depression, everything seems dark. I feel like there is nothing to live for. It is a terrible low.

It is easy to wonder when talking with the survivors or reading the medical reports written about them how the same complaints can reappear so regularly, and social scientists are inclined as a matter of training and general experience to approach this degree of uniformity with a skepticism bordering on disbelief. But no matter how ruthlessly one probes, there is no getting around the conclusion that the survivors have responded to the disaster and have suffered from it in much the same way. We are obviously dealing here with what physicians call a "syndrome"—a group of symptoms that occur together in a kind of package and affect whole populations of individuals similarly—and our eventual task will be to inquire where it comes from.

Before we turn to that subject, however, let us listen for a moment to another survivor. The remainder of this report will present snatches of conversation from interviews and from depositions, mere instants picked from moving reels of tape, to illustrate the various themes that seem to figure in that "syndrome"; but the following comments constitute something closer to a narrative, serving to remind us of business already dealt with and to introduce us to business yet to come. The speaker here is called Wilbur. That is not his name, but it does not matter because the story he tells is representative of the Buffalo Creek experience in everything but detail. It could have happened to anyone there. In a very important sense, it *did* happen to everyone there. The narrative itself is pieced together from a number of different interviews, the first of them dated a year and a half after the disaster and the last of them two and a half years afterward. Wilbur's wife joins the conversation from time to time, although her comments come from a separate source.

Wilbur was born in Kentucky in 1922. He has a strong mountain face, streaked here and there with thin scars and a little out of line. "I was caught under a slate fall," he says matter-of-factly, "and it busted my face up." His breathing is measured, labored, not as if he is gasping for air, but as if he is carefully rationing his intake, making every lungful count. He is one of five brothers, all of whom worked underground, all of whom have black lung in one degree or another, and all of whom had retired on a disability pension by their early fifties. Wilbur, like many of the men his age on Buffalo Creek, is a combat veteran of World War II. He landed in Normandy on D-day, served with Patton's army all the way through France, Belgium, Germany, and Czechoslovakia, and was then sent to the Asian theater of war for another tour of duty in the Philippines, all of which makes his several decorations easy to understand. He went to Buffalo Creek twenty-three years before the disaster and helped raise six children there. I have met Wilbur's wife only once, and that in passing, so I will not risk a description; her contributions to the following were taken from a legal deposition.

Four of Wilbur's children were at home in Lorado when the disaster struck, and in order for the following description to make sense, one needs to know that the wall of water roaring down Buffalo Creek swept a good deal of seepage before it like an enormous broom. That is why a yard could be overrun with water and small debris before the wave itself arrived.

For the sake of a little cigarette, I guess, is the reason we're here today. I woke up to get me a cigarette and my pack was empty. I got up and just put on my trousers and went out of the bedroom—me and my wife was sleeping downstairs with the baby, and the rest of the girls were upstairs. I come through the living room, through the hall, into the kitchen, and got me a pack of cigarettes. For some reason, I opened the inside door and looked up the road—and there it came. Just a big black cloud. It looked like twelve or fifteen foot of water. It was just like looking up Kanawha River and seeing barges coming down four or five abreast.

Well, my neighbor's house was coming right up to where we live, coming down the creek. It was a row of houses, bringing everything as it came. It was coming slow, but my wife was still asleep with the baby—she was about seven years old at the time—and the other kids were still upstairs asleep. I screamed for my wife in a bad tone of voice so I could get her attention real quick—of course I never talk hasty to my wife, but I had to get her attention real quick—and when I screamed at her she knowed something was wrong. She sat up on the side of the bed, pulled the drapes apart, and it was washing cans and tires and everything right over into our yard. I don't know how she got the girls downstairs so fast, but she run up there in her sliptail and she got the children out of bed and downstairs.

Wilbur's wife—Deborah, we'll say—said of that moment:

I don't know when Wilbur got out of bed, but the next I knew I heard him scream, "Oh, Lord have mercy! We've got to get out of here." And when he screamed, I threw the curtain back and looked out the window by the bed, and all kinds of debris was coming across the highway into the yard. My children was upstairs in bed asleep. When I saw that, I grabbed my housecoat as I run through the living room to get upstairs. I run up there screaming for them to get up. How I got to them so fast, I don't know.

And Wilbur continues:

Now I had a car parked out in back of the house. I looked around. Everything above us was acoming right on down, getting closer and closer, and we didn't have much time nohow. So we all got in that car and I was pulling out going up the valley. There was no way in the world out except going right into it. We had water in the yard all around, but none of the big stuff had got down there yet. We headed up the road. My wife was hollering, "Wilbur, you can't get through there," and my daughter Ann—she was twenty-one at the time—she said, "Yeah, Daddy, you can." Well, all the time the water and all those houses was coming right at us in a row.

Well, I don't know what happened. I just turned the key off, left it in the car, and we all rolled out one side, got in the water, run across over to the railroad tracks. And there were gons* for the Lundale mines sitting there to put coal in. My wife and some of the children went up between the gons; me and my baby went under them because we didn't have much time. My neighbor's house hit the gon that we was under while we were still under it and wrecked it, and that turned the big water down through the valley to give us a chance to get up into the woods. We got up into the woods and I looked around and our house was done gone. It didn't wash plumb away. It washed

---

* "Gon" is short for gondola, a railroad car.

down about four or five house lots from where it was setting, tore all to pieces.

At that time, why, I heard somebody holler at me, and I turned around and saw Mrs. Constable. She lived up there above us. Her husband was a wheelchair patient, got hurt in the Lorado mines, and they had four kids. She had a little baby in her arms and she was hollering, "Hey, Wilbur, come and help me; if you can't help me, come get my baby." Well, there was a railroad gon between me and her and I couldn't have got back to her anyway. But I didn't give it a thought to go back and help her. I blame myself a whole lot for that yet. She had her baby in her arms and looked as though she was going to throw it to me. Well, I never thought to go help that lady. I was thinking about my own family. They all six got drowned in that house. She was standing in water up to her waist, and they all got drownded.

Well, the lady that lived in the second house above me, and her oldest son and her daughter, got drownded. I saw them go down. They hollered at me too—they just hollered, "Hey, Wilbur"—but I don't believe they asked me to come help them. And Mr. Connor, I saw him go down with his house. And Clemmer, who lived five hundred feet above me, I saw two of his daughters, teen-age daughters, and one of his daughter-in-laws and her children go down in their house.

The first five houses above me, there was about fourteen drowned, and I saw every one of them in their homes as they floated by where I was at. Well, I looked back on down the valley, and everything had done washed out and gone. I didn't know where my daughter was who lived down below me. And about that time I passed out. I just slumped down. It was around maybe nine o'clock, in that vicinity somewheres.

Deborah, of course, saw this from her perch on the slope:

We were all up there on the hill, but there were so many people trying to get on the hill, and everybody screaming and carrying on—I don't know. We were up on the hill, that's all

I know, and my husband, he just passed out. I turned around and looked down the hill, and there he was on the ground. Me and my two daughters and one of our neighbors, we run to him and got him up off the ground and took him down to a house that was setting by the railroad track. This gentleman's car was parked in an alley and we put him in the car and wrapped him up in a bed blanket or quilt or something that was in the car. We had to wrap him up in that because he was barefooted. He didn't have no shirt on and it was raining and it was real cold. I don't know how long he stayed there before he finally realized where he was at or anything.

Wilbur recovered shortly and began to take stock of the situation:

My house was washed down about five lots from where it had been setting. It had washed up against another big two-story house, leaning on about a forty-five-degree angle, tore all to pieces. The whole back side of it was torn off, the porch was gone, the bathroom was gone, and mud and water and stuff up to the upstairs window. I decided to go over there. I had eight or nine hundred dollars of my money there at the house. I knew where I had it, and I thought maybe I could go in and maybe it wasn't washed away and maybe I'd get some valuable papers and so forth. I got over there and there was a little child had washed up in mine and my wife's bed, and it was torn in half. It was laying there in the bed, looked like eight or ten years old by the size of it. There was a truck, a pickup truck, setting in our living room, and it had a dead body in it. There was two dead bodies washed up with the debris that was laying outside of our house, and I had to step over them to get into the house. I just turned and went back.

Deborah, meantime, had taken refuge in a neighbor's home farther up the slope:

Well, we stayed at the Caldwell's house till just before dark on Saturday evening. We had three injured persons in the house with us. One of them was George Hardy. The other two was Mike Phillips and his little boy, Kenneth. Mike's wife and baby was already killed. Little Kenneth was bruised and muddy and we didn't have any water to clean him up. We had to use Q-Tips to get the mud out of his eyes and ears. George Hardy, he was mashed in here [indicating lower chest]. He had a real large concussion to the top of his head. His hand was all bashed and cut up, and he was just out of his head. He wasn't unconscious or nothing like that, but he was just wild because he had rode that water for half a mile. Mike Phillips said he had jumped out a window and glass had cut the main artery in his arm. He was about to bleed to death. He had a tourniquet or something around his arm.

Wilbur again:

They had a temporary morgue set up over at South Man Grade School. Well, they brung those bodies over there and I went in. Some of them I knew, some I didn't. Some of them you couldn't tell, 'cause they'd be beat up and banged and bruised and cut up and they would be beyond recognition, that's all. Some of them were never identified by nobody.

A fellow by name of Willard Dingess, he asked us was we in the flood and we told him we was. And he asked us where we was going to stay and we said we didn't know. He said, "Well, I've got a little wash house up here, just one room, and you're welcome to it. I've got a little gas heater in it, and you can make your bed down on the floor." So we stayed in that man's wash house, six of us, for nineteen days—a one-room wash house about twelve by twenty. We would eat cold cereal for breakfast of a morning, do without dinner, and then we would go walk about a mile over to the high school and get us a hot supper. We had a little gas-burner stove in that wash house, but we had nothing to cook in.

So that is what February twenty-sixth was like for Wilbur and Deborah and their four unmarried children. The narrative above does not tell us very much about their feelings during the events of that day, probably because they were too numbed at the time to feel much of anything and too overwhelmed later to think that a few words could begin to convey the horror of that scene. But two years after the disaster, they knew their feelings very well indeed. Wilbur talked about his continuing fear of water and storms and any other shift in the weather that hints even vaguely of trouble, and this despite the fact that the family had since moved to a new house so high up a hillside that it would take a flood of Biblical proportions to reach it.

I have the feeling that every time it comes a storm it's a natural thing for it to flood. Now that's just my feeling, and I can't get away from it, can't help it. Seems like every time it rains I get that old dirty feeling that it is just a natural thing for it to become another flood.

Why, it don't even have to rain. I listen to the news, and if there's a storm warning out, why I don't go to bed that night. I set up. I tell my wife, "Don't undress our little girls; just let them lay down like they are and go to bed and go to sleep and then if I see anything going to happen, I'll wake you in plenty of time to get you out of the house." I don't go to bed. I stay up.

My nerves is my problem. Every time it rains, every time it storms, I just can't take it. I walk the floor. I get so nervous I break out in a rash. I'm taking shots for it now.

I live up on a hill now, but that doesn't take away my fear. Every time it rains or goes to come up a storm, I get my flashlight—if it's two o'clock in the morning or if it's three. Now it's approximately five hundred feet from my house to the creek, but I make me a round about every thirty minutes, looking at that creek. And then I come back to the house, light me a cigarette or maybe get me a cup of coffee, and carry my coffee cup with me back down the hill to see if the creek has raised any.

What I went through on Buffalo Creek is the cause of my problem. The whole thing happens over to me even in my dreams, when I retire for the night. In my dreams, I run from water all the time, all the time. The whole thing just happens over and over again in my dreams.

And Wilbur had other complaints, too, which he attributed to the disaster:

This just puts on me a load I can't carry. It seems like I just got something bulging out my chest. I can't breathe like I should, and it just makes me feel that my chest weighs a hundred pounds. Just a big bulge in there.

I can remember back from 1932 up until 1972 much plainer than I can the past two years. In other words, I've got a mental block of some kind. In the past two years, there've been weeks or months went by, and I don't know where they went, what I've done, or what's happened to them.

I don't want to get out, see no people. I despise even going to town, going to the supermarket. I just want to be by myself, and the longer I stay there by myself, the better satisfied I am. I just sit there and whittle. Don't want to see nobody. If anybody comes, I'll be good to them, just as good as I can, offer them the best I got. But as far as going visiting, I don't. Why? I don't know. I'm just a different person. I just don't want to associate with no people. It bothers me. It makes me nervous.

I didn't even go to the cemetery when my father died [about a year after the flood]. It didn't dawn on me that he was gone forever. And those people that dies around me now, it don't bother me like it did before the disaster. It don't bother me no more. I just don't realize that they're really dead. They're just laying there and may be back some day. So I don't know. It just didn't bother me that my dad was dead and never would be back. I don't have the feeling I used to have about something like death. It just don't affect me like it used to.

What kind of person would feel so numbed inside that he could not mourn his father's death? One who has grieved so long that he is almost entirely drained of whatever inner material grief is fueled by, which may be another way of saying, one who thinks himself half gone already. The dead have no warrant to mourn the dead.

Death seemed to figure prominently in Deborah's mind, too:

I'm neglecting my children. I've just completely quit cooking. I don't do no housework. I just won't do nothing. Can't sleep. Can't eat. I just want to take me a lot of pills and just go to bed and go to sleep and not wake up. I enjoyed my home and my family, but outside of them, to me, everything else in life that I had any interest in is destroyed. I loved to cook. I loved to sew. I loved to keep house. I was all the time working and making improvements on my home. But now I've just got to the point where it don't mean a thing in the world to me. I haven't cooked a hot meal and put it on the table for my children in almost three weeks.

I got to the point where I just didn't think I had anything to live for. I just didn't want to live. I thought my family would be better off without me. I just cried all the time. I'd come home from work in the evening, and I'd just sit there and cry. I couldn't do nothing. I didn't want to see people. I got to the point where I hated them. I didn't want nobody around me.

I haven't told anyone this before, but at one point, on a Saturday morning, I was so depressed that I just didn't want to live. I just took a notion that I'd end it. I got the car keys and stepped out the trailer door, but my husband and my oldest daughter at home, they had been watching me, I reckon. When I got in the car and started it, my husband grabbed the door on the driver's side and my daughter ran to the door on the opposite side. I had intended to put that car over Kelly Mountain with me in it. So they drug me back out of the car and took me back in the house and gave me some nerve medicine. I didn't feel as though I was any benefit to my family.

As other people on Buffalo Creek were to discover, even the closest family groups had trouble maintaining their old intimacy in the wake of the flood. Deborah said:

My family is just different. We were always a happy family and a close family. We worked together, my girls and I. We did our housework together. We did our baking together and our cooking together, and we done our sewing together. Just everything we done together. But since this all happened, it seems like one is one way and one's another. They want to pull one way and me the other. I can't get nowhere with them. I can't do nothing with them.

And Wilbur added:

My whole family is a family of fear. Fear of rain, storms, wind, or hail. If it will just cloud up, my family all want to get to higher ground, but there's no place around that I can go to that'll beat where I am. And my wife, she's about to run us all off. She is so nervous and she is so upset, she don't take no interest in what we've got. It's not there. In other words, our house is just a place to stay. It's not a home. And we don't have no neighbors, that's the whole lot of it.

". . . no neighbors, that's the whole lot of it." Deborah and Wilbur have lost a home to which they were attached, lost whatever tone and rhythm kept the family intact, lost a feeling that they were secure in their surroundings, lost the sense, even, that they were fully alive. And a crucial feature in that pattern of loss seems to be the absence of a meaningful community setting. What had it been like before? Wilbur:

We all just seemed, in that vicinity, like one big family. We raised our children with our neighbor's children, they was all raised up together, and if your children wasn't at my house on a weekend from Friday to Sunday, mine was at your house with your children. And that's the way we raised our children, we raised them together, more or less like brothers and sisters. The whole community was that way.

Back before this thing happened, you never went up the road or down it but what somebody was ahollering at you. I could walk down the road on a Saturday morning or a Sunday morning and people would holler out their door at me, and maybe I would holler back at them, maybe go sit down and have us a cup of coffee or a cigarette or something. And there'd be half a dozen families would just group up and stand there and talk. But anymore you never see nobody out talking to one another. They're not friendly like they used to be. It's just a whole different life, that's all.

Now I've moved around from place to place in my time, but there was nothing like this. When I moved to this community, I had neighbors the very next day. The things we did up there, the whole community, we played horseshoes, we went to church together, we would group up when they had holy revivals, and then on Sunday evenings, maybe even on Saturday evenings, we'd come back from service and have our sports. We would play badminton or we'd play horseshoes. Not just one or two of us; we would have the whole bench setting full.

At the time these interviews took place, Wilbur and Deborah had a new home perched high on the hills surrounding the town of Man, but they were obviously pondering the idea of moving away from the Buffalo Creek area and all its terrible memories entirely. Wilbur, in fact, had done a fair amount of searching for likely spots:

What I plan on doing, I plan on going over to the country somewheres and deserting the whole valley so I won't come into contact with nothing that went on before and trying to see if I don't do better. I've been thinking on that for a right smart bit, but I don't yet know that I will. Now property is hard to find and I can't live just anywheres. I have to be kind of choosy. I've been over to Kentucky two trips and I couldn't find nothing to suit me. I went over to Charleston yesterday, and I wouldn't go there if they give me the whole place. I don't want nothing to do with it. I'd just be on edge all the time. I just don't believe I could take it. There's nothing around you other than just buildings. It's all level. There's not a wind-

breaker nowheres, and if there happen to come a windstorm through there and if you were in an area where it was going, why you'd go right with it.

Now there's lots of good river bottoms over in Kentucky, but I don't want to be near water under no circumstances. I've had all the water I want.

I'd like to live in a country type of place, but not at the head of no hollow. I don't want to live in the head of a hollow. I wouldn't mind living in the outskirts of a town, what you'd call a suburb or something like that, if I could find a suitable place. But I wouldn't have just any place regardless of whether it cost a large amount or a small. I just wouldn't have a place in the middle of town. Don't want it.

We will return to the themes suggested by this narrative, trying to see if we can identify some of the sources of the acute discomfort experienced by Deborah and Wilbur and the hundreds of others like them.

In the two years following the disaster, people like the two above were trying to come to terms with the horror of the flood and with their own inability to build a new life. Most of them still seemed dazed by what had happened—wounded might be a better term—and they could not mobilize the energy or the conviction necessary to stabilize their own lives or to rebuild the communities in which they had invested so much.

Part of the problem, as we shall see, had to do with the lack of a sound communal base, and this difficulty was compounded enormously by several new developments on Buffalo Creek that came in the wake of the flood.

The first of these developments had to do with the trailer camps provided by HUD. We noted earlier that the survivors who found themselves without shelter after the flood were scattered more or less at random into thirteen trailer camps, some of them on Buffalo Creek itself and others in nearby hollows. No effort was made to group people according to old neighborhood patterns, and as a result most people had to look across the narrow spaces dividing their new quarters at relative strangers. One young woman wrote thoughtfully about her experiences in the camps:

Perhaps the communities people were placed in after the disaster had a lot to do with the problem. If there had been time enough to place people [near] the same families and neighbors they were accustomed to, it might have been different. Instead, they were haphazardly placed among people that were strangers with different personalities. I have conflicts with people I don't even know. It seems like everyone's on edge, just waiting for trouble to happen. Things like that just didn't happen in Lundale. Everybody knew you and your personality.

Life in the trailer camps presented a number of other difficulties as well. The mobile homes were small and cramped, so small that families of more than four or five could hardly manage to eat meals together, never mind inviting friends or kin for larger gatherings. "The last meal our family had together was on February 25, 1972," said a mother of five. The trailers were poorly insulated, too, hot in the summer and cold in the winter, and they furnished almost no protection from the noises of a crowded refugee center. Being made of metal, they amplified the sounds of bad weather; raindrops landed like hammer blows and even moderate winds made the entire structure rattle.

We just can't seem to rest. Those trailers are just continuously cracking and popping. You'd think they're on fire. Heat will cause something to either contract or expand or something like that and all through the night you can hear them trailers apopping and acracking and you got to go check 'cause you don't know when they're on fire.

And there was little privacy. Family quarrels could be heard five or six doors away, and such everyday sounds as bedsprings moving or glassware breaking or toilets flushing were broadcast not only to everyone within the trailer itself but to half the neighbors as well. There were almost no play areas in the camps, no space to move around in; there were no front porches to act as a zone of transition between the privacy of the inside world and the communality of the outside world. In most of Appalachia, where life is centered on the front stoop, one's door forms a sensitive boundary between the interior and the exterior, but those trailer doors did not work properly at all from either a symbolic or a practical viewpoint. They opened outward, for one thing, which meant that one could not affix screens in the summer to keep out insects or storm doors in the winter to keep out rain and snow. And they opened out on to nothing.

Buddy, you don't want my opinion about those HUD trailers or no other trailer. I wouldn't give a dime for every one of them. I just don't like them. They're hotter than a firecracker and you just can't do nothing. You can't get out. You can't get out the front door without you're looking at another man's door and he's the same way to you.

So there was virtually no privacy inside to guard and virtually no community outside to make contact with.

There isn't one family in this trailer camp that I'm acquainted with. The people living here are very different in living habits than what I consider to be community living. There is no such thing here as a neighbor.

And these problems were sharply aggravated by the strained relations that developed between the residents and the HUD personnel. Trailer camps like these are bound to become encrusted with rules, all the more so if they are managed by a Federal bureaucracy; and the impersonality of those rules, in turn, is bound to annoy a mountain people who distrust governments anyway and dislike discipline imposed from the outside.

Well, I don't like to be told what to do like you would tell a baby or someone who is confined to an institution or jail. I like to be my old self, doing what I want to when I want to.

Moreover, a number of the residents, already sensitive to the fact that they were becoming more and more dependent upon a form of Federal charity, came to feel that they were being patronized by HUD officials and treated without the dignity they deserved. One highly respected couple returned from a visit to the HUD office with the report that they had been "treated like beggars," and a neighbor of theirs complained:

We all seem to have our problems with HUD personnel. They make only problems for us people. They harass us folks all the time. We feel like poor white trash every time we have any dealings with them.

In general, then, the residents of the trailer camps shared a sense of being pressed in on all sides, hedged in by the hardships resulting from the disaster, the narrowness of their new living arrangements, and the elaborate superstructure of rules imposed on them. For people used to a freer set of rhythms, this was almost a form of suffocation.

Now there is nothing. We can't even have a family reunion anymore because there is no space in this trailer. I feel like I am living in a box and my disposition gets so bad sometimes that I have to get out and take a walk to feel like I can breathe again.

We are closed in like a pack of sardines. I have had rats, mice, roaches, ants, things I can't get rid of. I have no privacy. There is a family that lives across from me and they have wild parties all the time. It is noisy. I cannot get out. There's no place to go. You cannot get out in the yard. You just have a little space for a yard, no porch, no screen door, no storm door. I can't get any fresh air.

I'm living in a HUD trailer, and I feel like I'm in jail. We always had a house, you know, with room to move, but I told my husband that I was going crazy being cooped up. Sometimes I could just scream, you know, because it seems like I'm so closed in. It just feels like you're going to smother in a trailer.

In everyday conversation, the trailer camps were likened to "concentration camps" and the mobile homes to "prisons" or "sweatboxes." "We are all like animals in a cage," said one resident bitterly.

The trailer camps contributed significantly to the discomfort of the survivors, but there were other complications as well, the main one being a decision by the state of West Virginia to build a fine new highway right up the middle of Buffalo Creek. Plans for some kind of road construction had been on and off the drawing boards for several years, although nothing of any real consequence had been done to implement them; and now it seemed as if the state had decided to take advantage of the flood's thorough demolition work and lay new pavement in its path. There were many arguments in favor of the highway, of course. It might bring new industries and new opportunities into the hollow as well as increase the value of the land. But there were arguments in opposition, too, some of them expressed and others not. For one thing, a project of that size was bound to absorb much of the available land, and this meant that large numbers of survivors were to discover that the torn lots on which their homes had stood, the last remnant of their former holdings, were being commandeered by the State Department of Highways. Moreover, roads are a very important part of the social setting in Appalachia. Major routes are called "arteries" in many sections of the country, but in places like Buffalo Creek, served by a single strip of asphalt, they are exactly that. A road is the channel along which the life of the community flows, the thread holding the disparate parcels of neighborhood together. People sit and watch the traffic drift along, identifying the vehicles of friends, waving to them as they meander by, speculating on the nature of their errands, and thus participate in the tides of communal life. A road, then, is almost like a civic square, a village green; but a highway is something else altogether, and a good deal of the distress caused by those construction plans may very well have stemmed from a feeling that the hollow was about to lose some of its special temper and pace.

In any event, the long intermission spent in trailer camps and the continued uncertainty about the road left survivors in a critical position, stranded, as it were, on the very spots to which they had been washed by the flood. And many survivors, dissatisfied by the meager attempts of the coal company to compensate them for their losses, spent those two and a half years waiting for legal proceedings to bring them what they took to be their due. The coal company set up a claims office shortly after the disaster, offering to repay survivors for the actual value of property destroyed, but many people thought that they were being treated shabbily by the company attorneys and turned elsewhere for relief. One of those lawyers, trying to describe the progress of negotiations with the survivors, is reported to have said: " 'A lot of water has passed over the dam.' "[1]

So conditions on Buffalo Creek in the years following the disaster were not conducive to rapid recovery, but these were aggravations of old injuries rather than the source of new ones, and the root cause of the troubles experienced on the creek was still the flood itself and the many traumas it inflicted.

I want to propose that the trauma experienced by the survivors of the Buffalo Creek disaster can be visualized as having two closely related but nonetheless distinguishable facets—"individual trauma" and "collective trauma."

By *individual trauma* I mean a blow to the psyche that breaks through one's defenses so suddenly and with such brutal force that one cannot react to it effectively. This is what clinicians normally have in mind when they use the term, and the Buffalo Creek survivors experienced precisely that. They suffered deep shock as a result of their exposure to death and devastation, and, as so often happens in catastrophes of this enormity, they withdrew into themselves, feeling numbed, afraid, vulnerable, and very alone.

By *collective trauma,* on the other hand, I mean a blow to the basic tissues of social life that damages the bonds attaching people together and impairs the prevailing sense of communality. The collective trauma works its way slowly and even insidiously into the awareness of those who suffer from it, so it does not have the quality of suddenness normally associated with "trauma." But it is a form of shock all the same, a gradual realization that the community no longer exists as an effective source of support and that an important part of the self has disappeared. As people begin to emerge hesitantly from the protective shells into which they have withdrawn, they learn that they are isolated and alone, wholly dependent upon their own individual resources. "I" continue to exist, though damaged and maybe even permanently changed. "You" continue to exist, though distant and hard to relate to. But "we" no longer exist as a connected pair or as linked cells in a larger communal body.

The two traumas are quite closely related, of course, but they are distinct in the sense that either of them can take place in the absence of the other. A person who sustains deep psychic wounds as the result of an automobile collision, for example, but who never loses touch with the rest of his community, can be said to suffer from a form of individual trauma. But a person whose feelings of well-being begin to deteriorate because the surrounding community is stripped away and can no longer supply a base of support—as often happens in slum clearance projects, for instance [2]—can be said to suffer from a form of collective trauma. In most human disasters the two traumas occur simultaneously and are experienced as two halves of a continuous whole, but it is worth insisting on the distinction in a study like this one because it alerts us to the possibility that the psychic injuries observed in a place like Buffalo Creek can be attributed to the second trauma as well as the first and because it lends emphasis to the point that people find it difficult to recover from the effects of the individual trauma so long as the community around them remains in shreds. It is a general theory in psychiatry that time heals all but the most devastating traumatic wounds, but there is a good deal of experience to argue that time can work its special therapy only if it acts in concert with a nurturing communal setting.

One must look for scars, then, not only in the survivors' minds but in the tissues of their social life as well.

Individual Trauma: State of Shock

THE FIRST CHAPTER of this report tried to suggest what the disaster *looked* like to the people who experienced it. We should now try to imagine what the disaster *felt* like, and the only responsible way to approach that objective is to quote the survivors at some length and allow them to carry the main burden of the discussion. Some of the quotations to follow may seem unnecessarily grisly and others may seem unnecessarily repetitive, but one has to become immersed in the overwhelming mass of detail to gain even a dim notion of what happened. The words we will be reading were uttered by solo voices, each of them expressing a private grief in a private way; but they are drawn from a vast chorus of similar voices, and together they tell of experiences common to a whole community.

First, a few figures. Some 615 survivors of the Buffalo Creek flood were examined by psychiatrists a year and a half after the event in connection with the legal action described earlier, and at least 570 of them, a grim 93 percent, were found to be suffering from an identifiable emotional disorder. Now a skeptical neighbor from another of the behavioral sciences may want to make some allowance for the fact that psychiatrists looking for mental disorder are more than apt to find it, but even so, the sheer volume of pathology is horrifying. Pittston also conducted a round of psychiatric evaluations and found a similar incidence of disorder, although the physician in charge of those examinations thought that the disturbances he was noticing could not have been a result of the flood. The medical names for the conditions observed in both sets of examination are depression, anxiety, phobia, emotional lability, hypochondria, apathy, insomnia; and the broader syndrome into which these symptoms naturally fall is post-traumatic neurosis, or, in a few cases, post-traumatic psychosis. But the nearest expressions in everyday English would be something like confusion, despair, and hopelessness. Listen to these voices for the profound pain they reflect.

As for myself, every time I go to Buffalo Creek I start to cry because it is like visiting a graveyard. I left there crying after the flood on Sunday and I wake up all through the night crying. I can see the water from the dam destroying my house, clothing, furniture, cars. We lost everything we had saved all our lives in a very few minutes. I can see my friends drowning in the water and asking for help. I will never be the same person again.

I think we will have to leave Buffalo Creek before we can get any peace. I have been a resident of this place for forty-five years and now I am unhappy, dissatisfied, and disturbed. The disaster has left me very nervous. When something like that happens and all the friends you have had down the years— some are living and some are dead and some you don't know where they're at—you don't forget something like that. As we stood in the rain and snow and saw what we saw coming down the hollow—houses washing down Buffalo Creek, people crying and getting out of the creek naked and almost frozen to death, people begging for help which we could not give. I had about twenty or more of my kin killed in the disaster, and if these things won't crack a person up they sure are strong people.

Well, you can't think straight. Your mind is muddled and you can't reason things out. People who went through this thing up there are so confused and so frustrated and so torn up that their lives will never be the same again. Nothing will ever be the same again. There's no way to describe the horror of that day. That would upset anybody, as cool as you are, buddy. It changed their lives. It changed everything about them.

Well, I've just about given up all hope. I don't know what to do. I don't know which way to turn. It seems like it's useless to even want to go on and try again. It's so hard to try to start a new life with nowhere to start from. It's enough to drive you insane, I suppose. I don't believe I'm insane, but it wouldn't take much to put me there the way things is going. I just lay there and study and worry and think and try to figure a way to live a life again that's peaceable. I wonder if I'm ever going to make it or not. I just about lost all hope of ever making it anymore. I've just about give up on it. It just don't seem to matter no more to me.

It seemed like people afterwards, they just went completely wild. They just wasn't the same. Living from day to day. Now, myself, there was months and months and months where I felt I was just sitting around waiting to die. That's the way I felt. I thought there's nothing to live for. And at that time I just didn't care, either. And I believe a lot of these people was the same way. Everything's changed. Nothing's the same.

My husband said he saw live wires on fire as he ran and had fear that he would be electrocuted by them. The water missed him by seconds. He saw our house go and then he said that's all he can remember. He has a mental block of it all floating by. He said he doesn't know how long he sat there or what he saw. There were twenty or more bodies went by him. He found a woman that day of the flood, hanging in the old tipple between Lorado and Pardee. He had known that woman all his life and grew up with her children. Her daughter and three sons floated by him as he sat on the bank, too. He said he lives in fear that he will remember some day.

Most of the survivors responded to the disaster with a deep sense of loss, a nameless feeling that something had gone awry in the order of things, that their minds had been bruised beyond repair, that they would never again be able to find coherence, that the world as they knew it had come to an end. These feelings, of course, were experienced as a generalized, pervading sense of gloom, and the men and women of the hollow did not try to catalogue the various strains that contributed to it. But there are recognizable themes in the stories they tell that give us some idea what the sources of their pain might be, and we should try to isolate a few of them.

ON BEING NUMBED

In the first place, almost everybody who survived the disaster did so by the thinnest of margins, and the closeness of their escape, combined with the relentless savagery of the water, left them feeling numbed and depleted, almost as if the rush to safety had consumed most of their energy and the sheer force of the waves passing below them had somehow drawn off what reserves were left. "When you get caught out there in that water," a middle-aged woman explained, "it will make you feel like that—washed away, just about washed away."

There were some dramatic escapes. The only survivor of a family of six, the young man mentioned earlier, dove into the bed of a pickup truck as the waters engulfed his home and then rode the current several miles down the stream before grabbing an overhead branch and pulling himself to safety. A young woman, having waved goodbye to her husband and child as water filled the room in which they were imprisoned, was somehow blasted through the wall by a collision and thrown onto an air mattress that carried her to safety. An elderly couple managed to scramble into the cab of their truck seconds before the water carried them off down the hollow, dry in their night-clothes despite the fact that the cab was totally submerged part of the time. There were many escapes of this kind, and the stories will be told for years. But most survivors had a less dramatic if equally frightening time of it.

There were those who had a moment's notice and made it up the side of a hill in time to see the black current sweep by below them.

Down below there was a huge amount of water. It looked like a river passing by so fast. It was going so fast I couldn't believe what was happening. I could see houses—some were broken up and some looked like whole houses still in good shape—just floating down this water. Some were going real fast, smashing into each other, and people were screaming.

There were those who saw the wave coming and barely escaped its path.

We walked out on the porch. Suddenly we could hear something that sounded like rolling thunder, only it was about ten times louder. I looked back and saw the thick black waters cover over the neighbor's house. We began grabbing the children and threw them into vehicles and started up the hill. I started screaming and lost control of my legs. For a minute there I couldn't get that car to move at all.

There were those who got caught in the water and managed somehow to wade or swim or thrash their way to the slopes.

I ran to the front porch and paused for a second or two to try and visualize where the sidewalk was beneath the black water. I began to run, but after the second stride the current knocked me off balance and I fell into the cold black murk, drenched. I scrambled to my feet, frantically running, stumbling, slinging my arms around to hold my balance, with no sense of direction except to get out of that black mess. I just did make it.

And there were those who did not have time to leave their houses at all and had to sit in terror as the water bore down on them and the world came apart all around them.

I walked to the back porch and saw my neighbors running and screaming. I heard one say "the dam." I then came running through the house and told my wife to head for the hills. When I got to the living room I saw the water rolling by the window. I knew then there was no way out of the house, and all hope just vanished. My wife started crying and praying. I saw a housetop going by with a friend of mine on top. Then I heard a big crash and saw the big wave of water coming with houses and trash in it. There was nothing we could do but watch and pray for the best and wonder how long our house would stand. I saw four or five of our neighbors' homes go by. I tried to think of a way out, but there just wasn't any. The water was thirty or forty minutes passing, but it seemed like it would never pass. Then finally it was gone and left a dead body lying on the hood of my car.

No sooner had they escaped, however, than people began to feel that they were unable to move, caught in a sluggish bank of fog, held back, as in a dream, by forces that slackened the muscles and paralyzed the will. A number of people remembered having gone limp or having lost control of their limbs, as was the case, for example, of the woman who could not persuade her legs to take command of her car. And another woman recalled:

After I looked back down the hollow and saw what that black water was doing and saw people struggling to get something to hold on to and not being able to help anyone, I just lost all control over my body. It seemed my body worked without my mind helping.

Quite a few others compared their reactions to a dream state.

I will never be able to explain my feelings, never. It was like— Did you ever dream about trying to get out of a building and something was holding you back and you just couldn't hardly make it? That was my feelings exactly. That's the best way I can explain it to you.

And some simply went blank in mind as well as limp in body.

I just didn't—I really didn't feel anything. Inside, you know, I didn't. Things just wasn't connected. Like I couldn't remember my telephone number. I couldn't remember my brother's or sister's telephone numbers. I couldn't remember where I lived. It's just—I don't know how to express it. I was just standing there and it seemed like I really didn't have anything on my mind at the time. Just everything disappeared.

In effect, then, people seemed physically overwhelmed by the brutality of the scene being enacted a few feet below them. Drawn tight by the narrowness of their escape, stunned by the ferocious energy of the water, horrified by the death and destruction, they simply went numb, as if yielding to the enormity of what was happening. One woman reached the knoll of a nearby hill several minutes before the wave struck and was looking straight down on her own neighborhood when the carnage began.

During the initial shock, we just stood there so helpless. We just stood and stared, nobody talking, just like we were in a trance, just numb. A house would go by, a car would go by, and you would wait for yours to go by. You'd see your neighbor's house go by, everything they had worked for for so long.

And we stood there so helpless, couldn't do nothing. We were there watching people trying to get out of the way, and the water just swept them right down. At first we couldn't cry. We couldn't cry. We were just appalled at the horror.

One of this woman's closest neighbors was standing on the same knoll a few feet away and looking down on the same scene.

I went to the edge of the hill and saw boards blocking the bridge and people in the bottom running. The black water came then. There were cars trying to back out of it. I saw three houses raise and float down to the railroad trestle and break up, and the water came down the bottom that we lived in. I couldn't stand any more. It was like something was wiped over me and left me different.

What made her and so many of her fellows "different" was something akin to an anesthetization of the senses, a closing of some inner valve so that no more horror could reach to the seat of their being. Most of us use the expression "I can't stand it" so many times in the course of an everyday existence that we scarcely recognize the signs when that condition becomes a simple fact of the psychological economy. The scene is so intolerable that one screens it out of one's line of vision. The screams for help are so wrenching that one scarcely hears them, postponing their desperate message for a later reckoning in daydreams and in nightmares. And the assault on one's person is so fierce and unrelenting that one has no choice but to yield. Social scientists who have done research on disaster have noted for some time that survivors tend to regard the attacking force as something directed at them individually, an enemy whose motive is personal malice. William James happened to have been in the vicinity of San Francisco at the time of the 1906 earthquake, and his initial reaction was that the blow had been aimed at him personally by a vaguely human agent.

First, I personified the earthquake as a permanent individual entity. . . . It came . . . directly to *me*. . . . Animus and intent were
never more present in any human action, nor did any human activity
ever more definitely point back to a living agent as its source and
origin.
All whom I consulted on the point agreed as to this feature in their
experience.[1]

Against all that force and animus, the person has no defense
other than to make himself small, to draw a curtain over his
sensory organs, to take his inner self out of the field of combat
so that there is less of him to be wounded and less of him to
be implicated in the insanity of what is happening. This
process of retreating into a limp slump has been noted again
and again in disaster research. Robert Jay Lifton calls it "psychic numbing," and Anthony F. C. Wallace gives it a prominent place in his notion of the "disaster syndrome."[2] But on
Buffalo Creek the process appears to have been somewhat
exaggerated by the extraordinary power of the flood and by
the helpless state in which it left its victims. To be drained of
energy, to be emptied of motive and self, is to be on the verge
of death itself, and that is how many of the survivors viewed
their own condition later. "I feel dead now. I have no energy.
I sit down and I feel numb."

THE FACES OF DEATH

In the second place, virtually everyone on Buffalo Creek had
a very close encounter with death, either because they felt
doomed themselves or because they lost relatives and friends
or because they came in contact with dead bodies. The upper
half of the valley, where most of the worst destruction took
place, was strewn with the signs of a terrible tragedy: "There
were people in trees and on the railroad tracks, on porches,
on the road." But people who lived downstream were not
spared the agony of this scene either, for the current carried
it to them.

I looked up the road and saw it coming, the water. I said, "Here comes a big old doll." But when it got to me, I said, "Lord, that's a kid," and I took off down the creek after it. Just muddy. It was naked, didn't have no clothes on. But the water was running faster than I could run. I couldn't keep up with it.

So death seemed to be everywhere, overhead, underfoot, crouched in every pile of wreckage.

As soon as the water went down, I began to work digging the bodies out of the debris. I worked for eight days after the flood looking for bodies, and I recovered twenty-two of them. The last one I found was a little five-year-old boy. It reminded me so much of my own little boy that I could not take any more. That is when I went to pieces.

On Sunday evening I walked to the Lundale company store to see if I could get some water and milk. They had just found my best friend. She was washed up against the side of the store. I can't forget the horrible expression in her eyes and on her face. She looked as though she was scared to death, not drowned.

Many of the men on Buffalo Creek were combat veterans who had seen dead bodies before, and everyone in the coal fields has a fair notion of what death looks and feels like. But this was wholly different. Death on the battlefield or in the mines offers at least a thin layer of insulation, if only in the sense that one's nerves are braced in anticipation and one's imagination has had a chance to rehearse the possibilities. But death at home—an ugly death that crashes in when one's defenses are relaxed and one's children are nearby and one's clothing is down both figuratively and literally—is quite another matter.

I have been in the mines and seen people killed, drug people out from under slate falls. I'm pretty hard to touch. But this—this is too much to cope with.

In one respect, perhaps, the people of Buffalo Creek might be said to have been "prepared" for the disaster and to have already done a fair amount of what Irving L. Janis calls "the work of worrying." [3] They live in a land where calamity is far from uncommon and they had been apprehensive about the dam looming above them for years. When disaster strikes right out of the blue, however, it is almost easier to face than when it appears as a grotesque exaggeration of something expected. Floods are not unexpected in places like Buffalo Creek, any more than bombing was unexpected in wartime Hiroshima or Dresden; but what happened was so far out of reasonable scale, so far beyond what the mind could have imagined, that people were unable to mobilize the emotional resources they had placed in reserve for emergencies. They were unable to respond, even to grieve.

Moreover, the faces of death on Buffalo Creek were badly disfigured ones. People spoke of these faces in matter-of-fact tones (or so it seems when their words are transferred from tapes to transcripts), but there was deep emotion behind such comments by both young and old. A sixteen-year-old girl: "Bodies? They were naked and messed up and scarred, stuff like that. You know, missing parts." A sixty-five-year-old miner: "We waded through that slurry mud and debris on the way up. I passed a good friend of mine up in a brush pile. He looked like he had been sandblasted." And others said:

Those bodies were distorted. You couldn't tell who they was. One of the corpses that I helped unload was a good friend of mine and I didn't even know who he was, he had so much muck and stuff on him. All the corpses I seen that day, none of them had any clothes on. They was all swelled up. Like I say, they was black with muck and mud. It was hard to distinguish who they was or anything about them.

I think the strain of trying to find and identify my brother and his wife had an effect on my nervous system. Neither of them was found for some days, and almost every day I made a trip to the morgue. My sister-in-law was found on March fourth, more than seventy miles downstream from here. My brother was found at about the same time, but neither my wife nor I could identify him for several days because he didn't look like himself.

Two young men. I don't know who they were. I picked the bodies up, put them in my truck, and kept them overnight. They was just black hulks. You couldn't tell who they were or what they were.

I went over to the post office and a smell was coming from the woodpile. I went over and started taking pieces of wood, and I found a body. It was Sarah Barlow. I picked up the back of her hair, what hair she had left. She didn't have no clothes on, and I turned her over and the blood and mud and water came out of her eyes and nose and mouth and ears. I had to go set down.

I saw them piled in the back end of a pickup truck. I walked by and looked at them and thought maybe I might recognize some of them, but you couldn't. They just looked like somebody that had been drug out of a sludge hole or something, clothes tore off and face skinned up. One kid had all the hide tore off the top of his foot, toenails and all. Looked like about ten years old, hair all full of coal dirt. You wouldn't have recognized any of them because they was in such bad shape. Their clothes was all tore off and they were skinned up and part of their scalps gone and— It was a horrible thing, I'll tell you it was. A man will never forget it. If I live to be a hundred years old, I will never forget it.

What people remembered most vividly, however, were the children.

Walking out to get to my neighbor's house there was a baby. I could just see the top part of it. It looked like a boy, the way his head was made and his hair, but it was unrecognizable because it just looked like somebody had peeled the top layer of skin off. It was just red and that old coal mud all in his hair.

They was muddy all over and had muck in their hair. Their little eyes were open, the kids' were, and there was dirt in their eyes and their mouths was open and full of dirt. It looked horrible.

Just as I come off the hill, I was fixing to step over something, and I looked down and I thought at first, "Oh, that looks like a doll." And a friend of mine says, "Huh-uh, that's not a doll, that's a child." So he moved the plank and it was a boy. He looked to be about five or six years old. You know those dolls with the big legs all bent out? His legs was like that. And I grabbed my whole body and hugged myself together.

My son was crushed up so bad, I went about four times trying to identify him. His head was just smashed to jelly. He had just a little bit of sideburn left, where you could tell it was him. All the bodies had swelled up so bad, you had to just keep looking and looking. . . .[4]

It is understandable, then, that there would be a good deal of what Robert Jay Lifton calls "death anxiety" on Buffalo Creek, a preoccupation with the forms death can take and a constant reliving of those moments in which it occurred.[5] The survivors were still trying to come to terms with that gruesome reality. Schoolchildren drew pictures of bloated bodies in oceans of ink-black water; adults found themselves reviewing the old scenes again and again in their minds. And if their interest in the topic almost seemed to approach a macabre attraction, a perverse compulsion, it only indicates that the task of resolution is very hard.

The house was right across the street from the grade school, and that's where the temporary morgue was set up. I would sit there on the porch sometimes and watch the bodies being brought in. Then I'd watch cars pulling up and people getting out and going in, women crying, men holding on to them. They would come back out screaming from trying to identify people they loved. That bothered me a lot. I did not break down, but I would sit there like it was a magnet. I felt I had to watch it and I'd sit there maybe all day long.

Death like this does not retreat into some discrete compartment of the mind, emerging now and again to haunt one's dreams. It remains with one, becoming a part of the very air one breathes and a dominating figure in one's imagery. Most individual deaths, of course, take place in the privacy of a home or behind the walls of a hospital, where they are screened from view and sanitized, muffled, tidied up. But collective deaths like those at Buffalo Creek do not permit the setting up of screens. Death lies out there at its inescapable worst. There are no wreckers to rush the crushed vehicle away, no physicians to shroud death in a crisp white sheet or to give it a clean medical name, no undertakers to wash away the evidence of death and to knead out the creases of pain or fear. It's all there—an advance look at hell. And the sight does not go away easily.[6]

They thought perhaps that she was a black person. Come to find out later on all the people looked like that, greasy and black, and the look on their face was just horror. If you've ever seen anybody die a violent death, it's not like going to a funeral home and seeing people all dressed and prepared. Instead, you see the fear in somebody's open eyes, mouths awry. It's just a horrible thing.

SURVIVAL AND GUILT

In the third place, where one finds death on so large a scale, one also finds guilt. It is one of the ironies of human life that individuals are likely to regret their own survival when others around them are killed in what seems like a meaningless and capricious way, in part because they cannot understand by what logic they came to be spared. People who sense the hand of God in it have many hard questions to ponder, and none of them are very comforting. One woman on Buffalo Creek, for instance, was deeply puzzled by the fact that she, an indifferent worshiper, should have lived through the flood while her devout sister did not. But people who sense nothing more calculating in it than luck or good fortune have a difficult time of it too, for when one person lives and another perishes in circumstances like these, the mind must confront some awkward realities. It is a reminder to the survivor how vulnerable he is and how uncertain life can be, and it is a sign to him that he has gained substance from his fellow's death, if only in the sense that he is the recipient of his fellow's share of grace and good luck. There may be a world of difference between the state of "having survived" and the state of "having killed" in law and in public morality, but that difference does not seem so obvious in those regions of the mind where old doubts and old guilts are stored away. The process begins right after the event:

The women started praying and some of them were crying and people were getting sick all over again [when rumors of a second dam break began to circulate on the hillsides]. There was just panic in the air. I kind of had the feeling like, "Well, it didn't get me the first time, it's bound to this time." But I wasn't worried about it for some reason. I just felt like it was due me, they owed me because I had lived through it the first time. So I just sat there and waited on it. I sat there patiently and waited for the water to come.

And it continues for years afterward:

Sometimes when you go to sleep and start to relax, the nightmares start. The water comes down again; you lay there and

*can't move, screaming for help. I believe that everyone con-
cerned would have been better off if everyone had been killed
that morning of February 26, 1972. Then you wouldn't have
to be sorry that your friend was killed and you were not.*

*I worry about such things as: Was it my big triple-glass mir-
ror that cut off one of my dear friend's head? This worries me
to death. These may seem like silly things to you, but just try
sleeping with such thoughts on your mind.*

*One of our very close friends stayed drunk for almost five
months because he could still hear his brother and sister
screaming for their mother and his mother screaming "God
help us" when the water hit them. Sometimes he talks with me
about it and I get the impression that he feels bad because he
lived through it all. He is only twenty years of age, but I guess
sometimes he feels like a thousand years old.*

One source of guilt, then, is a generalized feeling—often
found among combat troops, by the way—that the death of a
neighbor or a buddy has contributed to one's own survival.
Each death seems to pare down the odds against surviving, to
help satisfy the grim quota asked by the fates; each death
seems to enhance one's own chances. The human mind has its
own probability theories, and while they do not work out
mathematically, they have a certain elementary logic. Note
this account, for instance, of why someone in fear of his life
should avoid crowds.

*I don't like to be in a crowd of people no more. If I can
avoid them, I'll go on home. Now I couldn't tell you why to
save my life. I'm a church member, and I always loved a big
crowd. But now I just feel like I'm penned up when I'm in a
building where a crowd is. My feeling is, if there was twelve
of us standing out here talking and something happens, well
some of us is going to get hurt, maybe killed. But if I was there
by myself, why I would have a much better chance to escape.*

There would just be a better chance of some of us getting hurt if there's twelve of us out there than there would be if there was just one. If there's just going to be two escapes, it might be two other people and the other ten of us gone. But if there's just two there, then both are going to escape.

When one calculates the odds of survival in that way, one is almost bound to recognize at some level of consciousness that the neighbor who drowned was making a sacrifice on your behalf, tilting the scales of probability just enough for you to be among the quota of people who escaped. Whatever else this implies to a people of such fundamentalist religious leanings, it means, at the very least, that one's life has become the principal in a huge debt.

The counterpart to guilt, of course, is blame, and those survivors who had thought the matter through and consulted the stirrings of their inner selves often found that they were privately holding others to account for what happened, and this realization, in turn, became but another source of guilt.

At that time I had tremendous feelings of guilt over the death of my mom and dad. I felt like it was my fault. And then I blamed my husband, I guess, in a way, because his mom and dad both got out and mine didn't. And I didn't even want him near me. That's why I can understand some of those couples breaking up, you know.

As you know, my wife and I had a most crucial time in our marriage as a result of her father's death. Our marriage was on the verge of breaking up, our sex life had completely diminished. She was very hostile and had taken on a hardened attitude that I couldn't understand. At the visit with Dr. Lee, we discovered that she was holding me responsible for her father drowning in the flood. Since that time, things are a lot better between us.

Now both of these speakers are unusually insightful and both had had the benefit of a round or two of professional counseling, but much the same thought was expressed by others in a somewhat more muted way.

Well, I'm irritable, I know that. So is my wife. We have had disagreements in the past, of course, but now we're both irritable and we fight at each other a lot. And I think the flood's the very cause of it, because it never happened before. Sometimes I get the impression she thinks I caused the flood.

Since the disaster there have been many separations and divorces. I have had to live the last seven and a half months without my family. We have separated and have filed for divorce. Since the disaster my wife has acted very strange toward me, like I was the one who caused the disaster.

Ever since that flood, I drink a pretty good bit. Me and my wife, all we do is argue. I've even accused her—I said, "Why didn't you get my mom out?" Her family got out of the flood, see, and they got some more people out, but not my mom. So I was drinking and everything and I ran my wife off. And then her mommy came to talk to me about it and I ran her off, too.

I hated my husband at first. I just thought, as a man, he should have known more about dams around the mines. More or less, I just kind of blamed him for my sister's and her children's death.

And so the circle closes. People punish themselves for not being able to protect their families, for not being able to rescue their neighbors, or, worse, for not being able to recall that they even cared enough to attempt a rescue; and those awful moments of self-doubt are easily converted into a readiness to blame others. It is a hard burden to carry, all the more so for a people who do not have much in the way of psychiatric advice and would not be sure how to use it if they did, and it eats away at the sense of communion that once held people together.

THE FURNITURE OF SELF

In the fourth place, quite a number of people not only lost everything they owned but had to witness the loss from a point of vantage on the hillside only a few yards away. It is almost impossible to appreciate what this meant to the people of the hollow. In the best of circumstances it would be something of a shock to return to one's home after so narrow an escape and find that it was totally, finally, irretrievably gone.

There wasn't nothing left. It was plumb washed off the lot. You couldn't see nothing of it. All that was standing was the tree beside where the house had been.

Nothing. There wasn't nothing left. Even the topsoil was washed away, you know. And even the big sycamores around the creek banks—it just cleaned those out too. There wasn't nothing there.

It is important to remember that the people of the creek had invested a great deal of time and money and pride in the process of converting the old company shacks into comfortable new dwellings. The flood cleaned out some ragged housing as it made its way down the hollow—more than the residents like to remember—but the average home had been renovated in a hundred ways. "It was just a three-room house when we bought it," said one homeowner of seventeen years, "and it was in very bad condition, run-down." So the family refinished the existing three rooms with pine flooring, put Sheetrock on all the walls, built two additional bedrooms as well as a bathroom, added cement porches on the front and back, redid the now enlarged interior with wood paneling, replaced the roof, installed running water, put on aluminum siding, built a garage, rewired the entire house, put in a chimney, replaced every one of the windows, installed a new heating system, and planted hedges around the entire lot. A good deal of labor goes into projects like these, and the miner who said, "Look, mister, everything I earned in forty-five years in the mines was in that home; you tell me what it was worth"—that man was speaking for the majority of his neighbors.

A refurbished house on Buffalo Creek served as the emblem of one's rise out of poverty. It was a measure of security, an extension of self, a source of identity. It was not just the outer shell in which one lived out one's life but a major feature of that life. "To me," said one man, "it was the same thing as a hundred-thousand-dollar home or a million-dollar home. It was mine." Another explained:

I have a new home right now, and I would say that it is a much nicer home than what I had before. But it is a house, it is not a home. Before, I had a home. And what I mean by that, I built the other home. I took a coal company house, I remodeled it, I did the work on it myself. I put many a drop of sweat and drove many a nail into it, and I labored and sweated and worried over it. And it was gone. I left home Saturday morning and I had a home. On Saturday evening I didn't have nothing.

Moreover, people lost possessions of considerable meaning to them, not only trucks and cars and appliances with an established trade-in value, but mementos of no measurable worth which were highly cherished. Objects such as family Bibles or photographs, a father's favorite gun or a mother's proudest embroidery, had a place in the household almost like holy relics, and their loss was deeply mourned. They were a link with the past.

Well, I'll tell you. I had a lot of stuff I wouldn't have traded the world for, and I just didn't declare them at all. I had an old shotgun my daddy gave me when I was just a kid. It wasn't worth more than ten or twelve dollars when it was new, so what's it worth now? I had a silver dollar minted the same year my daddy was born, 1888. He gave me that, too, and his daddy gave it to him. What's it worth? A dollar? Things like that is priceless. You just can't ever get them back.

And they were a link with the future.

My fourteen-year-old daughter had things she had saved since before she had even started grade school, things she treasured and was hoping to pass on to her children in the future. But now it is all gone.

Considering the size of their homes and the size of their incomes, the people of Buffalo Creek sometimes had a remarkable number of personal belongings. One attorney representing the coal company was understandably dubious when he interviewed a miner who lived in a modest home and put in claims for three washing machines, four television sets, four record players, five hundred recordings, five hundred "whatnots," fifty wall decorations, seventy-five scatter rugs, four complete sets of dishes and glassware, eighty pots and pans, one hundred dish towels, eleven wristwatches, and two sets of encyclopedias. Perhaps these figures grew somewhat in the telling as the plaintiff tried to calculate the real meaning of his loss, but the idea of people having so huge a store of possessions, piled away in trunks and drawers and cupboards, is not so improbable at all. That is where a miner's pay often goes. And these goods are more than a form of decoration or a cushion against want; they are a measure of one's substance as a person and as a provider, truly the furniture of self.

Urban dwellers who occupy several different homes in the course of a lifetime rarely have the experience of feeling so attached to a particular set of rooms or a particular set of belongings that they become a part of one's personal world, the natural setting for one's life. City people may decorate their existence with new wallpaper or familiar old hangings, but they are not likely to confuse their own history, their own identity, with that of the structure housing them. A home that has grown along with one, however, literally been built around one, is not simply an expression of one's taste; it is the outer edge of one's personality, a part of the self itself. And the loss of that part of the self, as researchers have noted in other disaster situations, is akin to the loss of flesh. Compare Buffalo Creek, for example, to the scene of a devastating tornado in Texas:

> One of the outstanding impressions from our study . . . is the importance of the home as a symbol. When the home was intact, the family was intact; when the home was destroyed, the family was in peril. Further, and interestingly, new houses did not mean new homes. Several informants had houses they felt were as good as their old homes or better, but they were far from being satisfied with them. [People seemed to feel that] they had lost part of themselves.[7]

It may seem odd to think of people mourning a house or a familiar old shade tree, but when the people of Buffalo Creek stood there and watched their possessions crash down the hollow, they were watching a part of themselves die. One can find this sort of connection elsewhere, as the brief report from Texas indicates, but it takes on a special tone and urgency in Appalachia, for there is a sense in which the old mountain attachment to land reappears in the coal camps as a deep emotional investment in man-made—but natural—objects. To lose a home or the sum of one's belongings is to lose evidence as to who one is and where one belongs in the world.

ORDER AND DISORDER

In the fifth place, the disaster on Buffalo Creek had the effect of reducing people's already brittle confidence in the natural and, especially, in the social order, and while we will have reason to return to this topic later, a few words may be appropriate now. Losing faith in the very idea of order is one of the classic symptoms of chronic traumatic neurosis, being expressed, according to Irving L. Janis, as "a generalized form of apprehensiveness and timidity that seems to extend to the whole social and physical environment, indicating that the traumatized person now regards his entire world as an unsafe place."[8] Yet here, again, the more general finding from other research sites takes on a special meaning in the particular historical and ecological circumstances of Appalachia and of Buffalo Creek.

The ways of nature are uncertain in the mountains of Appalachia, and the people who make their home there have always kept a wary eye on them. Exactly because they are so tuned to the shiftings of the physical world, people know the difference between natural and man-made disasters, and the one on Buffalo Creek, to their way of thinking, was most assuredly man-made. An official of the coal company, obviously seeking to deflect responsibility for the tragedy, described it as " 'an act of God.' " The dam, he explained to a persistent reporter, was simply " 'incapable of holding the water God poured into it.' "[9] No scriptwriter hired for the purpose could have composed a line better calculated to irritate the people of the hollow. In Appalachia, God is not blamed lightly for the mistakes of men. To do so is to risk something very close to blasphemy, not just because it employs the name of the deity too casually, but because it seems to accuse God Himself of a terrible wrong.

The big shots want to call it an act of God. It's a lie. They've told a lie on God, and they shouldn't have done that. God didn't do this. He wouldn't do that.

People in the coal fields, of course, must rely heavily on the world around them. They count on the mountains looming over them to stay intact; they count on the water moving in on them from all sides to drain off; they count on the earth to yield coal and to protect them as they gouge it out; they count on their own physical sturdiness to cope with all the odd whims of nature; and, above all, they count on other people to respect the vulnerability of their condition. They have been disappointed many times, to be sure, because both men and nature seem to violate their own rules so often, but a catastrophe like this does more than disappoint. It makes people doubt whether there is order in the universe at all, and, further, it makes people distrust the workings of their own bodies.

The Buffalo Creek survivors, without saying so directly, have clearly lost much of their confidence in the workings of nature. They are troubled about the condition of the mountains, now scraped out inside and slashed with strip-mine benches; they are troubled about the water poised over their heads in other dams both real and imaginary; they are troubled about tornadoes and avalanches, floods and rock slides, earthquakes and explosions; and they are troubled about the capacity of their bodies and spirits to handle all the emergencies of life. Wilbur was quoted as saying, ". . . every time it rains I get that old dirty feeling that it is just a natural thing for it to become another flood"—and that expresses the mood exactly. It is "natural" now for things to go wrong.

We all walk the floor when it rains a lot. Of course a little old shower, why we don't pay it no mind. But if it starts raining all day hard, then we all start. There ain't no sleep. So I am afraid of rain. I am afraid there will be something come down someplace. There's always going to be a doubt there, always.

They are so scared when it rains. If you go down the road in the nighttime, and if it is raining, everyone on this creek is standing in the door with their lights on, watching. They are afraid it will be another flood, or maybe a mountain slide, because the hills are all stripped up.

Well, my wife, she just wants to get out of here. The mountain is tore all to pieces, and every time it rains, them strip mines and everything, why water comes out of everywhere.

No, I'm just going to get out of here. I can't get the idea out of my mind that this whole damn place is going to fall apart one of these days.

Among the problems with the land is that it still hides the remains of seven flood victims, and people up and down the hollow live in fear that those remains will suddenly reappear one day. The strongest man I know on Buffalo Creek once admitted in a quiet moment that he stiffens every time he looks out at the creek because he half expects to see a decomposed hand reaching out of it. A woman living nearby, once devoted to gardening, has simply given it up altogether because on her first attempt to plant a rosebush after the flood she dug up a bone that someone assured her was human. And a boy of nine, helping his father plant shrubbery, dug up what he took to be a set of false teeth and has suffered from terrifying nightmares ever since. In that sense, too, the terrain has become undependable.

Moreover, the people of Buffalo Creek have lost their confidence in Pittston. This may be a difficult point to explain because most readers of this report, in common with its author, will have no difficulty at all understanding why they might resent the company. But Pittston was part of the life of the creek. It employed hundreds of people and was represented locally by officials who lived in the area, were known by first names, and were merged into the community as individual persons. The residents knew that Pittston was a giant corporation with headquarters in New York, but they continued to visualize it as a kind of manorial presence at the head of the hollow that was implicated somehow in the affairs of the community. It was a proprietor, a patron, and it had obligations to fulfill.

Pittston violated those felt obligations, first, by building an unworthy dam, and, second, by reacting to the disaster in the manner of a remote bureaucracy with holdings to protect rather than in the manner of a concerned patron with constituents to care for. The heart of the company turned out to be located hundreds of miles away, and its first reflex was to treat the survivors—many of them company employees with decades of loyal service—as potential adversaries in a court action. One of the first persons I met on Buffalo Creek, a disabled miner with more than forty years' experience underground, kept saying over and over again, "They don't know what they've done to us; they don't know what they've done," almost as if he thought the company would have acted more compassionately if its officials had seen or felt how people were suffering. Another veteran of the mines was interviewed by a reporter a day or two after the flood, and he recalled having said:

> *He asked me, "Do you have any hard feelings against Pittston?" I said, "No, I don't have any hard feelings against them." And he said, "Do you believe they'll talk to people?" And I said, "I sure do. I believe they will. I believe they'll talk to the people because I worked with them and they've been good to me and I can't say anything against them."*

He was recounting the interview almost two years later, and by that time he had come to feel that his original confidence had been misplaced. Pittston did not really "talk to the people," at least not in the way they had expected, and the resentment generated by that seeming air of indifference came close to ranking with the flood itself as a source of irritation. The survivors had thought it would be otherwise. A seventy-year-old man who was stripped of everything by the flood said to one of the Pittston attorneys:

> *I've often thought some of this stuff could have been avoided if somebody would have come around and said, "Here's a blanket and here's a dress for your wife" or "Here's a sandwich. Could I give you a cup of coffee?" But they never showed up. Nobody showed up to give us a place to stay. . . . The Pittston Company never offered me a pair of pants to put on, no shirt. . . . That's what gets you kind of riled up.*

Another man who had spent his entire life in the hollow said almost a little apologetically:

I have a deep-seated resentment against Pittston which probably isn't normal, but I just cannot help it. I resent the fact that no one even bothered to come to see if we were well, needed anything, offer to help clean up, or seem to care what happened to us. This is probably the wrong way to feel, but I just cannot help it.

The people who speak for Pittston would not come out into the light, would not take the risk of establishing eye contact, would not expose themselves even for the purposes of finding out how the residents of the hollow were faring; and if this situation provoked a gentle annoyance in people like the one above, it provoked a bitter indignation in others. The following statement is unusually harsh for Buffalo Creek, but it expresses a mood shared by many of the men and women who survived the disaster.

I was going to jump on three policemen over there. I mean they was guarding that damn stockholders' meeting there. I said I was going to kill all of them sonabitches, and I would have killed every damn one of them. I could have whipped them, I believe, because it built up in me so damn strong. I couldn't right now, but I ain't angry now. It was built up so much in me I believe I had the strength of ten men, I tell you the truth. I don't know what it is. Maybe it's because I haven't met the people at Pittston that gets me angry. They're hiding, you know, and that bothers me. I can't see them.

So the prevailing feeling is of a bitterness so sharp that it seems to speak of betrayal as well as of personal injury.

The one thing I do not understand is how the officials of the company could let a thing like that happen. Surely someone should have known that the dam would not hold. The lives that were lost, the homeless, the hell that people have and are still going through—to me it was no less than murder.

We have bitterness toward the coal company. They washed us out, killed all those people. I don't think they thought of us as human beings.

All I can call the disaster is murder. The coal company knew the dam was bad, but they did not tell the people. All they wanted was to make money. They did not care about the good people that lived up Buffalo Creek.

In one sense, at least, the coal company had a paternal relationship with the people of the hollow. It was not necessarily a warm and benevolent relationship, to be sure, but it at least implied a certain interest in the fortunes of the community and a certain obligation to the people who lived there. The sins of this father were that he ravaged the land—the mother earth—and that he betrayed the trust of his dependents. The problem was not simply that he had failed to take proper care of them, for he had been neglectful in that department any number of times. The problem was that he had allowed them to suffer without warning them in advance and without even seeming to mourn the dead or aid the living afterward. When the people of Buffalo Creek speak of "murder," the idea that may be lurking vaguely in the back of their minds is something closer to "filicide."

So these were some of the effects of the individual trauma, that first numbing moment of pain and shock and helplessness. A few paragraphs of description can scarcely begin to convey what the tragedy must have felt like to the survivors or how it has influenced their lives, but many of the themes noted here correspond closely to ones noted in reports of other disasters, and to that extent, at least, what happened on Buffalo Creek is similar to all those other floods and bombings and hurricanes and earthquakes that interrupt the flow of human life.

But there are differences, too. Two years after the flood, Buffalo Creek was almost as desolate as it had been the day following, the grief as intense, the fear as strong, the anxiety as sharp, the despair as dark. People still looked out at the world with vacant eyes and drifted from one place to another with dulled and tentative movements. They rarely smiled and rarely played. They were not sure how to relate to one another. They were unsettled and deeply hurt.

Under normal circumstances, one would expect the survivors of such a disaster to convalesce gradually as the passage of time acted to dim old memories and to generate new hopes. It is a standard article of psychiatric wisdom that the symptoms of trauma ought to disappear over a period of time, and when they do not, as was generally the case on Buffalo Creek, a peculiar strain of logic is likely to follow. If one has not recovered from the effects of trauma within a reasonable span of time, or so the theory goes, then it follows that the symptoms themselves must have been the result of a mental disorder pre-dating the event itself. This is exactly the logic employed by the Pittston psychiatrist, as it happens, and it has a good deal of support in older literature on the subject. Irving L. Janis, describing that older view, refers to

> numerous clinical surveys that support two important conclusions: (1) Most persons who develop the symptoms of acute traumatic neurosis following exposure to accidents or disasters spontaneously recover quite rapidly, usually within a few weeks; and (2) the persons who fail to recover spontaneously are more likely than others to have a history of emotional disorder.

But, Janis goes on to say, "this highly optimistic view concerning the complete reversibility of the symptoms is now being seriously challenged." [10]

Unless we are ready to entertain the possibility that virtually all the people on Buffalo Creek suffered from a palpable emotional disorder on the morning of February 26, 1972, one has to look elsewhere for a way to explain their distress. The fact is that the amount of human damage done on Buffalo Creek is far more extensive than that reported in other disasters studied by social scientists, and this, too, requires explanation.

The argument I want to make in the next chapter is that a second trauma followed closely on the first, immobilizing recovery efforts and lending a degree of permanence to what might otherwise have been a transitional state of shock.

Collective Trauma: Loss
of Communality

THE DISASTER stretched human nerves to their outer edge. Those of us who did not experience it can never really comprehend the full horror of that day, but we can at least appreciate why it should cause such misery and why it should leave so deep a scar on the minds of those who lived through it. Our imagination can reach across the gulf of personal experience and begin to re-create those parts of the scene that touch the senses. Our eyes can almost see a burning black wave lashing down the hollow and taking everything in its path. The ears can almost hear a roar like thunder, pierced by screams and explosions and the crack of breaking timbers. The nostrils can almost smell the searing stench of mine wastes and the sour odor of smoke and death and decay. All this we can begin to picture because the mind is good at imagery.

But the people of Buffalo Creek suffered a good deal more that day, for they were wrenched out of their communities, torn from the human surround in which they had been so deeply enmeshed. Much of the drama drains away when we begin to talk about such things, partly because the loss of communality seems a step removed from the vivid terror of the event itself and partly because the people of the hollow, so richly articulate when describing the flood and their reaction to it, do not really know how to express what their separation from the familiar tissues of home has meant to them. The closeness of communal ties is experienced on Buffalo Creek as a part of the natural order of things, and residents can no more describe that presence than fish are aware of the water they swim in. It is just there, the envelope in which they live, and it is taken entirely for granted. In this chapter, then, as in the preceding ones, I will use quotations freely, but one must now listen even more carefully for the feelings behind the words as well as registering the content of the words themselves.

I use the term "communality" here rather than "community" in order to underscore the point that people are not referring to particular village territories when they lament the loss of community but to the network of relationships that make up their general human surround. The persons who constitute the center of that network are usually called "neighbors," the word being used in its Biblical sense to identify those with whom one shares bonds of intimacy and a feeling of mutual concern. The people of Buffalo Creek are "neighbor people," which is a local way of referring to a style of relationship long familiar among social scientists. Toennies called it "gemeinschaft," Cooley called it "primary," Durkheim called it "mechanical," Redfield called it "folk," and every generation of social scientists since has found other ways to express the same thought, one of the most recent being Herbert Gans's concept of "person orientation."

What is a neighbor? When you ask people on Buffalo Creek what the term means, they try to remember that you come from the city and they illustrate their answer with the kind of concrete detail that makes mountain speech so clear and direct.

What's a neighbor? Well, when I went to my neighbor's house on Saturday or Sunday, if I wanted a cup of coffee I never waited until the lady of the house asked me. I just went into the dish cabinet and got me a cup of coffee or a glass of juice just like it was my own home. They come to my house, they done the same. See?

We was like one big family. Like when somebody was hurt, everybody was hurt. You know. I guess it was because it was the same people all the time. I don't know how to explain it. It's a good feeling. It's more than friends. If someone was hurt, everybody was concerned, everybody. If somebody lost a member of their family, they was always there. Everybody was around bringing you something to eat, trying to help. It's a deeper feeling.

Here, if you have a neighbor, it's somebody you know, it's somebody that maybe you take them to the store. I mean, to us neighbors are people that we have. We just know each other, that's all.

Neighbor? It means relationship. It means kin. It means friends you could depend on. You never went to a neighbor with a complaint that they didn't listen to or somebody didn't try to help you with. That's a neighbor. When you wanted a baby-sitter you went next door and they'd baby-sit. Or you did something for them. They'd either need something or we'd need something, you know. When you see somebody going down the road, it's "Where are you going?" "To the store." "Well, bring me back such and such."

A neighbor, then, is someone you can relate to without pretense, a familiar and reliable part of your everyday environment; a neighbor is someone you treat as if he or she were a member of your immediate family. A good deal has been said in the literature on Appalachia about the clannishness of mountain life, but on Buffalo Creek, as in many coal camps, this sense of tribal attachment reaches beyond linkages of kin to include a wider circle, and the obligations one feels toward the people within that circle are not unlike the obligations one normally feels toward one's own family.

In good times, then, every person on Buffalo Creek looks out at the larger community from a fairly intimate neighborhood niche. If we were to devise a map representing the average person's social world, we would capture at least the main contours by drawing a number of concentric circles radiating out from the individual center—the inner ring encompassing one's immediate family, the next ring encompassing one's closest neighbors, the third encompassing the familiar people with whom one relates on a regular basis, and the fourth encompassing the other people whom one recognizes as a part of the Buffalo Creek community even though one does not really know them well. Beyond the outermost of those rings is the rest of the world, the terrain populated by what an older generation called "foreigners." Given the size of Buffalo Creek, it is obvious that the community contained people who were relative strangers to one another. Yet there was a clear sense of kinship linking even those relative strangers together— although, as we shall see shortly, that sense of kinship turned out to depend to a greater degree than people realized on the security of one's neighborhood niche.

Communality on Buffalo Creek can best be described as a state of mind shared among a particular gathering of people, and this state of mind, by definition, does not lend itself to sociological abstraction. It does not have a name or a cluster of distinguishing properties. It is a quiet set of understandings that become absorbed into the atmosphere and are thus a part of the natural order. The remarks below, for example, are separate attempts by a husband and wife to explain the nature of those "understandings."

Braeholm was more like a family. We had a sort of understanding. If someone was away, then we sort of looked after each other's property. We didn't do a lot of visiting, but we had a general understanding. If we cooked something, we would exchange dishes. It was sort of a close-knit type of thing.

Before the disaster, the neighbors, we could look out and tell when one another needed help or when one was sick or something was disturbing that person. We could tell from the lights. If the lights was on late at night, we knew that something unusual was going on and we would go over. Sometimes I'd come in from work on a cold day and my neighbor would have a pot of soup for me. There was just things you wouldn't think about. I would look forward to going to the post office. If my car wouldn't start, all I'd have to do is call my neighbors and they woud take me to work. If I was there by myself or something, if my husband was out late, the neighbors would come over and check if everything was okay. So it was just a rare thing. It was just a certain type of relationship that you just knew from people growing up together and sharing the same experiences.

And the key to that network of understandings was a constant readiness to look after one's neighbors, or, rather, to know without being asked what needed to be done.

If you had problems, you wouldn't even have to mention it. People would just know what to do. They'd just pitch in and help. Everyone was concerned about everyone else.

I don't think there was a better place in the world to live. People was there when you needed them. You got sick, they helped you. If you needed help of any kind, you got it. You didn't even have to ask for it. Now I'm a person that didn't make friends easy. I wasn't hard to get along with, I just didn't mix. But I knew everybody, and— Well, I just don't know no way to explain it to you, to make you see it.

You'd just have to experience it, I guess, to really know. It was wonderful. Like when my father died. My neighbors all came in and they cleaned my house, they washed my clothes, they cooked. I didn't do nothing. They knew what to do. I mean it's just like teamwork, you know. If one of the kids was sick, they'd drop every what they were doing, take the kid to the hospital or sit up all night with him. It was just good. How did they know when you needed help? I don't know how to explain it, really. The morning my daddy died—he died in Logan—my aunt called me and told me on the phone at about ten o'clock in the morning, and I had just got time to get off the phone and go set on the bed and in come three of my neighbors. They knew it that quick. I don't know how. They just knew.

The difficulty is that when you invest so much of yourself in that kind of social arrangement you become absorbed by it, almost captive to it, and the larger collectivity around you becomes an extension of your own personality, an extension of your own flesh. This means that not only are you diminished as a person when that surrounding tissue is stripped away, but that you are no longer able to reclaim as your own the emotional resources you invested in it. To "be neighborly" is not a quality you can carry with you into a new situation like negotiable emotional currency; the old community was your niche in the classic ecological sense, and your ability to relate to that niche is not a skill easily transferred to another setting. This is true whether you move into another community, as was the case with the first speaker below, or whether a new set of neighbors moves in around your old home, as was the case with the second.

Well, I have lost all my friends. The people I was raised up and lived with, they're scattered. I don't know where they're at. I've got to make new friends, and that's a hard thing to do. You don't make new friends and feel towards them like you did the people you lived with. See, I raised my family there. We moved there in '35 and stayed there. I knew everybody in the camp and practically everybody on Buffalo, as far as that is concerned. But down here, there ain't but a few people I know, and you don't feel secure around people you don't know.

Neighbors. We used to have our children at home, we didn't go to hospitals to have children. The one on this side of me, them two in back of me, this one in front of me—they all lived there and we all had our children together. Now I've got all new neighbors. I even asked my husband to put our home up for sale, and he said, "What do you think we're going to do? We're old people, we can't take to buy another home." And I said, "I don't care what you do with it, I'm not staying here. I can't tell you in words what's the matter." I said, "I don't care if we go to the moon, let's just get out of here. I'm just not interested enough anymore. You go out the back door here and there's a new neighbor. In front of me is a new neighbor and on the other side of me is a new neighbor. It's just not the same home that I've been living in for thirty-five years. It's just not the same to me."

A community of the sort we are talking about here derives from and depends on an almost perfect democracy of the spirit, where people are not only assumed to be equal in status but virtually identical in temperament and outlook. Classes of people may be differentiated for certain purposes—women from men, adults from children, whites from blacks, and so on—but individual persons are not distinguished from one another on the basis of rank, occupation, style of life, or even recreational habits. This is not hard to understand as a practical matter. The men all work at the same jobs; the women all command domestic territories of roughly the same original size and quality; the children all attend the same schools as an apprenticeship for the same futures; and everybody buys the same goods at the same stores from equivalent paychecks. Yet the leveling tendency goes even beyond that, for the people of the hollow, like the people of Appalachia generally, do not like to feel different from their fellows and tend to see status distinctions of any kind as fissures in the smooth surface of the community. Good fences may make good neighbors in places like New Hampshire, where relationships depend on cleanly marked parcels of individual space, but they are seen as lines of division in places like Buffalo Creek.

In most of the urban areas of America, each individual is seen as a separate being, with careful boundaries drawn around the space he or she occupies as a discrete personage. Everyone is presumed to have an individual name, an individual mind, an individual voice, and, above all, an individual sense of self—so much so that persons found deficient in any of those qualities are urged to take some kind of remedial action such as undergoing psychotherapy, participating in a consciousness-raising group, or reading one of a hundred different manuals on self-actualization. This way of looking at things, however, has hardly any meaning at all in most of Appalachia. There, boundaries are drawn around whole groups of people, not around separate individuals with egos to protect and potentialities to realize; and a person's mental health is measured less by his capacity to express his inner self than by his capacity to submerge that self into a larger communal whole.

It was once fashionable in the social sciences generally to compare human communities to living organisms. Scholars anxious to make the kind of distinction I am wrestling with now would argue that persons who belong to traditional communities relate to one another in much the same fashion as the cells of a body: they are dependent on one another for definition, they do not have any real function or identity apart from the contribution they make to the whole organization, and they suffer a form of death when separated from that larger tissue. Science may have gained something when this analogy was abandoned, but it may have lost something, too, for a community of the kind being discussed here *does* bear at least a figurative resemblance to an organism. In places like Buffalo Creek, the community in general can be described as the locus for activities that are normally regarded as the exclusive property of individuals. It is the *community* that cushions pain, the *community* that provides a context for intimacy, the *com-*

munity that represents morality and serves as the repository for old traditions.

Now one has to realize when talking like this that one is in danger of drifting off into a realm of metaphor. Communities do not have hearts or sinews or ganglia; they do not suffer or rationalize or experience joy. But the analogy does help suggest that a cluster of people acting in concert and moving to the same collective rhythms can allocate their personal resources in such a way that the whole comes to have more humanity than its constituent parts. In effect, people put their own individual resources at the disposal of the group—placing them in the communal store, as it were—and then draw on that reserve supply for the demands of everyday life. And if the whole community more or less disappears, as happened on Buffalo Creek, people find that they cannot take advantage of the energies they once invested in the communal store. They find that they are almost empty of feeling, empty of affection, empty of confidence and assurance. It is as if the individual cells had supplied raw energy to the whole body but did not have the means to convert that energy back into a usable personal form once the body was no longer there to process it. When an elderly woman on Buffalo Creek said softly, "I just don't take no interest in nothing like I used to, I don't have no feeling for nothing, I feel like I'm drained of life," she was reflecting a spirit still numbed by the disaster, but she was also reflecting a spirit unable to recover for its own use all the life it had signed over to the community.

I am going to propose, then, that most of the traumatic symptoms experienced by the Buffalo Creek survivors are a reaction to the loss of communality as well as a reaction to the disaster itself, that the fear and apathy and demoralization one encounters along the entire length of the hollow are derived from the shock of being ripped out of a meaningful community setting as well as the shock of meeting that cruel black water. The line between the two is difficult to draw, as one survivor suggested:

We can't seem to put it all together. We try, but it just isn't there. It may be the shock of the disaster or the aftermath of it all. I don't know. It's hard to separate the two.

But it seems clear that much of the agony experienced on Buffalo Creek is related to the fact that the hollow is quiet, devastated, without much in the way of a nourishing community life. What is Buffalo Creek like now? The shorter answers were crisp and to the point:

It is almost like a ghost town now.

It has changed from the community of paradise to Death Valley.

Some reason or other, it's not the same. Seems like it's frozen.

I don't know. A dreary hollow is how it seems to me.

It's like a graveyard, that's what. A cemetery.

And the longer answers seemed almost to fuse together into a long litany of despair. There is something missing, something gone; and that something is very hard to pin down.

I have found that most of the people are depressed, unhappy, mournful, sick. When you go up Buffalo Creek the only remains you see is an occasional house here and there. The people who are living in the trailers have a depressed and worried look on their faces. You don't see children out playing and running as before. Buffalo Creek looks like a deserted, forsaken place.

What I miss most is the friendliness and closeness of the people of Buffalo Creek. The people are changed from what they were before the disaster. Practically everyone seems despondent and undecided, as if they were waiting for something and did not know what. They can't reconcile themselves to the fact that things will never be the same again.

The best I could tell you, what lives on Buffalo Creek lives in sorrow. I've talked to so many people and they are so tore up. Some of them just don't care anymore. There's a part of us all missing somewhere.

It's kind of sad around there now. There's not much happiness. You don't have any friends around, people around, like we had before. Some of them are in the trailer camps. Some of them bought homes and moved away. Some of them just left and didn't come back. It's like teeth in an old folk's mouth down there now.

This whole thing is a nightmare, actually. Our life-style has been disrupted, our home destroyed. We lost many things we loved, and we think about those things. We think about our neighbors and friends we lost. Our neighborhood was completely destroyed, a disaster area. There's just an open field there now and grass planted where they were many homes and many people lived.

We did lose a community, and I mean it was a good community. Everybody was close, everybody knowed everybody. But now everybody is alone. They act like they're lost. They've lost their homes and their way of life, the one they liked, the one they was used to. All the houses are gone, every one of them. The people are gone, scattered. You don't know who your neighbor is going to be. You can't go next door and talk. You can't do that no more, there's no next door. You can't laugh with friends. You can't do that no more, because there's no friends around to laugh with. That don't happen no more. There's nobody around to even holler at and say "Hi," and you can't help but miss that. You haven't got nobody to talk to. The people that is there are so busy trying to put back what they have lost.

And so it goes. The observer listening in on all this has to confront two related problems. The first of those problems, of course, is that the words people are accustomed to using in everyday speech seem pale and insubstantial when assigned the job of conveying so immense a subject. This is true for survivors who are trying to find ways to express their sense of loss, but it is also true for observers who are looking for ways to pose questions. At one point in the study, realizing that I would never have time to interview everyone in the plaintiff group, I sent a questionnaire to some five hundred persons asking for a few brief answers to a few crisp questions. Some of those answers have appeared in the material presented so far, and others will appear later. But most of the answers reached so far beyond the questions that I did not really know what to do with them. It was as if I had asked people to compress a world of grief in the space reserved for a sentence or two. "What do you miss most about the old community?"

All my family were killed here. My old home is gone and I can't tell where it used to be. I don't know where any of my friends are now. I never see anyone anymore.

Once the observer gets over his embarrassment at having tried to confront so deep a pain with so casual an inquiry, he begins to recognize the futility of trying to convert everything into the coin of words. And yet the emotion behind the words seems easy enough to detect if one searches for it. One must look for the particular in a comment as general as this:

Everything has changed. Nothing is the same. The people that were left up there has changed. They don't seem like the same people I once knew. It don't look like the same place.

And one must look for the general in a comment as particular as this:

I miss my house and furnishings and clothing, which I have very little of now. I had a large yard, two shade trees. I miss it very much. I miss the pictures from the school yearbook. A lot of things. It's hard to explain.

The second problem has to do with the extraordinary repetitiveness of the comments people make, a problem we have already encountered. This study is based on thousands of pages of transcript material, whole packing boxes full of it, yet a researcher is very apt to conclude after rummaging through these data that there is really not very much to say after all. This is not because the material is contradictory or difficult to interpret but because it is so bleakly alike. I noted earlier that the psychiatric evaluations seem to indicate that virtually everybody who managed to survive the flood has suffered at one time or another from anxiety, depression, apathy, insomnia, phobic reactions, and a pervasive feeling of depletion and loneliness. What makes these data so frustrating is that one reads and hears the same remarks again and again, almost as if a script had been passed around the creek. At first glance, it does seem logical that something of the sort may have happened; phrases that do a particularly apt job of capturing a feeling common to many people may have circulated up and down the hollow, expressions that strike a common chord may have come to serve as a group explanation for what are otherwise individual emotions. But this theory, common in disaster research, will not serve entirely. For one thing, the survivors are scattered all over the area and do not keep in close touch with one another, and for another thing, those who do keep in touch generally make a point of talking about something else.

So the only reasonable conclusion one can reach is that the second trauma involves a syndrome as general and as encompassing as the first, and that we are dealing with a phenomenon stretching across the whole of the community.

Certain features of that syndrome, of course, must be understood as local to the particular situation of Buffalo Creek, but others appear to be common to large-scale disasters in general, and we should pause here for a moment to consider the distinction between the two.

Virtually every study of a disaster in the social science literature reports that the first reaction of survivors is a state of dazed shock and numbness, and one of the reasons for that stunned reaction—the main one, according to researchers like Anthony F. C. Wallace—is a feeling on the part of survivors that the larger community has been demolished. Even when the individual has not suffered any serious personal loss and has not been exposed to any immediate danger, he is shocked by the "cultural damage" and is likely to drift around in a state of "stunned disbelief" at the sight of his home territory in shambles. Wallace studied Worcester, Massachusetts, in the period following a vicious tornado, and he concluded in part:

> The precipitating factor in the disaster syndrome seems to be a perception . . . that practically the entire visible community is in ruins. The sight of a ruined community, with houses, churches, trees, stores, and everything wrecked, is apparently often consciously or unconsciously interpreted as a destruction of the whole world. Many persons, indeed, actually were conscious of, and reported, this perception in interviews, remarking that the thought had crossed their minds that "this was the end of the world," "an atom bomb had dropped," "the universe had been destroyed," etc. The objects with which he has identification, and to which his behavior is normally tuned, have been removed. He has been suddenly shorn of much of the support and assistance of a culture and a society upon which he depends and from which he draws sustenance; he has been deprived of the instrumentalities by which he has manipulated his environment; he has been, in effect, castrated, rendered impotent, separated from all sources of support, and left naked and alone, without a sense of his own identity, in a terrifying wilderness of ruins.[1]

Wallace's point here is that the most prominent features of the "disaster syndrome"—the numbness and apathy and insomnia and depression—are in part a reaction to the thought that the community, and maybe even the whole world, has been obliterated altogether and can no longer serve as a source of personal support. We will see in a moment that many survivors of the Buffalo Creek flood felt the world had come to an end, and several of them, like the woman quoted below, were afraid for one terrible moment that they were the only persons left alive.

And so we got up there on the hill and I looked back and said, "It might have been the best if we'd all gone with it, because I don't see nobody else." I couldn't see nobody else nowhere. As far as we knew, we were the only ones alive.

The symptoms that make up the disaster syndrome, then, are the classic symptoms of mourning and bereavement. People are grieving for their lost friends and lost homes, but they are grieving too for their lost cultural surround; and they feel dazed at least in part because they are not sure what to do in the absence of that familiar setting. They have lost their navigational equipment, as it were, both their inner compasses and their outer maps.

Among the characteristics of the disaster syndrome, according to Wallace, is a "stage of euphoria"—a sudden and logically inexplicable wave of good feeling that comes over survivors shortly after the disaster itself—and this feature of the post-disaster experience, too, has been noted by a number of other observers. The following remark, for example, is from a study of tornado damage in Vicksburg, Mississippi:

Many observers have commented on the increased intimacy and solidarity which characterizes populations in the post-disaster period. There seems to be a general reaching out to others and a readiness to share one's resources and experiences that lasts for a considerable period of time after a disaster. We have found it helpful to think about this process of reaching out as being in part a means of reassurance after the crisis is over. It seems to be a way of achieving a sort of talismanic protection which comes from figuratively (and literally) touching one's fellows.[2]

Other researchers have indeed reported the same findings. S. H. Prince, studying a ship explosion in Halifax, talked about a "city of comrades." R. I. Kutak, studying a flood in Louisville, talked about a "democracy of distress." Charles E. Fritz, studying a tornado in Arkansas, referred to a "community of sufferers." Martha Wolfenstein, reviewing the literature on disasters in general, called the phenomenon a "post-disaster utopia," while Allen H. Barton, having surveyed much the same literature, spoke of an "altruistic community." [3]

Wallace attributes this stage of euphoria to a discovery on the part of survivors that the general community is not really dead after all. The energy with which rescue operations are pursued and the cooperation of neighbors act to reassure people that there is still life among the ruins, and they respond with an outpouring of communal feeling, an urgent need to make contact with and even touch others by way of renewing old pledges of fellowship. They are celebrating the recovery of the community they once thought dead, and, in a way, they are celebrating their own rebirth. [4]

I mention all this because nothing of the sort seems to have occurred on Buffalo Creek, even for a moment, and this raises a number of important issues. On the more general level, it may very well be that the emergence of a stage of euphoria depends upon the continuance of most of the larger community, so that survivors, digging out from under the masses of debris, can discover that most of the body is still intact and is mobilizing its remaining resources to dress the wound on its flank. In Buffalo Creek this was simply not the case. Most of the work of rescue was done by outsiders following plans and initiatives issued from distant headquarters. They were strangers, many of them in uniform, and they cleaned up the wreckage without consulting the owners, sealed off the resi-dents from their own homes, and generally acted more like an army of occupation than a local disaster team. No wonder that the suspicion of looting was so widespread.

The work of those outsiders restored order on Buffalo Creek, and most of the survivors were glad to acknowledge the help:

The first couple of days there didn't seem to be any organi-zation at all. You know, people running around, not knowing what to do. Then the National Guard came in and started tak-

ing people back out across the mountain. Things were begin-
ning to take on a little organization then. Up to then, it seemed
dark and unreal.

But the feeling was general, nonetheless, that the people of
the hollow had lost control of their own home territory, and
this could only add to the perception that the immediate community had disappeared.

In most disasters, according to available reports, the initial
state of shock wears off quickly. Two of the most experienced
students of human disasters state flatly that "disasters do
not generally have disabling emotional consequences or leave
numbing mental health problems among any large numbers
of their victims." [5] One reason for this outcome, they suggest,
is that victims are invariably outnumbered by non-victims in
situations like this, leaving a more or less intact community
into which those affected by the disaster can be gradually
reabsorbed. On Buffalo Creek, of course, the victims outnumbered the non-victims by so large a margin that the
community itself has to be counted a casualty.

The lack of a discernible wave of euphoria, then, as well as
the inability of the survivors to recover from the initial effects
of the "disaster syndrome" had something to do with conditions local to Buffalo Creek; and in order to follow that line
of approach properly, we should again look for particular
themes in the larger syndrome.

Before doing so, however, one reservation should probably
be noted in passing. I am talking about a syndrome here, by
which I mean that the experience of the disaster and its aftermath was generally shared by all the survivors. But this does
not suggest that the suffering itself was quantitatively the
same for everyone, and, in reading the material to follow, it
may be worth keeping in mind that people living in the higher
reaches of the hollow saw a great deal more destruction than
those living farther down, and that women may be more distressed on the average than men, if only because the men can
fall back, if weakly, on the fellowship of work. These differ-

ences are not great, however, because everybody on Buffalo Creek, regardless of his or her exposure to the black water, was implicated in the loss of communality, and in that regard, at least, all were hurt in much the same way. This does not appear to have become a new basis for community, as has so often been the case in other disasters, but it has certainly contributed to the leveling tendency already pronounced along the creek.

One further note before we move on to the particular themes. It is quite likely that the survivors' memories of the old community are somewhat idealized, partly because it is natural for people to exaggerate the standard against which they measure their present distress, and partly because the past always seems to take on a more golden glow as it recedes in the distance. It is important to remember and to make an allowance for that idealization, but it is also important to remember that the ideal tone of those memories, whatever its basis in fact, has now become the only relevant reality to the people of Buffalo Creek. One way to convey the sharpness of one's pain is to contrast it with a climate that may never have existed in quite the form it is remembered, but the need to do this is itself a strong indication of how deep that pain must be.

MORALE AND MORALITY

The Buffalo Creek survivors face the post-disaster world in a state of severe demoralization, both in the sense that they have lost much of their individual morale and in the sense that they have lost (or fear they have lost) most of their moral anchors.

The lack of morale is reflected in a weary apathy, a feeling that the world has more or less come to an end and that there are no longer any compelling reasons for doing anything. People are drained of energy and conviction, in part because the activities that once sustained them on an everyday basis—working, caring, playing—seem to have lost their direction and purpose in the absence of a larger communal setting. They feel that the ground has gone out from under them.

People don't know what they want or where they want to go. It is almost as though they don't care what happens anymore.

My husband and myself used to enjoy working and improving on our home, but we don't have the heart to do anything anymore. It's just a dark cloud hanging over our head. I just can't explain how we feel.

I don't know. I just got to the point where I just more or less don't care. I don't have no ambition to do the things I used to do. I used to try to keep things up, but anymore I just don't. It seems I just do enough to get by, to make it last one more day. It seems like I just lost everything at once, like the bottom just dropped out of everything.

I don't have the heart to work. I don't know. I just don't feel like it. It used to tickle me to get ready to go to work, but now it seems like I've got a dread on my mind or something.

The clinical name for this state of mind, of course, is depression, and one can hardly escape the conclusion that it is, at least in part, a reaction to the ambiguities of post-disaster life in the hollow. Most of the survivors never realized the extent to which they relied on the rest of the community to reflect back a sense of meaning to them, never understood the extent to which they depended on others to supply them with a point of reference. When survivors say they feel "adrift," "displaced," "uprooted," "lost," they mean that they do not seem to belong to anything and that there are no longer any familiar social landmarks to help them fix their position in time and space. They are depressed, yes, but it is a depression born of the feeling that they are suspended pointlessly in the middle of nowhere. "It is like being all alone in the middle of a desert," said one elderly woman who lives with her retired husband in a cluster of homes. As she talked, the voices of the new neighbors could be heard in the background; but they were not *her* neighbors, not *her* people, and the rhythms of their lives did not provide her with any kind of orientation.

This failure of personal morale is accompanied by a deep suspicion that moral standards are beginning to collapse all over the hollow, and in some ways, at least, it would appear that they are. As so frequently happens in human life, the forms of misbehavior people find cropping up in their midst are exactly those about which they are most sensitive. The use of alcohol, always problematic in mountain society, has evidently increased, and there are rumors spreading throughout the trailer camps that drugs have found their way into the area. The theft rate has gone up too, and this has always been viewed in Appalachia as a sure index of social disorganization. The cruelest cut of all, however, is that once close and devoted families are having trouble staying within the pale they once observed so carefully. Adolescent boys and girls appear to be slipping away from parental control and are becoming involved in nameless delinquencies, while there are reports from several of the trailer camps that younger wives and husbands are meeting one another in circumstances that violate all the local codes. A home is a moral sphere as well as a physical dwelling, of course, and it would seem that the boundaries of moral space began to collapse as the walls of physical space were washed down the creek. The problem is a complex one. People simply do not have enough to do, especially teen-agers, and "fooling around" becomes one of the few available forms of recreation. People have old memories and old guilts to cope with, especially the seasoned adults, and drinking becomes a way to accomplish that end. And, for everyone, skirting the edges of once-forbidden territory is a way to bring new excitement and a perverse but lively kind of meaning into lives that are otherwise without it.

A widow in her forties speaking of her sixteen-year-old daughter:

And then she started running with the wrong crowds. She started drinking. She started taking dope. And feelings wasn't the same between her and I. Before the flood it wasn't like that at all.

A retired miner in his sixties speaking of himself:

I did acquire a very bad drinking problem after the flood which I'm doing my level best now to get away from. I was trying to drink, I guess, to forget a lot of things and get them moved out of my mind, and I just had to stop because I was leading the wrong way. I don't know what the answer is, but I know that's not it. I don't want to drink. I never was taught that. I've drunk a right smart in my life, but that's not the answer.

And a woman in her late twenties who had recently moved out of the largest of the trailer camps:

There was all kinds of mean stuff going on up there. I guess it still does, to hear the talk. I haven't been back up there since we left. Men is going with other men's wives. And drinking parties. They'd play horseshoes right out by my trailer, and they'd play by streetlight until four or five in the morning. I'd get up in the morning and I'd pick up beer cans until I got sick. The flood done something to people, that's what it is. It's changed people. Good people has got bad. They don't care anymore. "We're going to live it up now because we might be gone tomorrow," that's the way they look at it. They call that camp "Peyton Place," did you know that? Peyton Place. I was scared to death up there. I don't even like to go by it.

Yet the seeming collapse of morality on Buffalo Creek differs in several important respects from the kinds of anomie sociologists think they see elsewhere in modern America. For one thing, those persons who seem to be deviating most emphatically from prevailing community norms are usually the first to judge their own behavior as unacceptable, even obnoxious. Adolescents are eager to admit that they sometimes get into trouble, and those of their elders who drink more than the rules of the hollow normally permit—a couple of beers exceeds the limit for most—are likely to call themselves "alcoholics" under circumstances that seem remarkably premature to jaded strangers from the urban North. To that extent, the consensus has held: local standards as to what qualifies as deviation remain largely intact, even though a number of people see themselves as drifting away from that norm. Moreover, there is an interesting incongruity in the reports of immorality one hears throughout the hollow. It would seem that virtually everyone in the trailer camps is now living next to persons of lower moral stature than was the case formerly, and this, of and by itself, is a logistical marvel; for where did all those sordid people come from? How could a community of decent souls suddenly generate so much iniquity? It probably makes sense to suppose, as the last speaker quoted above did, that quite a few of the survivors are acting more coarsely now than they did before the disaster. But something else may be going on here too. The unfamiliar people who move next door and bring their old styles of life with them may be acting improperly by some objective measure or they may not, but they are always acting in an unfamiliar way, and the fact of the matter may very well be that relative strangers, even if they come from the same general community, are almost by definition less "moral" than immediate neighbors. They do not fall within the pale of local clemency, as it were, and so do not qualify for the allowances neighbors make for one another on the grounds that they know the motives involved ("we don't worry none about that, it's just the way Billy is"). One can find a strong hint of this in the following comment:

I think that morals have degenerated. I think that is a characteristic of the whole society of Buffalo Creek now. Things which I didn't notice before. I have been in all areas of Buffalo Creek and it has never manifested itself as it has now. It is much more open. I have lived on Buffalo Creek all of my life.

Before, you had the town drunk and that sort of thing. You knew which family did what. Everyone knew everyone's business. But now it seems it is much more open. No matter where you go, this type of thing is going on where it didn't before.

Clearly, the speaker is lamenting the apparent rise of immorality on her home turf, but she is also suggesting that the old communal order of the hollow had niches for some forms of deviation, like the role of the town drunk, and ways to absorb others into the larger tissue of everyday life. But the disaster had washed away the packing around those niches, leaving the occupants exposed to the frowning glances of new neighbors. So the problem has two dimensions. On the one hand, people who had not engaged in any kind of misbehavior before were now, by their own admission, doing so. On the other hand, the unfamiliar manners of a relative stranger seem to hint darkly of sin all by themselves, and personal habits that once passed as mild eccentricities in the old neighborhood now begin to look like brazen vices in the harsher light of the new neighborhood. A resident in one of the smaller trailer camps said:

Well, living there was an intolerable situation for me because my children were exposed to people that I didn't want my children to be around. There were drunkards. There were fights, vulgar language. And all of these were situations to which my children had never been exposed. This is not the type of home life we have nor our friends and families have. Even the small children used language which I didn't approve.

And another person living a short distance away echoed the same thought.

The people of Buffalo Creek tended to group themselves together; therefore the breaking up of the old communities threw all kinds of different people together. At the risk of sounding superior, I feel we are living amidst people with lower moral values than us.

Perhaps so. There is no question but that "immorality" is on the rise, and there is a clear hint in some of the complaints along these lines—although not in the one above, as I happen to know—that the protesting voices issue from white mouths and are referring to black manners. But the people of "lower moral values" who populate the various trailer camps come from the general community too, and if some of them really are less well behaved in fact, the rest, in their turn, appear to have their own doubts about the new neighbors across the way. Everyone appears to be scanning a sea of unfamiliar faces and sensing that a fair amount of evil lurks out there.

"Morality" is a curious notion anyway. Theories of human nature generally assume that moral posture is shaped not only by the voices of conscience from within but by the voices of authority from without. Most of those outer voices have disappeared on Buffalo Creek for the good reason that people do not pay that much attention to one another anymore, but the inner voices, even, seem to have lost much of their force— as if they were wilting from lack of nourishment. In the long run, perhaps, morality is a form of community participation. To be moral is to keep faith with the generality of one's fellows, to be in tune with the values of the larger collectivity. No matter how stern and unrelenting one's inner voices may turn out to be, they rarely outlast the community structures that molded them and gave them tone.

DISORIENTATION

It has been noted many times that the survivors of a disaster are likely to be dazed and stunned afterward, unable to locate themselves in time and place. Time stops. Places and objects seem transitory. Survivors have trouble finding stable points of reference in the surrounding terrain, both physical and social, to help them fix their position and orient their behavior.

The people of Buffalo Creek responded to the events of February 26 in just that way. Many of them reported that the flow of time seemed to stop all at once: "everything has stopped," "the end is here," "there can be no tomorrow," "time stopped for us," "our lives are over." For a long time after the disaster, people were uncertain as to where they belonged in the universe and how they should behave in relation to it: "I didn't know where I was. I didn't know what I was doing. I didn't know anything."

Now all of this can be understood as a natural result of shock, but the fact is that people continued to experience that same sense of disorientation for months and even years after the flood had passed. "We find ourselves standing, not knowing exactly which way to go or where to turn," said one survivor. "They should call this whole hollow the Bureau of Misplaced Persons," said another; "we're all just lost." The hollow is changed, of course, and people continue to live unsettled lives. But the familiar hills are still there. The old road, though damaged and scarred, curves its way up the narrow valley as before. The schools have reopened, the stores are back in business, the churches are functioning, the men have returned to work. By now, it would seem, a certain equilibrium should have been restored. But, no. Along the entire length of Buffalo Creek, people continue to feel that they are lost in "a strange and different place."

Part of the trouble is that the terrain *is* different.

Amherstdale just doesn't look like it used to. I've lived here all my life and it's hard for me now to remember the way some of the houses looked and where they used to be. Half of the people have not come back and it just doesn't look like the coal-mining town I grew up in.

When I get back to visit, which is quite frequently, I miss seeing the houses and landmarks. At one time I knew where everybody lived, but now it's hard for me to point out where anything was.

Well, I go right by where we used to live every night on my way to work. There's only a few people lives there and you can only see a couple of lights. It just don't seem right. It ain't the same or anything.

But the problem clearly reaches beyond the change in physical appearance, for the spiritual mood of the hollow, if that is the correct phrase, has changed even more drastically, and people are just not sure how to relate to those changes.

Our own yard was a gathering place for the neighborhood children. There are children here, but we aren't even acquainted with them. There isn't one family in our trailer park that we were really close to. So we feel like we're in a strange land even though it is just a few miles up Buffalo Creek from where we lived.

We don't have a neighborhood anymore. We're just strange people in a strange place. I feel our lives have been completely turned inside out by what has happened.

My lonely feelings is my most difficult problem. I feel as if we were living in a different place, even though we are still in our own home. Nothing seems the same.

Such feelings of disorientation are difficult to talk over because the language does not lend itself to that kind of complaint. Once one has said that one feels "strange" and "out of place," one has almost exhausted the available vocabulary. But these feelings are reflected in other ways, too—in the frequency with which survivors will simply forget the names of people close to them, for example, or the frequency with which they will lose track of persons or events or places. Professional visitors who have gone into the hollow since the disaster have noticed that survivors often answer factual questions about time—their own age or their children's grade in school—as if history had indeed stopped on the date of the flood. One psychiatrist remarked at the end of an exhausting clinical interview:

I might say at this point in the interview, for reasons that are not altogether clear, Dr. Michaelson and I both became slightly confused about sequences and what was going on. It is possible that we were tired at this point in the day and that this contributed to our confusion, but it is also possible that Mrs. Hemphill was contributing to our confusion too, because . . . there are some indications here in terms of Mrs. Hemphill's uneasiness regarding dates that she may have stopped in time as far as the flood is concerned.

This was those psychiatrists' first exposure to the problem, but visitors who had spent more time on Buffalo Creek had become used to it. Even two years after the disaster, it was a common occurrence for survivors to give vital statistics about themselves as of the date of the flood, as if that were the last day on which they had measured their existence in that way, as if that were the last day they knew themselves to be living at all. Every person in the hollow understands when another says, "That was, you know, before." There was history before, an orderly and calculable sequence of time, but there has been nothing since other than a blurring of logic and a collapse of meaning.

So, in general, people all over the hollow live with a lasting sense of being out of place, uprooted, torn loose from their moorings, and this feeling has long outlasted the initial trauma of the disaster itself. Each of the following remarks, for example, was recorded more than a year after the flood.

I just don't know what we are all going to do. The pressure is on and I just don't understand what is happening. My mind is a blank.

People here are not like they used to be. Only people who were in the flood realize that it's not rudeness when you have to ask them to repeat something simply because you weren't listening, your mind was somewhere else. Or you forget to ask them to come back again when they leave after a visit.

Or, as happens every day, you start to say something and for-
get what it was, or just walk away while someone is still talking
to you. Or you start looking for something you know you have
and then remember, "That was before."

    My nerves have been and are so bad. Sometimes I feel like I
hate myself. My body is one big pain, so stiff when I get up in
the morning. And I feel like I am going to fall. I feel like the
flood has brainwashed me.

    I mean I can be out doing something and go into the house
after something to do it with and by the time I get in the house
I forget what I went after, and I have to stop and study. After
a while it will come back to me what I was going after and
I'll go get it. I forget easy and I get real nervous.

    Sometimes like I'll be in the yard working and want to go
in the house. I'll want to get me a drink of water, but when I
get there I think, "Now, what did I come in here for? What was
I after?" Or if I'm in the house and I go out to my toolhouse.
I'll get there sometimes and I'll study and I'll say, "I came out
here for something, now what was it?" I've got to study.

    I forget, see. I forget what happens to me. I mean odd things
happen. To me it seems like I can remember but three hours
later I don't remember what happened. And these things worry
me. I go places, I don't even know where in the hell I'm at,
you know. I have to sit down and think, "What the hell am I
doing down here, where am I at?" 'Cause I'm in a strange
place. I don't know how I got there and what I'm doing there,
you know.

People normally learn who they are and where they are by
taking soundings from their fellows. As if employing a subtle
form of radar, they probe other people in their immediate
surround with looks and words and gestures, hoping to learn
something about themselves from the return signals. But when

there are no reliable objects out there to receive those explora-
tory probes, people have a hard time estimating where they
stand in relation to the rest of the world. They come to feel
that they are not whole persons because they have no con-
firmed place in the general drift of humanity. One woman,
speaking for her neighbors, put the case well:

*I feel that the disaster has affected almost everyone on Buf-
falo Creek emotionally. People have no sense of belonging
anywhere. There are no existing community identities left,
only desolation and indecision. People are not sure yet of what
to do or where to turn.*

And a couple of those neighbors described their own feelings.

*Well, I just don't feel like the same person. I feel like I live
in a different world. I don't have no home no more. I don't
feel normal anymore. I mean, sometimes I just wonder if I'm
a human being. I just feel like I don't have no friends in the
world, nobody cares for me.*

*I lived all my life at Buffalo Creek, and I hesitated every
time I spoke of the place because I knew if I mentioned where
I come from that they was going to ask what happened and
such. And it seemed like every time I tried to remember anything in my past, it bothered me tremendously—because the
flood in its own way destroyed my past in the mental sense. I
knew everybody in the area. That's where I lived, and that's
what I called home. And I can't go back there anymore, I can't
even think of it. I have no past.*

LOSS OF CONNECTION

It would be stretching a point to imply that the neighborhoods strung out along Buffalo Creek were secure nests in
which people had found a full measure of satisfaction and
warmth, but it is wholly reasonable to insist that those neigh-

borhoods were like the air people breathed—sometimes harsh, sometimes chilly, but always a basic fact of life. For better or worse, the people of the hollow were enmeshed in the fabric of their community; they drew their being from it. When that fabric was torn away by the disaster, people found themselves exposed and alone, suddenly dependent on their own personal resources.

And the cruel fact of the matter is that many survivors, when left to their own mettle, proved to have meager resources, not because they lacked the heart or the competence, certainly, but because they had always put their abilities in the service of the larger community and did not know how to recall them for their own individual purposes. A good part of their personal strength turned out to be the reflected strength of the collectivity—on loan from the communal store—and they discovered that they were not very good at making decisions, not very good at getting along with others, not very good at maintaining themselves as separate persons in the absence of neighborly support.

Words like "lonely" and "lonesome" appear again and again in local conversations.

I can't get used to the way it is. It is very lonesome and sad. I'm disgusted. I'm moving out of this valley.

A lot has changed. Nothing is the same. It is just a big lonesome hollow to me, and I hope I don't ever have to go back up there.

People are "lonely" in the sense that old and trusted neighbors have moved away, leaving them isolated; but the word "lonesome" means something else as well. The people of the hollow are lone some-ones, left to themselves, out of touch even with those they see every day. Despite the obvious fact that most of them are surrounded by other people, they feel as if they have been cast on a distant beach, drenched and bruised and frightened beyond measure, but suffering mainly from the feeling that they are in a land of strangers, with no one to talk to about the past, no one to share what is left of the future, and no one from whom to draw a sense of who they are. One elderly woman who moved several miles from Buffalo Creek into a nearby town crowded with people has already been quoted: "It is like being all alone in the middle of a desert." And a man of about the same age who continued to live in his damaged home after the flood put it:

Well, there is a difference in my condition. Like somebody being in a strange world with nobody around. You don't know nobody. You walk the floor or look for somebody you know to talk to, and you don't have anybody.

Many survivors fear that they are beginning to suffer the kind of disorientation and even madness that can come from prolonged stretches of isolation.

I just stay mad. Sometimes I think they have brighter people in the nut house than I am. I haven't had a real good night's sleep in nine months. Sometimes I wake up and have a big fear inside of me. It feels like something has chased me for miles. I feel numb, my heart feels like it is jumping out of me. My mind is just a blank.

One result of this fear is that people tend to draw farther and farther into themselves and to become even more isolated. This is the behavior of wounded animals that crawl off to nurse their hurts. It is also the behavior of people who string rough coils of barbed wire around their lonely outposts because they feel they have nothing to offer those who draw near.

I don't know. I'm a different person since the disaster. People get on my nerves. They irritate me. People that I always liked prior to the flood, I've alienated myself from them now. I like to be in seclusion. I seldom have a civil word for people now. I'm rather sarcastic and sometimes I'm a bit too smart. It's mostly because I don't want to fool with anyone.

I took nervous fits all the time. I went crazy. I got real upset and started shaking all over, and I would just forget about everybody. I couldn't remember nobody. I didn't want nobody around me. I didn't want nobody to speak to me or even to look at me. I wanted nobody even ten miles around me to call my name, I got like that. I just wanted to hit them and make them leave me alone.

Seems like everything in you just curls up in knots and you want to explode. I've always been an easygoing man all my life and good to everybody. But here lately I'm as ill as a copperhead. I'm just ready to explode on anybody right there.

Well, I can't hold a conversation like I once could, I can't give people a good word. I was always a quiet-termed man, you know, but I could always hold a conversation with any man I met. But I ain't been able to do that since this thing has happened. I'm just a different man. I don't have the same attitude towards people that I had. It used to be that I cared for all people, but anymore I just keep myself alive. That's the only thing I study about.

So the lonesomeness increases and is reinforced. People have heavy loads of grief to deal with, strong feelings of inadequacy to overcome, blighted lives to restore, and they must do all this without very much in the way of personal self-confidence. Solving problems and making decisions, those are the hard parts.

Yes, I think the whole society of Buffalo Creek has changed. The people are more depressed and despondent. Uncertainty seems to rule their lives. They aren't sure of how to make decisions. If they make a decision, they aren't sure they have done the right thing. My parents can't decide whether they want to move somewhere else, whether they want to build on their lot. They don't know what to do. They don't know what is going to happen. And I know my in-laws have already pur-

218 | *Everything in Its Path*

chased one house and sold it because they didn't like it. They are in the process of buying another, which they aren't sure they want to buy. That's the type of thing. People don't know where to go.

Well, I'm disorganized. It's like I lost my life and I've never been able to find it again. That's the way I feel. I want to find it. I try to find it, but I don't know how. In a way, I gave my life up in the flood, and it's like I'm not repented. Since then, everything has been disorganized. I can't organize anything anymore. If I pound a nail, I'll scar myself all up. Anything I do, I do it wrong. I wanted to get away from people, so I thought I'll get me some animals or something to raise. So I got me some dogs to take care of and chickens to take care of and the damned dogs killed my chickens. It's all simple, but I can't seem to solve the problems. I mean there are so many problems I've got to look at and try to solve, but I can't seem to solve any of them. I used not to make mistakes in decisions, and I do today on about everything.

The inability of people to come to terms with their own isolated selves is counterpointed by an inability to relate to others on an interpersonal, one-to-one basis. Human relations along Buffalo Creek took their shape from the expectations pressing in on them from all sides like a firm but invisible mold; they had been governed by the customs of the neighborhood, the traditions of the family, the ways of the community. And when the mold was stripped away by the disaster, something began to happen to those relationships. This was true of everyday acquaintances; it was doubly true of marriages.

No act in life seems more private, more intimate, than the decision by two people to get married, particularly in this age when we celebrate the distance we have come since the times of arranged marriages. It is true, of course, that people "select" their own mates now, whatever that may mean. But there are other ways to arrange marriages than becoming a formal partner to the contract—spoken and unspoken encouragements

and friends beforehand, as well as a
…ggestions that become a part of the
…. While we do not know very much
…tries, it is clear enough that marriage,
…mmunity affair. It is validated by the
… the community, commemorated by
y married couple in the world knows
…sures exerted on that union by inter-
sense, then, a marriage between two
gravitational field. The human parti-
… are held together by interpersonal
charges passing between them, but they are also held together
by all the other magnetic forces passing through the larger
field; and when the outer currents and tensions lose their force,
the particles find that the inner charge, the interpersonal bond,
begins to fade as well. Wholly devoted husbands and wives
were to discover on Buffalo Creek that they did not know how
to care for each other or to work together as a team or even
to carry on satisfactory conversations when the community was
no longer there to provide the context and set the cadence.

So some of these marriages limp along, the particles remaining in a kind of proximity even though the charge seems entirely exhausted. "My marriage? It's just like a job," said one
woman bitterly. Said another:

*Our marriage is just there. We care for each other, but it's
like a fixture in life. We're married, and that is it. We don't
seem to have the time for each other anymore. If I sit down
and try to tell him something, he turns the TV on and me off.
We're just not a close unit like we were.*

But other marriages—a large number of them, apparently—
are breaking up altogether, the particles drifting farther and
farther apart.

*It's tore up I don't know how many marriages. The divorce
list is as long as your arm. There's been hundreds of them, I*

bet, and remarriages and things. Like I said, I had a cousin to divorce her husband and then my other cousin married him. And now she's seeing him again. I don't know, people are just going around in circles.

Many marriages have broken up that seemed secure before the flood. My husband and I can agree on only one thing: we won't go back to Lorado. When the time comes to buy us a house, we both agree that we will face a major problem in our marriage. I hope we can agree on where to live. If not, then we may have to come to a parting of the ways after twenty-six years of marriage.

My husband and I, we was happy before the flood. We got along real good, other than just a few quarrels that never amounted to nothing. But after the flood we had fights, and it was constantly we were quarreling about something or other. We had fights. He would hit me and he would choke me and he would slap me around.

All of this is reflected, as one might reasonably expect, in a decreasing ability to get along sexually. Studies of emotional stress have suggested that a decline in sexual interest is only to be expected after moments of extreme dislocation, and the pattern has certainly held here. But it has held too long. As the people of the hollow prepared to commemorate the second and then the third anniversary of the flood, they were still reporting all manner of trouble in this sensitive area, and one has to conclude that the absence of viable community supports has helped prolong what might otherwise have been a transitory problem. The following comments of a young couple are a fair sample of what people from every part of the hollow said in formal interviews or in chance conversations.

You wanted to know how the disaster has affected our lives. Well, we haven't had much time for play since the flood. We have had to readjust to many new homes, and we didn't feel like having any fun. Really, we just haven't been a complete family since the flood. I was just unable to be a whole woman and wife to my husband for the longest time, and even now we don't seem to enjoy our relations like we once did.

I was robbed of my sex life, if that's what you're getting at. I enjoyed sex before the flood, but now I don't. I still feel for my wife. I don't want nothing to ever happen to her, and I think she feels the same way about me. Even though we sleep in separate bedrooms, there is never a night goes by that I don't go in to her and tell her good night. But I don't have any desire for sex with her.

Older couples, too, expressed the same complaints, although sometimes in the heartier language of people who have known the ways of bedrooms for thirty or more years.

Well, male and female—you have to get in a mood for something like that. He quarrels at me and he fusses at me. He says I got another man because it don't interest me whatsoever. The memories come back when I least expect them. So you might as well throw a bucket of ice water on me. It's no good.

The difficulties experienced by so many married couples in relating to each other spread to the rest of the family as well. In the same way that wives and husbands stare at each other across the breakfast table and wonder how to strengthen and reconfirm their relationship, other members of the family find that intimacy and gentleness are hard to sustain in an emotional atmosphere as dry as this one. The general community validated those bonds and gave them shape, and people do not really know how to keep them intact by deliberate expressions of affection or by conscious offers of support. For one thing, as we noted earlier, people are very absorbed in their own problems.

Each person in the family is a loner now, a person alone. Each of us is fighting his own battles. We just don't seem to care for each other anymore.

But even when heroic attempts are made, old familial bonds reaching across generations or within generations seem to break noiselessly as the various particles, drifting now in a dead gravitational field, slowly separate.

The family is not what they was. They're not the same people they was. Before—I don't know how you'd put this—but there was love in the home. Of course we had arguments like everybody else does once in a while, maybe over something that doesn't amount to anything. But now it seems like each one is a different person, an individual by himself or herself, and there's just nothing there.

My children are changed. I sit and try to talk to them, tell them they are a family and should love each other and treat each other like brothers and sisters. But most of the time they treat each other like enemies. They're always on the firing line at each other. It's always screaming and yelling.

My grandchildren. It used to be we was the loveliest people you ever seen. We was, together. Now my grandchildren won't hardly give me a look. I don't know what's wrong. They seem like they are moody or something. My grandson there, used to be he loved me better than anything, and now he won't even look at me. He don't want to be around me. One of the granddaughters, too, is about the same. She has spells that way. I don't know. I can't understand it.

The general problem people have in maintaining intimate ties with others extends beyond marriages, beyond families, across the whole hollow. The complaint is heard everywhere that people can no longer get along warmly. Whether people feel distressed because old neighbors seem reluctant to approach them or because they themselves cannot mobilize the energy or confidence to approach others, the situation is difficult.

Well, it was a very close-knit, friendly neighborhood, and we all had fellowship with each other and cared about each other. It was just a nice place to live. But now you could compare it more to living in a city. We're all so busy trying to take care of our own business and it seems like everybody is a little bit hurt or something. It's just not the same. All roots were pulled out.

And you just be stuttering, you just don't feel right among people. You'd just rather not be around them, you know. You'd just rather be by yourself instead of being with somebody. Since the flood, well, it just seems like I'm someone different. It seems like I'm a different person.

Well, before the flood I was happy. I was never depressed. I was always cheerful. I could have conversations with people and I could get along with them very well. But after the flood I couldn't hold a conversation and it seemed like it was hard for me to make friends with someone. Anymore it just seems to me like I am interfering with people or I bother them or something like that. I just don't feel like I have any use having conversations with them.

When one asks why this sense of alienation should exist, a number of theories are proposed. In part, of course, old attachments have dissolved because people have drifted apart physically.

The people there were like a closely knit family. But now people are scattered all over the state and neighboring states. You can ask for anyone left and no one knows where they are.

But that only begins to explain the difficulty, for most of the survivors are still in the general vicinity of Buffalo Creek, strewn around the area, to be sure, but still within reach of one another. There are those who seem to maintain a permanent storm alert and hesitate to let others wander too far away from the safety of home.

The people who are here don't get out and do things like they used to. Before the flood, the men worked on old cars or got together and talked for hours at a time. Now it's just for a few minutes at a time, and it seems everyone wants their children to stay close to home.

Well, my children. When I let them go anyplace I expect them back at a certain time, and if they are late, I panic. I always worry that something will happen to them while they are gone. I fear for the safety of my children. I used to be a reasonable person, but now I magnify those fears a hundred times more than I used to.

There are those who seem so preoccupied, so dulled in spirit, so drawn in on themselves that they are incapable of anything but the most perfunctory encounter anyway.

People don't visit or associate with each other. Most just speak and go on about their business. They seem to be in a daze, having deep thoughts or pressing problems with which they cannot cope.

For the most part, people don't care for each other the way they did before. Everybody went through their own agonies and are more concerned with their own problems. You hardly see a smiling face anymore.

I am now back in the community that I lived in before the flood, but most of my close friends have moved. No one is the same. No one visits, no children come to play. Everyone seems to be selfish now, living only for themselves and no one else. Before, they were kind and helpful.

There are those who feel that they are no longer fit for human company of any kind, either because they have fallen to so low an estate or because they sense some kind of anger or blame in the reactions of their neighbors and worry that the world looks upon them with a sharper glance than before.

I have the impression that people say, "Well, just looky yonder, what's he doing up here?" or "What's he doing in this gathering or in this community?" Like I was casted out. I just get that feeling on my mind that people really don't want me there. I just can't get it straightened out that I'm still one of the community.

They wouldn't come to visit me or come and say, "How are you doing?" or anything. And I just didn't like that. I felt they could stop by and see how I was doing or if I was faring all right or if I was sick or something. I just felt rejected or something. I felt that nobody wanted to be bothered with me. I felt at a distance.

And then I'm hurt in the way I think people feel toward me. I can't go places like I once did. It seems to me that some people dodge me, peoples not friendly with me on the street when they pass me or when they meet me. They just look at me [as if to say] "Well, you ain't got nothing, I don't want to speak to you." It seems to me like they just want to shun me and get away. And it hurts deep down, buddy, I'll tell you that. The way people act toward me, I don't desire to go anywhere. I don't feel that I'm welcome. I just sit around the house all day, and if something don't change, I'm just going to dry up.

And there are those who deliberately avoid relating to others as a matter of policy, ostensibly because they want to avoid the pain of further separations and refuse to invest any more than is absolutely necessary in bonds that may be shattered later. It seems clear, however, that this policy is based at least in part on a profound uncertainty as to how one goes about "making" relationships in any case. In places like Buffalo Creek, where attachments between people are seen as a part of the natural scheme of things—inherited by birth or acquired by proximity—the very idea of "forming" friendships or "building" relationships seems a little odd. Attachments like that are not engineered; they just happen when the communal tone is right. So people are not sure just what to do.

I have good new neighbors, but it's not the same. The neighbors I had before the flood shared our happiness when our babies were born, they shared our troubles and our sorrows. Here is the change. My husband has been sick going on three weeks. My old neighbors would ask about him or go see him or send him a get-well card. But he only got one card, and it was from someone away from here. The day the flood came, the people of Buffalo Creek started running, and they are still running inside their minds. They don't have time to stand and talk.

I have noticed that people do not visit each other as they did before the disaster. They don't seem to want to establish lasting friendships. Most people keep pretty much to themselves. You can drive through the trailer camps and see that most people stay inside with the doors closed. I do it myself. It is as though we have lost our own identity. We seem to be a forgotten people.

But the friends I have left on Buffalo Creek, it seems like they've turned cold-hearted against people and I just don't know how to explain it. It seems like they don't want anything in particular to do with you.

One result of all this is that the community, what remains of it, seems to have lost its most significant quality—the power it generated in people to care for one another in times of need, to console one another in times of distress, to protect one another in times of danger. Looking back, it does seem that the general community was stronger than the sum of its parts. When the people of the hollow were sheltered together in the embrace of a secure community, they were capable of extraordinary acts of generosity; but when they tried to relate to one another as individuals, separate entities, they found that they could no longer mobilize whatever resources are required for caring and nurturing. This story is certainly not a new one. Daniel Defoe wrote of the London plague:

> Indeed the distress of the people at this seafaring end of the town was very deplorable, and deserved the greatest commiseration: but alas! this was a time when every one's private safety lay so near them, that they had no room to pity the distresses of others; for every one had death, as it were, at his door, and many even in their families, and knew not what to do, or whither to fly. . . . It is not indeed to be wondered at; for the danger of immediate death to ourselves took away all bowels of love, all concern for one another.[6]

And that is what happened on Buffalo Creek—a loss of concern, a loss of human trust. "It seems like the caring part of our lives is over," one elderly woman said, and this thought was echoed over and over again by persons of all ages. The following speakers are, in order, a teen-age boy, a woman in her middle years, and a man in his seventies.

It used to be that everyone knew everyone. When you were hitchhiking, you just put out your thumb and the first car along would pick you up. But it's not like that now. They just don't care about you now. They got problems of their own, I guess.

The changes I see are in the people. They seem to be so indifferent toward their fellow man. I guess it's because they had to watch a whole lifetime go down the drain.

I'm getting old, too, and I can't get no help. Nobody'll help you do nothing. You have to pay somebody, and they'll come and start a project for you, but then they'll walk off and leave you. It's just too much.

Behind this inability to care is a wholly new emotional tone on the creek—a distrust even of old neighbors, a fear, in fact, of those very persons on whom one once staked one's life. A disaster like the one that visited Buffalo Creek makes everything in the world seem unreliable, even other survivors, and that is a very fragile base on which to build a new community.

I've just learned that you don't trust nobody. I just feel that way. You don't put no confidence in nobody. You believe nothing you're told. I don't know, you could have come along before the flood and told me you was going to give me the moon, and I'd have believed you.

That's it. Nobody trusts anybody anymore. You know, when we moved back home I was so scared I went out and bought a pistol. I don't know whether it was the place or the house or the people or what I was so scared of. And I'm still scared. I don't know what of, either. Why, my husband and I used to go to bed at night and leave our front door open, but now, of a day, those doors are locked. I'm scared to death.

This emptiness of concern, although he did not say so directly, may have been what a young miner had in mind when he said:

Well, it seems like everything just don't go right no more. There's a part of you gone and you can't find it. You don't know what part it is. It's just a part that's gone.

ILLNESS AND IDENTITY

I noted earlier that mountain people in general have lived along a cultural axis marked by a high degree of physical ability on the one pole and an equally high degree of physical disability on the other, and that the course of recent events in Appalachia has acted to tip the scales for many of them. Illness is one of the options open to people who need to define themselves by their disabilities because they no longer respect or derive a measure of selfhood from their abilities. This has always been true of people who live difficult lives, but it may be particularly true for Appalachia. Words are not really a major currency of exchange in the mountains. People talk, of course, but their main vehicles of self-expression are movement and activity. The mountain mind is oriented to concrete details rather than abstract states, and it is wholly possible that the large number of somatic complaints one hears within the privacy of the family circle or in the more public domain of the clinic is a mountain way of giving palpable form to troubles for which there are no satisfactory words. Mountain people do not talk easily about anguish, despair, or hopelessness, but they are quite familiar with the language of aching backs and stiff joints, of frayed nerve ends and malfunctioning organs.

Folk medicine still has a place on Buffalo Creek for some.

I had a sore on my ankle and it would spread and it would come up my leg plumb up to my belt, and my leg would swell fit to bust. The blood would run out of it, and I would stay as high as seven, eight, nine days in the hospital at a time, and they would run that disease down to my ankle, but they couldn't cure it. They said I would carry it to my grave. . . . So I was in the hospital one time and there was an old woman sitting there at the desk and I was on the bed. She told me, she said, "Mister, I don't know your name, but I can tell you something that will cure that." And I said, "I wish you would, this doctor here is wearing me out." She told me to get some bluevittle or bluestone and dissolve it up in lukewarm water and wash my leg in it. And I done so, and now my leg is as well as anybody's leg.

But most of the people of the hollow are quite at home with modern medicine and have come to depend upon it profoundly, so much so that visitors are often impressed by the volume of traffic passing through physicians' offices.

This may have something to do with the fact that the busiest local doctors are employed by the coal companies and are paid on a check-off system, with the result that patients are not normally charged by the visit; and it may have something to do with the fact that men who work in the mines need to apply for medical compensation through a physician's office. But coal mining is a hard occupation, and it takes a heavy toll both on those who work underground and those who never see the inside of a mine.

So the people of Buffalo Creek logged a considerable number of hours in physicians' offices even before the flood, but this flow of traffic, according to the testimony of all observers, has gone up dramatically since. One Pittston attorney blurted out after having participated in a number of exhausting depositions: "If you tell me that you haven't seen Dr. Craft or Dr. Long since the flood, you are going to be the only person on Buffalo Creek who hasn't." And, indeed, the woman being questioned visited one of those physicians, not once but several times.

A good deal of the new business being attracted to doctors' offices is for the treatment of symptoms that do not appear anywhere in traditional medical textbooks, symptoms that may originate somewhere in the tissues of the mind but are experienced as organic sensations nevertheless and must be counted as real disturbances in the ecology of the body.

There are people, as we have seen, who come to feel that their bodies are working improperly—that their joints are moving independently of their minds, that their reflexes are becoming sluggish, that the sinews holding the various parts of their bodies together have grown slack and unresponsive. "I just can't get this body of mine to do what I want," said one woman miserably. "I don't know," said another, "I sometimes feel like a puppet, like somebody else was pulling the strings."

There are people who cannot escape the thought that their bodies and the rest of the world around them are contaminated in some way, stained by the events of the past. This feeling begins with the memory of having been surrounded by mud and silt and sludge.

And I think I'm losing my mind. I hope I don't have to go through life like this all the time. I hope there's a better day for me. If I have to go through any more of this, I don't believe I can make it. The flood, the mud, I don't know what to think. Looking at all that mud will drive you nuts. It will almost drive you crazy if you have to crawl in it and work in it and smell it. Don't nobody know. All the mud. All the disaster.

And it grows into a conviction that all this black misery has worked its way into the hidden center of things. It is lodged between the walls, under the floor, behind the panels; and it seems to have become absorbed into the very machinery of the body itself. "Everything is contaminated," one person said. "I just feel dirty inside all the time."

There are those who feel as though they are always smothering, unable to draw a clean breath or to loosen the bands around their necks and chests. Miners who report this sensation, of course, are likely to be suffering from respiratory ailments connected with their work, but the complaint is common even among people who have never been exposed to coal dust.

Sometimes I take spells that I'm just choking half to death since I come through the flood, and I tell Dr. Harris and he just goes ahead and writes. It's just like something was wrapped around my neck. I'm short of breath all the time. It's just a choking feeling. Just like everything is a tightening up.

There are people who feel drained by the events of the immediate past, emptied of reasons for doing anything, emptied of explanations for their own feelings and motives, emptied of love or conviction or pleasure, emptied of self-esteem and an ability to relate to others. It is as if the wells of the spirit had suddenly gone dry.

I don't know. I just don't take interest in nothing no more like I used to. I used to live a happy life. Now I don't and I don't have no feeling for nothing. I feel like I'm drained of life.

None of these conditions, of course, has a recognizable name, but the most common complaint found on Buffalo Creek does have one—"bad nerves." Most people understand that "bad nerves" has something to do with emotional strain and originates in the mind, but they tend to visualize it as a palpable organic disorder. Nerves, after all, are a form of living matter, and when people insist that their nerves are "all tore up," they are suggesting that bodily fibers have been damaged in some way and need to be attended to. The condition is hard to describe, but everyone who suffers from it knows what it feels like.

Well, myself, I'm nervous. I'm not nervous on the outside, like when your hand is shaking or anything. I'm nervous on the inside. I've got something that wants out and can't get out. I don't know how I feel.

I was in such a shape that I was just all to pieces. It seemed like everything I went to do went wrong, and I was completely tore up inside. I felt like my insides was setting there just juggling like that. I kept feeling a roaring inside of me. I was just shaking all the time. I couldn't eat. I couldn't sleep. I was smoking one cigarette after another, and I knew I had to do something.

These, then, are some of the reasons why so many people along Buffalo Creek visit physicians, and given everything that has been said so far about the effects of the disaster, none of them should be surprising. The people of the hollow feel ill, out of sorts, disturbed, not quite whole. Their bodies and spirits have been damaged by the flood, and it makes sense to assume that people need therapy in the wake of a shock like that. But maybe there is more to be said than that, for the bodily sensations we have been talking about here and in other parts of the report are the symptoms of grief and abandonment as well as the symptoms of shock, and the volume of human traffic moving in and out of doctors' offices on Buffalo

Creek is not only a reflection on the state of individual health but a reflection on the state of communal health. Some people came close to recognizing this explicitly.

After the flood, I was sick about six months, real sick, but I didn't know what was wrong or anything. I just had fevers and chills and diarrhea every day and I couldn't get rid of it. I just got so weak I couldn't walk around and do my work. And then I took spells of crying and I would get depressed because I was in a strange place and didn't know nobody and had lost so many of my friends, my close friends. My sickness started when I lost my girl friend, I would say that was the biggest impact. I couldn't hardly ever get over it.

The above speaker, a woman in her early thirties, is almost suggesting that the loss of neighborhood and community is related in some way to the loss of bodily function. And there may be something to that, for there is a sense in which separation from the familiar linkages of community is itself a form of illness. When one's communal surround disappears, and with it a feeling of belonging and identity, one tends to feel less intact personally; and one also tends to turn to illness as a way of explaining one's own discontents. This is why illness and disorder can become a way of life, a source of self-identification, a central fact of everyday existence.

They offered me a trailer at Latrobe and that very morning I went all to pieces. I said, "I cannot go up this road no further. I won't have no friends. I won't have no neighbors. I can't get out and go to the doctor."

Now this person may in fact need the services of a physician more than most, since she suffers from an assortment of medical disorders; but her situation is far from critical and it seems evident on the face of it that being near a physician has almost become a form of communality in itself. Physicians, like the community in general, can accredit one's difficulties, give a name to one's distress, and help one find a place in the order of things.

Health has something to do with feeling whole and being in harmony with the larger physical and social environment. I have proposed above that the people of the creek often seem to feel that their own bodily integrity has been disrupted, that the spaces inside as well as the spaces outside have been contaminated, that the pressures of life have drawn in so tightly that they can scarcely breathe, and that they have been drained of vigor and spirit. And these missing qualities are exactly what a community can supply. It can offer a place, a rhythm, a coherence. It can protect one from contamination, help absorb the pressures of life, and serve as a source of meaning and energy. When that insulation is stripped away, most people are exposed and alone, and their own bodies become the tissue, as it were, on which disturbances in the surrounding world are recorded in painful detail.

THE ILLUSION OF SAFETY

Among the symptoms of extreme trauma is a sense of vulnerability, a feeling that one has lost a certain natural immunity to misfortune, a growing conviction, even, that the world is no longer a safe place to be. And this feeling often grows into a prediction that something terrible is bound to happen again. One of the bargains men make with one another in order to maintain their sanity is to share an illusion that they are safe even when the physical evidence in the world around them does not seem to warrant that conclusion. The survivors of a disaster, of course, are prone to overestimate the perils of their situation, if only to compensate for the fact that they underestimated those perils once before; but what is worse, far worse, is that they sometimes live in a state of almost constant apprehension because they have lost the human capacity to screen the signs of danger out of their line of vision.

All of the other difficulties experienced by the people of Buffalo Creek as a result of the disaster have been aggravated by that raw sense of fear, amounting almost to a conviction that death and destruction have now become an inevitable part of existence. "My whole family," said Wilbur in a passage quoted earlier, "is a family of fear," and many other people up and down the hollow have had to cope alone with the terrors crouched in their minds because they have forgotten how to reach out and offer one another solace.

The fear takes several forms. For many, it is a sharp concern that the black water will come again to finish them off completely, and this is expressed in a constant alarm over rain and storms and bad weather.

People used to love to sit on their porch and watch it rain, but now when it starts to rain they gather coats, blankets, plastic, anything that will shelter them from the weather and wait for the sign that they have to run for the hills. It can just cloud up and some of the people start walking the floor and watching the water in the creek.

For others, the fear is more generalized and diffuse.

There is something in the atmosphere around here—a fear, a fear of people, of things unknown. You're on the alert all the time, always expecting something bad to happen.

I seem to have a sense of urgency about everything. When I'm at home, I have an urgent need to leave. When I'm away, I have an urgent need to come home. It's like I'm always waiting and watching for something terrible to come along.

The fear experienced by adults can be measured in sleepless nights, troubled days, and heavy dosages of medication. The fear experienced by children, however, is beyond all measure —and perhaps even beyond all description. Each of them has a memory of the flood itself, even if he was not there to see it, and each of them has to make something of all that blackness, all that death, all that noise and excitement and terror, without any real technical understanding of what in fact happened. At school the pictures they draw of the flood are filled with people—people floating on the water, people waving matchstick arms on the sides of the hills, people washed up on the banks of the creek—and the dominant accent of those pictures is generally conveyed by a heavy black crayon. It is clear, then, that the scene has become a permanent part of most children's recollections. Yet the vividness of that scene has been sharpened by the conditions of life that now prevail in the hollow and by the anguish they see in their parents' eyes and hear in their parents' voices. They know, most of them, that the flood changed their world, and if they do not quite remember what life was like on Buffalo Creek before the tragedy, they are nonetheless aware that February 26, 1972, was a special moment in the only history that matters very much to them. So they, even more than the older people around them, have come to feel that the flood was not just a freak act of nature or a vicious act of men but a sample of what the universe has in store for them.

The feeling that something terrible is apt to happen (or maybe even that something terrible *should* happen) often began on the very day of the flood.

We picked up a little kid that morning and put him in the back of the truck. He looked at me—he was covered with mud from his head to his toe—he looked at me and said, "Mister, are you going to kill me?" And I didn't know what to do. We just put him in the back of the truck and put a blanket around him. He didn't have a stitch of clothes on and he was just covered with mud.

And it was still one of the main themes stalking those young minds a year and even two or three years later.

On the morning the dam broke, he kept asking his daddy, "Are we going to die too?" He saw the bodies of some of the people. Now, every time it rains, he asks us, "Are we going to get drowned now?"

My daughter, who was four years old at the time of the flood, has really had a time. She's very nervous. Right after the flood we were at my sister's house and everyone walked out of the room she was in. We heard her screaming and ran in there. She just kept screaming and was shaking all over, crying that everybody had left her there. We were a long time quieting her down. She still won't go in a room by herself. We have to sleep with her because she tries to run out and tries to climb the walls. If she's outside and hears a loud noise, we have to run to her because she goes all to pieces. When it rains she won't leave our side.

Both my children have changed since the flood. My son will not go to bed at night without plenty of clothes on because he says that if the dam breaks again he doesn't want to get cold. When it rains, he sets his shoes beside the door and asks me if we are going to go up on the hill. My daughter was small then, but she has a certain hostility toward everyone. She seems to want to hurt everyone. She is bright for her age, but she acts very much older than what she is. She liked to play with dolls before the flood, but now she punches out their eyes and pulls their arms off. She calls her daddy on her play phone now when it rains and tells him to come get her because the dam is breaking. They both seem to be carrying a burden too heavy for children their ages. They seem to be worried all the time.

My little girl, she wakes up at night and all you can do is sit and hold her, just hold her in your arms until she hushes screaming—not crying, screaming—"The water's going to get us, Mommy, the water's going to get us." My boy is the same way. At night you can be laying in the bedroom and him in his room and all of a sudden he'll hit the wall. You go in there and he's rolling all over the bed. Sometimes he goes onto the floor.

These children moved from infancy to childhood in the embrace of an elaborate network of aunts, uncles, grandparents, and other people, some of the latter attached by bonds of kinship but most of them attached only by ties of neighborhood. Communality, to them, meant a continuing atmosphere of warmth and concern, and their fears were obviously aggravated by the abrupt disappearance of that surround. Parents try to fill the vacuum, of course, but they are low on such resources themselves and cannot substitute for all the other people who once made up their children's social world.

The major problem, for adults and children alike, is that the fears haunting them are prompted not only by the memory of past terrors but by a wholly realistic assessment of present dangers. We noted earlier that the physical terrain of Buffalo Creek seems less reliable and less benevolent than it did in the past, and this is no trick of an oversensitive imagination. Many of the surrounding hills are hollowed out now and filled with black water, and the surface of those slopes is covered with mine wastes. Strip mining is on the increase too as underground reserves become depleted, and the sight of those cruel gashes high on the sides of the mountains can be awesome. One teen-age boy on Buffalo Creek told me that the people of the hollow never venture up the hills now without probing the ground ahead of them with a stick. I cannot quite credit this as a literal fact (although I may have misunderstood) because I have climbed the slopes several times in the company of local residents and have never seen anybody do it, yet the statement itself is a telling comment on the confidence people have in their surroundings. The land they have always counted on has proven to be dangerous.

Well, if I think there is going to be a serious rain, I am always thinking what could happen in a community like Buffalo Creek. It worries me what might happen because the hills are torn up with strip mines and I know what can happen. I've seen it happen. Take the place where I live. It's located be-

tween two hollows with very steep mountains in back of us. Strip mining has torn up the whole area in back, I don't know how much. And I know what can happen. Your home might be destroyed before morning.

The Lord, of course, reigns over all this insecurity, and there are signs that the doubts many people now feel about the natural world are easily converted into doubts about the nature of faith. One old Baptist minister said, "People are much more suspicious of God's justice," and one hears comments elsewhere in the hollow suggesting that people often find it difficult to fit their memories of the flood into the larger logic of their faith.

Well, I just lost the desire for everything. I don't care for nothing anymore. I don't even want to go to church anymore. I've been three times since the flood happened. Now I know I should go to church. I should be a better person—and still, when I go to church, it seems like I get hurt and can't stand it. The singing and stuff like that, I just can't stand it. So I guess I feel I've lost religion, yes. I don't cuss, drink, or carry on in any way, but I always had the feeling if you didn't associate with your church, why, you've lost your religion. . . . And I blame the flood for it. It was because it just tore us all up till we didn't care. I believed in the Bible real strong before the flood. I believed in going to church and stuff like that. But the flood just took all of the desire out of me. I don't believe in the Bible as much as I did, because they told us it was an act of God. And I set down and got to thinking it over that it could of been and it couldn't have been. So I just got messed up in my mind there. I don't know if it was an act of God or not.

So Buffalo Creek has become a strange and precarious place, not only because the terrain now seems erratic or because old faiths have lost their simplicity, but because the people of the community can no longer trust one another in the way they did before.

> *It's just awful. The people you know, you never see them. Everybody wants to stay right in their house. They don't want to go nowhere, they don't want to do nothing, they don't want to communicate with nobody. It's insecurity, I believe. You're afraid when you walk out the door that you don't know what's going to happen next.*

In general, then, the loss of communality on Buffalo Creek has meant that people are alone and without very much in the way of emotional shelter. In the first place, the community no longer surrounds people with a layer of insulation to protect them from a world of danger. There is no one to warn you if disaster strikes, no one to rescue you if you get caught up in it, no one to care for you if you are hurt, no one to mourn you if the worst comes to pass. In the second place—and this may be more important in the long run—the community can no longer enlist its members in a conspiracy to make a perilous world seem safe. Among the benefits of human communality is the fact that it allows people to camouflage what might otherwise be an overwhelming set of realities, and the question one should ask about Buffalo Creek is whether the people who live there are paralyzed by imaginary fears or paralyzed by the prospects of looking reality in the eye without the help of a communally shared filter. An old joke making the rounds some years ago had it that paranoids, far from being crazy, are the only people who really know what is going on around them. It might be hard to build a responsible psychiatric theory around that insight, but there is certainly something to be said for it in a context like this. One of the crucial jobs of a culture is to edit reality in such a way that it seems manageable, and that can mean to edit it in such a way that its perils are at least partly masked. It *is* a precarious world, and those who must make their way through it without the capacity to forget those perils from time to time are doomed to a good deal of anxiety.

And this is what the flood seems to have done on Buffalo Creek. It stripped people of their communal supports, and, in doing so, it stripped them of the illusion that they could be safe.

This is how the world can look when you are required to face it alone and have to reconsider your place in it.

No, this world's going to blow all to hell one of these days and it's not going to be long away. I believe in the Bible, and I believe what it said in the Bible is happening now. There ain't going to be a world very much longer. When you see things happening right before your very eyes, you've got to believe it. That's all there is to it. . . . Mostly I read Revelations and things like that to tell me what's going to come. It didn't seem so much to apply to the world and the way it was before the flood. You didn't think too much of the war in Vietnam and everything else before '72. But this destruction, this disaster that happened to us, I believe it opened up a lot of people's eyes. . . . I believe there will be wars, and there will be a bomblike thing that will just destroy this place to pieces. Somebody, some fool, is going to blow it all to pieces. It'll happen. Sure as I'm sitting here and you're sitting there, it'll happen. . . . So the flood has more or less opened up my imagination. It's got me thinking more about the way of life we're having to live, the way our kids is going to have to live, and things like that. I wasn't thinking about those things before the flood. I was just easygoing, come one day at a time. . . . It just seemed like it woke up a new vision, I guess you'd call it, of what is and what used to be. You know, you're almost halfway afraid to turn on the TV anymore. Afraid something's broke out in the United States, afraid some railroad car has broken open with poisonous gases running out right in your brother's face. . . . It scares the hell out of me. I ain't kidding. Sometimes I'll go to bed and think about it, you know—the end of time, destruction, what's going on in wars. It's like growing up, I guess. Before I wasn't thinking about nothing but making sure the house was kept clean, making sure my husband had things he needed for his dinner bucket, making sure the kids had the right clothes on, making sure they was clean, making sure I went to this place at the right time and that place at the right time.

The people of Buffalo Creek come from a land where dreams are thought to have special portent, so they may have been prepared for the fact that the black water would come back to haunt them at night. Most of those dreams are hazy re-enactments of scenes witnessed on the day of the disaster or general dramatizations of the horror they provoked.

Since the flood, I have dreams, you know. I dream like I'm running from death, and when I wake up the next morning, I'm just wore out like I run all night. I'm always running from death.

I was dreaming I was in black water and I was underwater holding my breath, and I liked to smother myself to death. I woke up and I was taking deep breaths.

Another time I dreamed of being in this hollowlike place and it was all muddy and all the trees were dead, and I was trying to get to the top of the hill. But I woke up before I got there.

As one might expect, children, both known and unknown, play a prominent part in those dreams.

My sister's got a baby about a year old, and I dreamed that we lived in the hollow and water was coming out of there. She had come down to the house and she was getting out of the car and she dropped the baby. She made it to the steps in the yard, but the baby went down and was trying to get hold of the fence. There's a wire fence there and the baby was trying to get hold of it and pull itself out. We never did find it.

I've had bad dreams, too. I had one dream three times about water. One time it would be black, and the next time it would be clear. I'd have a baby in my arms, and I'd go so far in this water and it would keep getting deeper, and then I would get fear. I'd start smothering and I'd head back the other way. And this baby were in my arms. I don't know whose baby it was.

And it is interesting to note, if only in passing, that one does not need to have been a participant in the disaster to remember it later in one's dreams, although that certainly fits the logic of the argument being made here. The following nightmare, for example, was reported by a man who was more than two thousand miles away from Buffalo Creek on the date of the flood, but he, too, has had to face a community in ruins, and in that sense he is a true witness to the event.

I have dreams that are hard to describe for the simple reason that they always got destruction in them. It's not of no one in particular. It is faces I've seen, but mostly it's just destruction of buildings or something of that nature. It's black, just real black water, all mucky-looking. It's not a real frequent dream. It usually comes after I've been real tensed up or depressed or something.

One theme that appears again and again in those dreams is the feeling that one is dead and is being buried by people who were once quite close. It is as if one's alienation from others is a form of death, a grim rehearsal for that final act of separation.

In the dream there is a big crowd at the funeral—the whole family is watching. I'm being buried. I'm scared to death. I'm trying to tell them I'm alive but they don't pay no attention. They act like I'm completely dead, but I'm trying to holler to them that I'm alive. They cover me up and let me down, but I can see the dirt on me. I'm panicked and scared. I become violent trying to push my way through the dirt. . . . I think I'll

*suffocate if I don't fight my way out. . . . I'm trying to shout
that I'm alive.*

The dreams of the night, then, relive the terrors of that day,
but they also serve to remind people that the fears and uncertainties derived from the events of February 26, 1972, are still
a part of their lives now. In dreams, the disaster becomes a
kind of vortex into which other problems are drawn, a repetitive drama in which the unsettled anxieties of the past and the
newer anxieties of the present fuse together in a chronology
that knows no time.

*I always dream of water, that muddy water. I'm either out
in it, you know, walking in sloppy, muddy water, or I'm in
a house. It's supposed to be my home, but the house I'm in is
not anything like my house. And I'm always sweeping water
out with a broom, and the more I sweep out, the water is still
there, you see. I had a brother that died about seven years ago,
and some of my children are always there, you know, in the
dream. I'm always telling them that if I can get the mud and
water out of here I'm going to cook dinner. I have the same
dream over and over again. I don't know why. It seems like
in the dream I am always trying to get something done.*

In many ways, the whole world of Buffalo Creek is reflected
in that dream. The woman is more or less at home, but it is
not quite her home (not quite her hollow) at all. The entire
place is full of black water and mud, and as soon as she can
dispose of that mess she will do what mothers in Appalachia
are supposed to do—look after her family and prepare dinner.
The meal, as it turns out, is not for persons who live in the
present but for a brother seven years dead and children long
gone from home. And, in the meantime, there is all that water
and muck spread like a black curse over her world, preventing
her from doing what she must, preventing her from joining
her people in an act of communion.
Almost everyone on Buffalo Creek could imagine themselves

in that scene. Like the woman, they are trying to sweep the memory of the flood out of their minds, worrying about their kin, overwhelmed by sludge and dirty water and contamination, wondering how to bring some sense of order back into their lives, and longing to sit down to a warm family meal once again.

Conclusion

I OPENED this report with the somewhat pale declaration that I did not want the Buffalo Creek flood to serve as one more "case" in the search for sociological generalization, one more "example" placed in the files to supplement our knowledge of disasters in general. Yet data from research on other catastrophes as well as general theorizing about the character of human culture have clearly played a role in the telling of this story, and perhaps the report should end with a further note on the theme introduced at its beginning.

There are at least two sound reasons for studying an event like the Buffalo Creek disaster. The first, of course, is simply to get the story straight, to order its details in such a way that one can follow it in the narrative sense. The flood on Buffalo Creek was a unique human event, a singular tragedy, and it resulted in wounds that can only be understood properly when they are seen in their own local context. In order to relate that part of the story—the task normally performed by dramatists or historians—one should focus on the particularities of the locale, the history of the persons involved, and the contours of the event itself. The second reason for studying an event like this, however, is to consider the way it contributes to our understanding of the anatomy of disasters in general. In order to relate that part of the story—the task normally performed by social scientists—one should focus on those details that seem to be found in other events of a similar kind occurring elsewhere in the world and pay less attention to those details that are local to the immediate cultural setting and to the particular persons involved. That is, one should look for themes reflected in other disasters as well as the one under study—earthquakes in Lisbon and San Francisco, hurricanes in Bristol and Charleston, tornadoes in Worcester and Vicksburg, air raids in Dresden and London, floods in Amsterdam and Louisville, and all the other instances that together constitute the "literature" on human disasters.

These two ways of approaching the story have been fused here, like threads appearing and disappearing in the fabric of the account. I spent a fair amount of time talking about the particularities of the Appalachian experience and the special nature of coal mining because they constitute the background necessary to understand the Buffalo Creek flood as a unique event. I have also spent a fair amount of time alluding to catastrophes that occurred elsewhere, using them as a point of comparison, because they constitute the background necessary to understand the flood as a generalized event.

In that sense, at least, the report has really had two themes, two points of focus, and it seems fitting that it should end with two separate conclusions. The first conclusion will be concerned once again with the mountain ethos and the "axes of variation" running through it. The second conclusion will reflect on the nature of disasters in general.

I

Although I have returned to Buffalo Creek several times since, this report brings the story only up to a day in late August, 1974, some two and a half years after the flood. On that occasion, a group of lawyers, legal assistants, and other persons connected with the litigation went to Buffalo Creek to distribute the plaintiffs' share of $13.5 million won from the coal company. In some ways, of course, it was a day of triumph. We wandered up and down the creek saying good-bye and bringing conversations that had been going on for two years to a close.

That evening, most of the adult participants in the suit gathered in the local school auditorium to hear a few announcements and to mark the end of the long ordeal. People shuffled awkwardly into the hall to the sounds of country music being played by a band (provoking more than one complaint that the moment was too solemn for such festivities) and then listened to a few speeches delivered from the stage, the speakers looking pale and remote in the glare of the television lights. Afterward, it was time for handshakes, expressions of thanks, and a few shy embraces. Small gifts were exchanged, addresses written down on scraps of paper, comments entered into personal journals, and promises made about the future. The gathering was too subdued to count as a joyous occasion, although it was affectionate and warm. A stranger might very well have mistaken it for a graduation exercise.

For the visitors, at least, it was a kind of graduation. All of us managed to leave a piece of unfinished business behind in order to have a reason to return, but all of us felt that we had come to the end of a very important episode in our lives and were about to move on to other personal and professional concerns. That sense of finality, in fact, is what makes it possible to write a book like this: the whole event is recorded in the mind as having an opening date and a closing date, a first chapter and a last.

For the people of Buffalo Creek, however, the day was little more than a somewhat brighter moment in the flow of their lives. It was a graduation in the sense that it ended a period of uncertainty, vindicated a decision to enter litigation, and furnished people with sufficient funds to realize whatever plans they were ready to make. But it was also a graduation in the sense that it propelled people into the future at the very moment it was placing a final seal on a portion of the past. The time had come to seek new housing, to make overdue decisions, to put the many pieces of a shattered life back together. A painful period of suspension was over, but that put people in the position of no longer being able to act as if their fates were hanging on an attorney's competence, a judge's sense of fairness, or a jury's compassion. So it was a cruel time as well as a comforting one, for the fact is that many of the people in the school auditorium did not really know what they would do next and had not really decided how to use their new resources. The most common emotion expressed that evening was satisfaction at having made the coal company pay a large penalty and having warned other coal operators to be wary of dams like the one in Middle Fork, the gain being that "other people won't have to suffer like we did." It was a generous thought, even a gallant one, but it was addressed to the past rather than to the future.

There is a sense, then, in which this report ends at the very moment it might have begun, for the main task of restoration is still ahead. The calendar on which the beginning and the end of this research are marked was not set by the natural sequence of events on Buffalo Creek but by the more arbitrary timing of a legal action. The story itself continues, and we can only guess how it will end.

What information we have gives us reason to suppose that the wounds received on Buffalo Creek will not heal quickly. The people of the hollow—some of them, in any event—have been compensated financially for the loss of their property and symbolically for the emotional injuries they had to bear. But they have not been compensated for the loss of their communal base, and to that extent they are still stranded in the same uncomfortable spot, suspended vaguely in midair.

I suggested earlier that Appalachian culture—or any culture, for that matter—can be visualized as a kind of gravitational field in which people are sometimes made more alike by the values they share in common but are sometimes set apart, differentiated, by contrary pulls built into the texture of that field. Every culture, then, is characterized by a number of continua, or "axes of variation," along which people are arrayed in all their differences and along which responses to social and cultural change are most apt to take place.

I have not been very precise in the way I introduced this notion because I mean it to serve as a "sensitizing concept," in Herbert Blumer's terms, rather than as a finished theoretical formulation. But I am proposing here that one can learn something about the cultural history of a people by watching the way they cope with the ambiguities built into their cultural terrain and by tracing the way they move along the axes thus formed.

To repeat, then. The old mountain culture was characterized by continuing tensions between a longing for individual freedom and a longing for conventional forms of authority, between a sense of assertion and a sense of resignation, between feelings of physical vigor and feelings of physical susceptibility, between a capacity for orderliness and a capacity for disorder, and, above all, between a need for independence and a need for dependency. Life in the mountains earned its coherence and integrity by the way those contrary tendencies were held in a kind of complementary balance, by the way they stayed poised on the edges of the cultural field and counteracted one another.

The people of Appalachia have been the victims of one long, sustained disaster brought about by the pillaging of the timber reserves, the opening of the coal fields, the emergence of the Depression, and the introduction of welfare as a way of life; and the effect of these and other developments in the life of the region has been to create a shift in the gravitational field and to destroy that old balance. If we had a chart to indicate the flow of change across that cultural field, it would be covered with arrows showing drifts away from individual freedom to enforced conformity, from self-assertion to passivity, from ability to disability, from tidiness to an almost sullen kind of slovenliness, and from independence to an ever-growing dependency. All of the vectors of change indicated on our chart would have to be counted as movements toward less satisfactory potentialities in the field, even if we used no other base line than the standards of the people concerned. One should also note a turn away from the old mountain self-absorption to a newer form of communality, as we have seen, but even that development turned out to be ambiguous in the long run considering how exposed people became in its absence.

The story of Buffalo Creek up until the winter of 1972 is the story of people who had begun to reverse those cultural drifts. There is no point in reviewing that development once again, but it is clear that the people of the hollow were in the process of recovering many of those old mountain strengths as they climbed out of the poverty that had been the lot of so many of their fellows elsewhere in Appalachia; and when one tries to calculate the size of their loss or the size of the problems they are likely to face in the future, one must keep all this in mind.

Now the traumatic symptoms we have been describing here as effects of the flood are similar to those noted in other reports of extreme human stress. But these symptoms have a special meaning on Buffalo Creek because they represent retreats— if that is the word—along the very axes we have been talking about. So our chart, already slashed with arrows moving backward and forward across the field, now becomes even more complicated: the arrows must be pictured as reversing themselves once again, indicating movement along the axes of variation toward the weaker ends of the scale. When the Buffalo Creek survivors report that they seem to have lost interest in keeping an intact household, they are warning us of a slide back to the disorder of depressed mountain hollows. When they report that they no longer feel in charge of their own destinies, they are warning us of a turn back to the fatalism of the old Appalachian ethos. When they report an increasing concern with illness and compensation, they are warning us of a return to the world of dependency. And so it goes across the whole of the chart.

When one lists the effects of the Buffalo Creek flood, then, one must note that it may very well have altered the currents of the larger cultural field and opened up potentialities for change that have always lurked in the shadows of Appalachia.

II

There is an extensive literature throughout the social and behavioral sciences on the subject of human disaster, beginning in the 1950's when the world took stock of the devastating effects of the Second World War. Government planners and university researchers shared a deep concern about the destructive energies unleashed by the war and particularly about the terrifying force of the atom bomb. The government planners were interested because it seemed important to know how well a civilian population could weather atomic attack, and the university researchers were interested because the subject was topical and offered insight into the human condition generally. One cannot drop experimental bombs on civilian populations in order to create a laboratory for study, so the best available research strategy was to turn to human situations that most closely approximated atomic attacks, and the obvious candidates were disasters of one kind or another. Nature has a way of providing such laboratories regularly, and thus, for a number of years, teams of social and behavioral scientists were dispatched to the scenes of fires, hurricanes, floods, tornadoes, tidal waves, and all the other visitations that disturb the peace of mankind.

Interest in natural disasters has continued over the intervening years, even though the bomb itself no longer seems to loom as so great a threat in the public imagination, and this may be the result of a growing conviction that the future —no matter how one envisions it—holds such a rich promise of creating disasters of the man-made variety. It is not just a question of specific horrors lying in wait (although it is no feat to compile a list of those) but a question of increased vulnerability to accident, malfunction, and sheer ill will.

The real danger is that, like some grotesque variation on

the Peter Principle, technological progress seeks its own level of incompetence. People are encouraged to think that they can control the best in nature and the worst in themselves, and they continue to think so until the momentum of some adventure carries them beyond the limits of their own intelligence or stamina. People do not usually know their limitations until they reach them, and when they are in charge of weapons and other contrivances with an almost infinite capacity to do harm, the probabilities that the future will be marked by periodic disasters are certainly increased. None of the celebrated advances in science and technology seem to have done much to arrest the force of natural disasters, although we can see them coming a few hours earlier and can measure their destructiveness more exactly afterward, but those advances have added decisively to man's catalogue of potential catastrophes.

But what is a "disaster" anyway? In social science usage as well as in everyday speech, the term refers to a sharp and furious eruption of some kind that splinters the silence for one terrible moment and then goes away. A disaster is an "event" with a distinct beginning and a distinct end, and it is by definition extraordinary—a freak of nature, a perversion of the natural processes of life. Disasters customarily leave a tremendous amount of damage in their wake, of course, but we are likely to classify that damage as an "aftermath" and assume that both the physical wreckage and the human wreckage will be repaired over a period of time. So the two distinguishing properties of a disaster are, first, that it does a good deal of harm, and, second, that it is sudden, unexpected, acute.

Disasters tend to inflict injuries on the minds of at least a few of the people who survive them, and those injuries are often diagnosed as "psychic trauma," meaning an assault on the person so sudden and so explosive that it smashes through one's defenses and does damage to the sensitive tissues underneath. The human mind (or so the theory goes) is normally equipped with a stimulus barrier or shield, an invisible membrane that protects it against sudden stress from the outside. This barrier acts like an outer layer of skin, and, like scar tissue, it becomes thicker and tougher over time as it is exposed to a constant bombardment of stimuli from the environment. In the ordinary course of events, the stimulus shield can be counted on to protect the ego from normal dosages of stress, but when the outside threat is too abrupt or too strong, the barrier is breached and the mental processes within are disturbed.

Something like this, at any rate, is what clinicians usually have in mind when they try to describe the dynamics of "psychic trauma," and the only reason I have taken a stab at defining those medical terms is to make the point that trauma is generally viewed as an *effect,* the result of a blow from the outside. When there is no blow, there is no trauma; and what this means for most practical purposes is that the presence of a disaster or some other source of immediate stress is necessary to the definition of trauma.

Suppose, however, that we were to reverse the logic of that sequence. We would begin with the same empirical observation: the events we generally identify as "disasters" seem to have the result of provoking a condition we generally identify as "trauma"—never mind for the time being whether the prevailing definitions of either term sound persuasive or prove easy to work with as conceptual tools. But instead of classifying a condition as *trauma* because it was induced by a disaster, we would classify an event as *disaster* if it had the property of bringing about traumatic reactions. According to the terms of this rule, any event or condition that could be shown to produce trauma on a large scale would have earned a place on the current roster of "disasters."

Were we to do this, either as a parlor game or as a serious intellectual exercise, we would presumably want to keep quotation marks around the term "disaster," because the intent of the exercise is not to offer a new dictionary meaning for an old word but to suggest that there are any number of happenings in human life that seem to produce the same effects as a conventional disaster without exhibiting the same physical properties. However we maneuvered around that linguistic obstacle, the rule just proposed would require us to add considerably to our list of disastrous events.

In the first place, we would be required to include events that have the capacity to induce trauma but that do not have the quality of suddenness or explosiveness normally associated with the term. For example, people who are shifted from one location to another as the result of war or some other emergency often seem to be traumatized afterward, and this is certainly the case for many of those who are evacuated from urban areas on the grounds that their old neighborhoods are scheduled for renewal. And one might add here that thousands of American Indians, confined to reservations for the better part of a century, continue to show the effects of traumatization. Our list might also have to include such slow-developing but nonetheless devastating events as plague, famine, spoilage of natural resources, and a whole galaxy of other miseries.

In the second place, now that we are working with new rules for identifying disasters, we have to note that we are edging toward the notion that *chronic conditions* as well as *acute events* can induce trauma, and this, too, belongs in our calculations. A chronic disaster is one that gathers force slowly and insidiously, creeping around one's defenses rather than smashing through them. The person is unable to mobilize his normal defenses against the threat, sometimes because he has elected consciously or unconsciously to ignore it, sometimes because he has been misinformed about it, and sometimes because he cannot do anything to avoid it in any case. It has long been recognized, for example, that living in conditions of chronic poverty is often traumatizing, and if one looks carefully at the faces as well as the clinic records of people who live in institutions or hang out in the vacant corners of skid row or enlist in the migrant labor force or eke out a living in the urban slums, one can scarcely avoid seeing the familiar symptoms of trauma—a numbness of spirit, a susceptibility to anxiety and rage and depression, a sense of helplessness, an inability to concentrate, a loss of various motor skills, a heightened apprehension about the physical and social environment, a preoccupation with death, a retreat into dependency, and a general loss of ego functions. One can find those symptoms wherever people feel left out of things, abandoned, separated from the life around them. From that point of view, being too poor to participate in the promise of the culture or too old to take a meaningful place in the structure of the community can be counted as a kind of disaster.

But the logic of our new rules may take us one step further. One does not need to visit the homes of the wretched to find symptoms of trauma, for there are ample indications that modern life itself can become a principal cause of traumatic reactions. One of the long-term effects of modernization as we know it has been to distance people from primary associations and to separate them from the nourishing roots of community, and the costs of this process have been heavy for certain portions of the population. This idea has been the subject of so many recent writings that I will not try to pursue it further here, but I would like to make one observation.

If it makes sense to assume that acute disasters are likely to occur in greater numbers, not because nature has become more malevolent but because men have learned so many ways to create their own havoc; and if it makes sense to assume that the processes of modernization often breed their own forms of chronic disaster; then it is reasonable to wonder whether traumatization is apt to become an increasingly common experience in human life.

Each historical age has its own particular problems and poses its own particular strains on the human nervous system, and each historical age, as a result, can be said to produce its own special brands of neurosis. In one sense, at least, the neuroses characteristic of any given period are a part of its signature, because they reflect the dilemmas and ambiguities to which people had to respond. A short psychiatric history of the twentieth century would presumably note that the sexual neuroses were an identifying signature of the earlier years of the century and that the character neuroses were an important signature of the middle years. What comes next? A sociologist may have no business trying to name various types of neurosis or to identify their basic psychological origins, but it is useful to speculate about the sources of strain people may have to cope with in the remaining years of the century.

In the first place, we may be entering an age of relativism in which people come to feel the lack of fixed moral landmarks and established orthodoxies. What was once an obscure intellectual discovery confined to the equations of physicists and the field notes of cultural anthropologists is now becoming a matter of general understanding, and this raises an important question: How will people develop a secure sense of self in the midst of a relativity that threatens to encompass everything? If the groups to which one belongs and the values to which one subscribes can no longer be experienced as morally special, ordained by God or history or nature, then one is very apt to feel adrift, charting a course for oneself across a largely indifferent terrain. A world without stable points of reference is a world in ruins for those who find themselves without the personal resources or the good luck to navigate effectively in it.

In the second place, we may be entering an age of impotence in which fewer and fewer people are able to derive meaningful satisfaction from the act of producing something that is both sanctioned and needed by the rest of the community—goods, offspring, or something else—and come to the conclusion that their presence on the planet does not make very much difference to anyone. They move onto the human stage, sulk around its edges for a few years, and then depart without having left a trace of their passage behind. One reaction to that state of affairs is to withdraw into a dulled silence, sitting out one's life in front of television sets, inventing a more active life in fantasy, nursing old resentments, and spending a good deal of time tending the aches and pains of one's own body with the help of a heavy diet of medications. This is a form of resignation, the passivity of the long-distance spectator, and it is particularly acute among people who come to feel that the world operates by a logic alien to their own instincts.

In the third place, we may be entering an age of sensory overload in which there is so much diverging information to absorb, so many moralities competing for one's attention, so many contradictory sensations to respond to, that people without the right kind of insulation run the risk of developing scar tissue from ear to ear. One result of all this is apt to be a flattening of affect, a sheer anesthetization of the moral and cognitive senses, as if one were suffering from a kind of psychological concussion.

And, finally, we may be entering an age of such diffuse apprehension that certain people will find it difficult to put faith in the motives of others or in the workings of nature. We do not need to discuss all the dangers that confront the modern mind in order to make the point. As one of the last voices we heard from Buffalo Creek put it, the list of potential calamities is all in Revelations anyway. But the feeling that something bad is bound to happen sooner or later and that the world has become an unreliable place is certainly not an image unique to survivors of an acute disaster.

A good deal more could be said about the future, of course, but the remarks above are sufficient for our present purposes. I have suggested that human reactions to the age we are entering are likely to include a sense of cultural disorientation, a feeling of powerlessness, a dulled apathy, and a generalized fear about the condition of the universe. These, of course, are among the classic symptoms of trauma, and it may well be that historians of the future will look back on this period and conclude that the traumatic neuroses were its true clinical signature. These dilemmas and ambiguities, of course, place differing strains on the people who are exposed to them; and, as in every age, one must ask which of those people are apt to prove most vulnerable.

This takes us a long way from Buffalo Creek, and maybe one should not try to find a way back at the last moment. Yet there is one final point to be made. I have proposed several times that the people of Buffalo Creek are now in the process of recovering from two disasters—the first being the gradual deterioration of mountain culture and the second being the events of February 26, 1972. If they are unable to restore at least a fair facsimile of the old community or to find secure places for themselves in neighboring ones, they may find themselves launched unwillingly into the larger scene I have just traced, skidding sideways, so to speak, into all the fluidities and uncertainties that characterize much of modern life. Few people in this country are less prepared for that transition. It would be dramatic beyond all reason for me to conclude this report with an assertion that modern life is a calamity, but it would be only prudent to notice in passing that those people who live out on the margins of the new America, who continue to live in communities and to think of themselves as folk, are likely to experience the world we are making for them as yet another disaster.

What happened on Buffalo Creek, then, can serve as a reminder that the preservation (or restoration) of communal forms of life must become a lasting concern, not only for those charged with healing the wounds of acute disaster but for those charged with planning a truly human future.

Notes

Introduction

1. James Watt Raine, *The Land of Saddle-bags: A Study of the Mountain People of Appalachia* (New York: Council of Women for Home Missions, 1924), p. 101.

I. *February 26, 1972*

1. For these and the following figures, see Hearings Before the Subcommittee on Labor of the Committee on Labor and Public Welfare, United States Senate, May 30 and 31, 1972 (Washington, D.C.: U.S. Government Printing Office, 1972); and Report of the Governor's Ad Hoc Commission of Inquiry into the Buffalo Creek Flood and Disaster (Charleston, W.Va.: State of West Virginia, 1972).
2. Harry M. Caudill, "Buffalo Creek Aftermath," *Saturday Review,* August 26, 1972, p. 16.
3. Testimony of Denny Gibson, Report of the Governor's Ad Hoc Commission, *op. cit.,* Vol. I, p. 189.

II. *Notes on Appalachia*

1. François André Michaux, "Travels to the West of the Allegheny Mountains, 1802," in Reuben G. Thwaites, ed., *Early Western Travels, 1748–1846* (Cleveland: Arthur H. Clark, 1904), Vol. III, p. 174.

2. Edgar Allan Poe, from a "minor tale" dated 1845. Quoted in Horace Kephart, *Our Southern Highlanders* (New York: Outing Publishing Co., 1913), p. 11.
3. Ellen C. Semple, "The Anglo-Saxons of the Kentucky Mountains: A Study in Anthropogeography," originally published in *The Geographical Journal*, London, 1901, and reprinted in the *Bulletin of the American Geographical Society*, 42:561–594 (1910). Present citation from the latter source, p. 561.
4. Kephart, *op. cit.*, pp. 17–18, 248.
5. Michaux, *op. cit.*, p. 247.
6. Meshach Browning, *Forty-four Years in the Life of a Hunter* (Philadelphia: Lippincott, 1928), p. 365.
7. Quoted in Muriel Earley Sheppard, *Cabins in the Laurel* (Chapel Hill, N.C.: University of North Carolina Press, 1935), p. 25.
8. Michaux, *op. cit.*, p. 249.
9. James Watt Raine, *The Land of Saddle-bags: A Study of the Mountain People of Appalachia* (New York: Council of Women for Home Missions, 1924), p. 191.
10. Harry M. Caudill, *Night Comes to the Cumberlands* (Boston: Little, Brown, 1963), p. 58.
11. Browning, *op. cit.*, pp. 111–112, 364.
12. Francis Asbury, *Journal* (London: Epworth Press, 1958). The excerpts are from Vol I, p. 197 (1776); Vol. I, pp. 576–577 (1788); and Vol. II, p. 411 (1803).
13. William James, "On a Certain Blindness in Human Beings," in *Pragmatism and Other Essays* (New York: Washington Square Press, 1963), p. 252. This essay was first published in 1907.
14. Roy B. Clarkson, *Tumult on the Mountains: Lumbering in West Virginia, 1770–1920* (Parsons, W.Va.: McClain Printing Co., 1964), p. 2; Michaux, *op. cit.*, p. 175.
15. The reigning expert on the subject says flatly: "By 1920 the original forest was completely depleted except for a few isolated areas of small acreage." Clarkson, *op. cit.*, p. 38.
16. Early sketches include the notes of seasoned travelers who spent long periods in the mountains: Ellen C. Semple, *op. cit.* (1901); Horace Kephart, *op. cit.* (1913); Samuel Tyndale Wilson, *The Southern Mountaineers* (New York: Presbyterian Home Missions, 1914); John C. Campbell, *The Southern Highlander and His Homeland* (New York: Russell Sage, 1921); James Watt Raine, *op. cit.* (1924); and Muriel Earley Sheppard, *op. cit.* (1935).
   Among those early sketches are works from a few long-time residents who hoped to rescue the reputation of the region from journalists who had discovered the appeal of feuds, moonshine, and mountain quaintness in general, for example: Josiah Henry Combs, *The Kentucky Highlanders from a Native Mountaineer's Viewpoint* (Lexington, Ky.: J. L. Richardson, 1913); and Fess Whitaker, *History of Corporal Fess Whitaker* (Louisville, Ky.: Standard Printing Co., 1918).

Works coming out of a more academic tradition include: S. S. MacClintock, "The Kentucky Mountains and Their Feuds," *American Journal of Sociology,* VII:1–28, 171–187 (1901); Mandel Sherman and Thomas R. Henry, *Hollow Folk* (New York: Crowell, 1933); Claudia Lewis, *Children of the Cumberland* (New York: Columbia University Press, 1946); Herman R. Lantz, *People of Coal Town* (New York: Columbia University Press, 1958); Marion Pearsall, *Little Smoky Ridge* (Birmingham, Ala.: University of Alabama Press, 1959); Thomas A. Ford, ed., *The Southern Appalachian Region* (Lexington, Ky.: University of Kentucky Press, 1962); Elmora M. Matthews, *Neighbor and Kin* (Nashville, Tenn.: Vanderbilt University Press, 1966); John Fetterman, *Stinking Creek* (New York: Dutton, 1967); John B. Stephenson, *Shiloh: A Mountain Community* (Lexington, Ky.: University of Kentucky Press, 1968); David H. Looff, *Appalachia's Children: The Challenge of Mental Health* (Lexington, Ky.: University of Kentucky Press, 1971); David S. Walls and John B. Stephenson, eds., *Appalachia in the Sixties* (Lexington, Ky.: University of Kentucky Press, 1972); and Robert Coles, *Migrants, Sharecroppers, Mountaineers* (Boston: Little, Brown, 1972).

The two most influential (and, in my opinion, the two best) works on Appalachia were written by a lawyer and a clergyman, respectively: Harry M. Caudill, *Night Comes to the Cumberlands* (Boston: Little, Brown, 1963); and Jack E. Weller, *Yesterday's People: Life in Contemporary Appalachia* (Lexington, Ky.: University of Kentucky Press, 1966).

17. Kephart, *op. cit.,* pp. 307, 253.
18. *Ibid.,* p. 231.
19. Semple, *op. cit.,* p. 583.
20. Weller, *op. cit.,* p. 49.
21. Semple, *op. cit.,* p. 569.
22. Weller, *op. cit.,* pp. 3–5; and Herbert J. Gans, *The Urban Villagers* (New York: Free Press, 1962).

III. *The Mountain Ethos*

1. See, in this connection, Anthony F. C. Wallace, *Culture and Personality* (New York: Random House, 1961).
2. Jack E. Weller, *Yesterday's People: Life in Contemporary Appalachia* (Lexington, Ky.: University of Kentucky Press, 1966), p. 83.
3. John B. Stephenson, *Shiloh: A Mountain Community* (Lexington, Ky.: University of Kentucky Press, 1968), p. 79.
4. George Santayana, *The Last Puritan* (N.Y.: Scribner's, 1936), pp. 128–129.
5. See David H. Looff, *Appalachia's Children: The Challenge of Mental Health* (Lexington, Ky.: University of Kentucky Press, 1971); Robert Coles, *Migrants, Sharecroppers, Mountaineers* (Boston: Little, Brown, 1972); and Weller, *op. cit.*

IV. *The Coming of the Coal Camps*

1. Samuel Tyndale Wilson, *The Southern Mountaineers* (New York: Presbyterian Home Missions, 1914), pp. 173–174. Reissue of work first published in 1906.
2. Horace Kephart, *Our Southern Highlanders* (New York: Outing Publishing Co., 1913), p. 383.
3. James Watt Raine, *The Land of Saddle-bags: A Study of the Mountain People of Appalachia* (New York: Council of Women for Home Missions, 1924), pp. 236–237.
4. Nettie P. McGill, "The Welfare of Children in Bituminous Coal Mining Communities in West Virginia," United States Department of Labor, Children's Bureau, Publication Number 117 (Washington, D.C.: Government Printing Office, 1923). Quotes scattered throughout report.
5. George Korson, *Coal Dust on the Fiddle* (Philadelphia: University of Pennsylvania Press, 1943), p. 235.
6. John Brophy, *A Miner's Life* (Madison, Wis.: University of Wisconsin Press, 1964), p. 48.
7. Raine, *op. cit.,* pp. 172–173.
8. Edmund Wilson, "Frank Keeney's Coal Diggers," in *The American Jitters* (Freeport, N.Y.: Books for Libraries Press, 1968), p. 151.
9. McGill, *op. cit.*
10. Bill Peterson, *Coaltown Revisited* (Chicago: Henry Regnery, 1972), p. 114.
11. Harry M. Caudill, *Night Comes to the Cumberlands* (Boston: Little, Brown, 1963), pp. 279–280.
12. Fyodor Dostoievski, "Notes from Underground," in B. G. Guerney, ed., *A Treasury of Russian Literature* (New York: Vanguard, 1943), p. 454.
13. See, for example, Lewis W. Field, Reed T. Ewing, and David M. Wayne, "Observations on the Relation of Psychosocial Factors to Psychiatric Illness Among Coal Miners," *International Journal of Social Psychiatry,* III:133–145 (1957).

V. *Buffalo Creek*

1. George T. Swain, *History of Logan County, West Virginia* (Kingsport, Tenn.: Kingsport Press, 1927), p. 81.
2. *Ibid.,* p. 114.
3. These figures are all drawn from the same source, although they are not wholly consistent with one another: Walter R. Thurmond, *The Logan Coal Field of West Virginia* (Morgantown, W.Va.: West Virginia University Press, 1964).

   For comparison, figures for a neighboring coal field in 1921 were: 16,200 mountain white, 2,300 Southern black, and 11,200 foreign-born. See Boris Emmet, "Labor Relations in the Fairmont,

West Virginia, Bituminous Coal Field," Bulletin of the United States Bureau of Labor Statistics, U.S. Department of Labor, Publication Number 361 (Washington, D.C.: Government Printing Office, 1927), p. 3.

As for the state of West Virginia in general, population estimates from the 1930 census were as follows: The total population was 1,729,205, and of these only 51,520 were foreign-born and only 115,000 were black, a considerable drop from the preceding census. The three largest groups of immigrants were, in order, Italians, Poles, and Hungarians. See Charles Henry Ambler, *West Virginia, The Mountain State* (New York: Prentice-Hall, 1940), p. 533.

4. George T. Swain, *The Incomparable Don Chafin* (Charleston, W.Va.: Ace Enterprises, 1962).
5. Thurmond, *op. cit.*, p. 55.
6. George T. Swain, *History of Logan County, West Virginia* (Kingsport, Tenn.: Kingsport Press, 1927), p. 156.
7. Winthrop D. Lane, *Civil War in West Virginia* (New York: B. W. Huebsch, 1921), p. 78.
8. Arthur Gleason, "Private Ownership of Public Officials," *The Nation*, 110:724–725 (1920), p. 725. Gleason followed up this first warning with a second: "Company-Owned Americans," *The Nation*, 110:794–795 (1920).
9. George T. Swain, *Facts About the Two Armed Marches on Logan County* (Charleston, W.Va.: Ace Enterprises, 1962).
10. Lane, *op. cit.*, pp. 32–33.
11. David S. Walls and John B. Stephenson, eds., *Appalachia in the Sixties* (Lexington, Ky.: University of Kentucky Press, 1972), pp. 6, 89.
12. Buffalo Valley Redevelopment Plan, Governor's Office of Federal/State Relations in Conjunction with Federal Regional Council (Charleston, W.Va.: State of West Virginia, 1973); and Environmental Impact Statement for the Buffalo Valley Redevelopment Plan, Governor's Office.
13. Cf. James S. Brown and George A. Hillery, Jr., "The Great Migration, 1940–1960," in Thomas A. Ford, ed., *The Southern Appalachian Region* (Lexington, Ky.: University of Kentucky Press, 1962); and Environmental Impact Statement for the Buffalo Valley Redevelopment Plan, *op. cit.*
14. Harry M. Caudill, *Night Comes to the Cumberlands* (Boston: Little, Brown, 1963), p. 331.

VI. *Looking for Scars*

1. Harry M. Caudill, "Buffalo Creek Aftermath," *Saturday Review*, August 26, 1972, p. 17.
2. Cf. Marc Fried, "Grieving for a Lost Home," in Leonard J. Duhl, ed., *The Urban Condition* (New York: Basic Books, 1963).

VII. *Individual Trauma: State of Shock*

1. William James, "On Some Mental Effects of the Earthquake," in *Memories and Studies* (New York: Longmans, Green, 1911), p. 212.
2. Cf. Robert Jay Lifton, *Death in Life; Survivors of Hiroshima* (New York: Random House, 1968); and Anthony F. C. Wallace, *Tornado in Worcester*, Disaster Study Number Three, Committee on Disaster Studies, National Academy of Sciences—National Research Council, 1956.
3. Irving L. Janis, *Stress and Frustration* (New York: Harcourt Brace Jovanovich, 1971), p. 101.
4. This quote is from a newspaper reporter's account of the disaster. See Tom Nugent, *Death at Buffalo Creek* (New York: Norton, 1973), p. 97.
5. Cf. Lifton, *op. cit.*
6. Cf. Allen H. Barton, *Communities in Disaster* (Garden City, N.Y.: Doubleday, 1969).
7. Harry Estill Moore, *Tornadoes over Texas* (Austin, Tex.: University of Texas Press, 1958), pp. 252–253.
8. Janis, *op. cit.*, p. 30.
9. Mary Walton, "After the Flood," *Harper's*, March, 1973, p. 82.
10. Janis, *op. cit.*, pp. 33–34.

VIII. *Collective Trauma: Loss of Communality*

1. Anthony F. C. Wallace, *Tornado in Worcester*, Disaster Study Number Three, Committee on Disaster Studies, National Academy of Sciences—National Research Council, 1956, p. 127.
2. Stewart E. Perry, Earle Silber, and Donald A. Bloch, *The Child and His Family in Disaster: A Study of the 1953 Vicksburg Tornado*, Disaster Study Number Five, Committee on Disaster Studies, National Academy of Sciences—National Research Council, 1956, p. 47.
3. S. H. Prince, *Catastrophe and Social Change* (New York: Columbia University Press, 1920); R. I. Kutak, "Sociology of Crises: The Louisville Flood of 1937," *Social Forces*, XVII:66–72 (1938); Charles E. Fritz, "Disaster," in Robert K. Merton and Robert A. Nisbet, eds., *Contemporary Social Problems* (New York: Harcourt Brace, 1961); Martha Wolfenstein, *Disaster: A Psychological Essay* (Glencoe, Ill.: Free Press, 1957); and Allen H. Barton, *Communities in Disaster* (Garden City, N.Y.: Doubleday, 1969).
4. See also Anthony F. C. Wallace, "Mazeway Disintegration: The Individual's Perception of Socio-Cultural Disorganization," *Human Organization*, XVI:23–27 (1957).

5. E. L. Quarantelli and Russell R. Dynes, *Images of Disaster Behavior: Myths and Consequences,* Disaster Research Center, The Ohio State University, 1973, p. 17.

6. Daniel Defoe, *History of the Great Plague* (London: H. Teape, 1819), pp. 234–235.

Index

Accoville, 22
  see also Buffalo Creek
action, importance of, 51, 60, 74, 78, 87, 229
  see also feeling and sensation
air pollution:
  in coal camps, 96, 100, 102
  mining and respiratory ailments, 98, 99–100, 137, 231
alcohol:
  drinking, 57, 62
    increase in, after flood, 171, 173, 205, 206, 207, 208
  whiskey (moonshine) made and sold, 57, 68, 85, 104, 116
alienation, sense of (after flood):
  in family life, 145, 146, 172, 173, 205, 207, 218–22
  as a form of death, 243–44
  toward neighbors, 222–27
  see also communality, loss of
American Indians, 132, 255
Amherstdale, 22, 29, 33, 41, 210
  see also Buffalo Creek

anxiety and tension, 60, 62, 74–75, 77–78, 83–93 *passim,* 113, 250
after flood:
  about health, 157, 217, 228–235, 251
  nervousness, 136, 142, 145, 146, 157, 213, 217, 232
  see also survivors, anxiety and fear
about health, 75, 76, 87–88, 111–12, 113, 228, 250, 257
see also nature, distrust and fear of
apathy, 257, 258
after flood, 42, 136, 142, 157, 194, 198, 204
Appalachia, 51–78
  18th century, 51–52, 55, 60–61, 65–66, 68, 69
  19th century, 52–53, 55–57, 61–62, 65, 66, 68, 69, 71
  20th century, 50–54, 57, 69–70, 71, 108–09
    Depression, 108, 109, 110, 117, 250

Appalachia *(cont.)*
World War II, 109
see also coal camps and
towns; migration
Appalachia—mountain ethos, contrasts and tensions in, 77–78,
83–93 *passim,* 250
change, lack of, 53–54, 71–72
see also traditionalism
changes, 74, 77, 83, 84
changes in coal camps, 102–07
from 1930's on, 108–09, 131,
259
changes after flood, 251–52
in moral standards, 203, 205–
209
see also individual feelings and
traits
Arnold and Porter: lawsuit against
Pittston on behalf of survivors,
9–16, *passim,* 118, 153, 156,
197, 198, 247–48, 249
Asbury, Bishop Francis:
on Appalachia in the 18th-19th
centuries, 66
authority:
governmental, distrust of, 57,
72, 84–85, 150–51
patriarchal family life, 76, 86,
89, 90–91

Barton, Allen H., 201
Becco, 22, 45
see also Buffalo Creek
birth rate, 52, 65, 76, 109, 126
blacks:
coal mining, 117, 118, 119, 123
migration, 117, 118, 119
and whites, relationship, 129,
209
Blair Mountain, battle of, 122–23
Blumer, Herbert, 250

Braeholm, 22, 33–34, 135, 189–
190
see also Buffalo Creek
Browning, Meshach: on Appalachia in the 19th century, 58, 65
Buffalo Creek:
blacks, 117, 118, 119, 123, 129,
209
coal mining, 23–24, 117, 118,
119, 123–30
changes in terrain and continued fears, 179, 238–39
see also coal mining; Pittston
Corporation—Buffalo Min-
ing Company
description of, before flood, 22,
23–24
highway proposed, 152, 153
migration and population shift,
23–24, 125, 126, 127
settlers, 115, 116
villages in, 22
see also individual villages
see also coal camps and towns;
Logan County
Buffalo Creek flood:
conditions and causes (mine
waste, black water), 25–27
attempts to alleviate pressure
and company's failure to
give warning, 27, 183
collapse of waste (dam), 28
responsibility for, according
to survivors, 178, 180–83
weather preceding flood, 27
damage to land and property,
40, 42, 45–46, 174–77, 198,
201
lingering traces, 135
deaths, 40, 41, 43, 45, 169
descriptions of flood and encounters with death, 28–34